# THE UNITED STATES
# AND IRAQ SINCE 1979

# THE UNITED STATES
# AND IRAQ SINCE 1979

Hegemony, Oil and War

Steven Hurst

Edinburgh University Press

© Steven Hurst, 2009

Edinburgh University Press Ltd
22 George Square, Edinburgh
www.euppublishing.com

Reprinted 2010

Typeset in Palatino Light by
Norman Tilley Graphics Ltd, Northampton,
and printed and bound in Great Britain by
CPI Antony Rowe, Chippenham and Eastbourne

A CIP record for this book is available from
the British Library

ISBN 978 0 7486 2767 7 (hardback)
ISBN 978 0 7486 2768 4 (paperback)

The right of Steven Hurst to be identified as author
of this work has been asserted in accordance with
the Copyright, Designs and Patents Act 1988.

# CONTENTS

# ACKNOWLEDGEMENTS

My greatest intellectual debt is to those whose ideas I have pillaged in the course of writing this book. All scholarship is an exercise in standing on the shoulders of others, and in this case the work of three individuals in particular has been critical. In no particular order, therefore, I would like to express my gratitude to Bruce Cumings, for his contribution to World Systems Theory, to Simon Bromley, for his writing on the international oil system, and to Toby Dodge, for his expertise on Iraq.

I also owe Toby thanks for the comments he made in a brief chat which helped to clarify some of the most recent developments in Iraqi politics. In addition, I would like to thank those who have commented on papers and articles produced in the course of writing this book, and in particular the regular participants at the American Politics Group Conference and the US Foreign Policy sessions of the European Consortium for Political Research. Special thanks should go to Tim Lynch for disagreeing with me about everything and forcing me to consider my arguments more carefully.

The British Academy provided funding that enabled me to secure access to the National Security Archive's *Iraqgate* collection. That support has contributed greatly to the book's coverage of the period from 1979 to 1990. I would also like to express my gratitude to the National Security Archive and its staff for the work involved in compiling this excellent collection of documents. The map of the Middle East (Map No. 4102, Rev. 3, United Nations, August 2004) is reproduced with the kind permission of the UN Cartographic Section. The map of Iraq is based on UN Map No. 3835, Rev. 4, United Nations, January 2004.

The editorial team at Edinburgh University Press, particularly Nicola Ramsey, Lianne Vella and Eddie Clark, responded helpfully to my various queries and were understanding of the slight delay in delivery of the manuscript, so my thanks to them, again.

Last, but never least, I would like to once more thank my wife, Sam Faulds, for everything else, which is actually the important stuff.

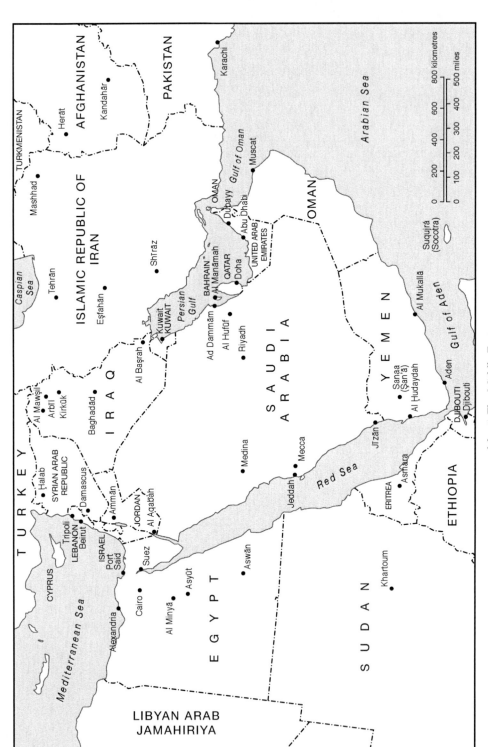

*Map 1.* The Middle East

*Map 2.* Iraq

# ACRONYMS

| | |
|---|---|
| ACC | Arab Cooperation Council |
| BNL | *Banca Nazionale del Lavoro* |
| BW | biological weapons |
| CCC | Commodity Credit Corporation |
| CENTCOM | United States Central Command |
| CW | chemical weapons |
| DOD | Department of Defense |
| GCC | Gulf Cooperation Council |
| IAEA | International Atomic Energy Agency |
| ISCI | Islamic Supreme Council of Iraq |
| NFZ | no fly zone |
| NMD | National Missile Defence system |
| NSC | National Security Council |
| OFF | 'oil for food' |
| ORHA | Office of Reconstruction and Humanitarian Assistance |
| P5 | the five permanent members of the UN Security Council |
| SCIRI | Supreme Council for the Islamic Revolution in Iraq |
| SOFA | Status of Forces Agreement |
| UAE | United Arab Emirates |
| UNMOVIC | UN Monitoring, Verification and Inspection Commission |
| UNSCR | United Nations Security Council Resolution |
| WCS | world capitalist system |
| WMD | weapons of mass destruction |

# INTRODUCTION

The American invasion of Iraq in 2003 has been widely attributed to a 'neocon coup',[1] in which a handful of individuals exploited the trauma caused by the events of 11 September 2001 to seize control of American foreign policy and persuade George W. Bush to implement their plan to eliminate Saddam Hussein.[2] Whilst there are various things wrong with this argument, perhaps the most fundamental is that it reduces the invasion and subsequent occupation of Iraq to a kind of historical accident – a consequence of the unforeseeable conjuncture of 11 September and 'neoconservative' influence in Washington. However, whilst such transient factors are always significant in any historical explanation (the invasion of Iraq is certainly impossible to imagine without the events of 11 September), they rarely represent the most important elements of that explanation. An emphasis on 11 September and neoconservatives serves to obscure the more important fact that the invasion of Iraq was a logical, though hardly inevitable, result of much longer term trends in American foreign policy and politics. In particular, it was a product of a long-established American determination to maintain the position of the United States as the dominant power in the Gulf and of the socio-economic and political transformation of the United States that brought the long-marginalised right wing of the Republican Party to a position of national power for the first time since the 1920s.

## WORLD SYSTEMS THEORY

In order to demonstrate this, and in so doing to place recent events in their proper historical context, this study employs a version of World Systems Theory (WST) developed by Bruce Cumings.[3] This approach locates American foreign policy and the individuals who make it within a set of interlocking structures which shape and constrain that policy and those individuals whilst avoiding the determinism of any single structure and represents a sophisticated attempt to address the fundamental problem of structure and agency in social and historical explanation.[4]

Specifically, Cumings posits three sets of structures within which the American state and its policy-makers must be located:

1. the world capitalist system (WCS);
2. specific regional subsystems of the WCS;
3. the American domestic socio-economic system.

Each of these structures is connected to, and shaped by, the others, but each also has its own autonomous dynamic. Of the three, the WCS is the most fundamental in terms both of its scope and its explanatory role. It is the fundamental axiom of all forms of WST that the position of a state within the WCS is strongly determinative of multiple aspects of its economic, social and political existence. States within the WCS are located in the core, the semi-periphery or the periphery. Core states are defined by their status as the most advanced states in the system, specialising in high-wage, high-profit capital-intensive activities. Peripheral states are characterised by relative under-development and low-wage, labour-intensive economies. The three sets of states are integrated within the WCS via the processes of trade and exchange which tend to transfer wealth from the periphery to the core thanks to the tendency of capitalism to reward money and skills more than raw labour power.[5]

The WCS is also characterised by a tendency toward hegemony – a condition which results from the dominance in production, finance and technology of a single core state to such an extent that it is able to order the international political and economic system according to its own preferences.[6] The preponderant political, economic and military power of the hegemon means that it plays a qualitatively different role to other core states. As the principal beneficiary of the WCS, the hegemon polices and maintains the system and provides public goods. It enforces global economic liberalisation, breaks down barriers to trade and investment, and ensures the other core states access to necessary inputs from the periphery, such as oil.[7] Hegemony does not, therefore, equate to mere dominance but, wherever possible, is characterised by consensual leadership. Whilst the hegemon benefits most, the WCS also operates to the benefit of the other core states and this, as well as the inculcation of an ideology that legitimises hegemony, helps secure the latters' consent to the hegemon's leading role.[8] Coercion is hardly absent from hegemonic practice, however. States and groups in the periphery periodically challenge the operation of the WCS and the dominance of the hegemon, necessitating the use of violence to maintain the system. Since the end of the Second World War, the United States has occupied the position of global hegemon, and its foreign policy has been driven by the imperatives deriving there from. It has consistently sought to defend and to extend its preferred version of market-democracy to as many states as possible. In so doing it has acted, for the most part, in cooperation with its allies in the core states of Western Europe and Japan, whilst frequently resorting to force in order to discipline the recalcitrant periphery.[9]

The second level of structure in Cumings' version of WST is the regional subsystem of the WCS. To some extent, the theoretical justification for the existence of this concept lies in the distinctive nature of the integration of different regions into the WCS. In the case of the Middle East, its role as the world's principal source of oil has produced a unique combination of dependency and impenetrability in its relations with the core states and the American hegemon. On the one hand, direct intervention and colonial rule by the European powers, followed by the carving up of the region into a series of artificial states after the First World War, created a series of weak, dependent states. The ruling elites of the regimes thus created generally lacked legitimacy and depended upon core allies for their security against threats both external and internal. In some cases, that perceived illegitimacy led to the emergence of radical nationalist movements which overthrew pro-Western regimes and sought to free their countries of Western influence. Such developments, however, served only to reinforce the dependence of the surviving regimes upon their core allies. By and large, therefore, Western intervention and the integration of the Middle East into the WCS created a situation where the economic interests, world views and threat perceptions of local elites largely coincided with those of their allies in the core and those elites depended upon those allies for their survival.[10]

At the same time, however, the oil states of the Middle East have been able to retain a significant degree of autonomy, certainly when

compared to other peripheral states, because of their ability to translate oil wealth into a means to resist both deeper integration into the
WCS and domestic demands for economic and political liberalisation.
Most oil states conform to the rentier-state paradigm, wherein the
wealth produced by oil 'rents' results in the development of an atypical
state which needs no tax base and thus no legitimation in the form
of democracy. Instead, the rentier state itself supports society with its
oil wealth and in doing so buys the acquiescence of society whilst
maintaining its autonomy from it. Moreover, whereas most peripheral
states have been forced to integrate ever more completely into the
WCS in order to gain access to bank loans and foreign direct investment, and thus to accept the dictates of the hegemon and its core
allies (as manifested in the rules and strictures of the International
Monetary Fund and the World Bank), the oil states of the Gulf have
not. Whilst the rest of the periphery was steadily forced to reform and
restructure along neoliberal lines from the late 1970s onwards (and
become ever more deeply penetrated by American capital – and
culture – as a result), much of the Middle East stood outside this
process because of its ability to generate its own revenue.[11] As a consequence, the United States has been unable to move its hegemony in
the region beyond the provision of security guarantees onto a more
stable and consensual footing through deeper economic integration
and the spread of hegemonic values. This failure has had significant
ramifications for the United States' policies, not least in the frequent
need to resort to coercion to maintain its dominant position.

The importance of regional subsystems does not rest solely on the
particular nature of their integration into the WCS, however. They
also have internal dynamics, peculiar to themselves, which are largely
autonomous from the operation of the WCS. Conflicts such as those
between the Arab states and Israel, or that between Iran and Iraq,
whilst ultimately rooted in Western intervention and the effort to
incorporate the Middle East into the WCS, nevertheless possess a
logic of their own which cannot be reduced to, or understood, simply
in terms of that origin. Moreover, whilst Western powers more or less
completely dominated the Middle East under colonial rule, independence brought a degree of autonomy to all regional states. The politics
of the Middle East is thus not simply a matter of the hegemon
imposing its will, but rather of an interaction between external powers
and forces on the one hand, and regional powers pursuing their own

objectives on the other.[12] Above all, in this particular case, American policy toward Iraq cannot be understood without a proper grasp of the role that Iraqi policies and objectives have played in shaping it.

Whilst the first two levels of Cumings' version of WST are located, in a sense, 'above' the state, the last is located 'below' it. Both the WCS itself, and the particular dynamics of the Middle East subsystem, create pressures to which American foreign policy must respond, but there is always more than one possible response, and which is chosen is in part a function of the nature of the elites in power at any given time and their particular interests and objectives. It is here that the level of the American socio-economic system enters the analysis, since it is from the operation of that system that different coalitions of interests emerge to dominate the American political system at different times.

Cumings' account of US foreign policy between 1945 and 1950 emphasises how that policy was shaped by the conflict between the dominant New Deal coalition based in internationally oriented business and organised labour, and a weaker Republican-led bloc dominated by nationally oriented business interests. In foreign policy terms, the former was characterised by support for the 'containment' of the Soviet challenge to American efforts to recreate and maintain the WCS, and the latter by a more aggressive demand for the 'rollback' of communism. The outcome of the struggle was a decisive victory for the internationalists and containment, with the support of the liberal, eastern wing of the Republican Party,[13] and the marginalisation of the Republican nationalist right.[14]

For several decades after this struggle, the right wing of the Republican Party would be a voice railing in the wilderness against the failures of American foreign policy, which it deemed to be multiple. It rejected the policy of containment as ineffectual: 'To try and contain [the USSR] is as futile as to try and stop a lawn getting wet by mopping up each drop from a rotating sprinkler . . . To stop the flow we must get at the source.' What was required, therefore, was 'a policy of liberation' or the 'rollback' of communist power.[15] To that end, the Republican right demonstrated an enthusiasm for the employment of force not shared by the containment internationalists. Indeed at times it seemed as though its foreign policy positions 'relied almost exclusively on military solutions'.[16] Conservative Republicans were also decidedly hostile to multilateralism in general and the United

Nations (UN) in particular, both of which the liberal internationalist advocates of containment viewed as useful devices for the maintenance of American hegemony, not least because of their contribution to the consensual dimension of American leadership.[17] When the conservative *National Review* was launched in 1955 it identified its two primary foreign policy goals as defeating communism and combating 'the fashionable concept of world government, the United Nations and internationalism'.[18] Multilateralism was an unwanted constraint on America's freedom of action and the UN was an institution which allowed third class nations with no business involving themselves in world affairs to obstruct American foreign policy.[19] For the best part of half a century, those holding these views were largely confined to the role of critics of those in power. In 2000, however, they gained power for themselves, with the election of George W. Bush. The militarism and unilateralism that this development brought to US foreign policy were significant causes of the 2003 invasion of Iraq, a comprehensive analysis of which therefore requires an understanding of how the Republican right made its way back to power.

Broadly speaking, the 'conservative ascendancy',[20] which reached its apotheosis in the victory of George W. Bush, was the result of two parallel and interrelated processes, namely the decline of the New Deal internationalist coalition and the transformation of the Republican Party. The first of these was precipitated by the defection of two core constituencies. Firstly, conservative white southerners began to transfer their allegiance to the Republicans in response both to the Democrats support for civil rights and rising prosperity across the south.[21] The Republican share of southern seats in the House of Representatives rose from 8 per cent in 1960 to 58 per cent in 2006. Secondly, the 1970s saw the defection from the coalition of large sections of American multinational business. Facing increasing foreign competition and threats to foreign direct investment as a result of Third World revolutions, corporations were attracted by the Republican promise of neoliberal reforms at home and a more aggressive foreign policy to protect American investments overseas.[22] As a result, the Democratic Party, which had dominated American politics since 1932, was reduced to a north-eastern rump of organised labour, liberals and minorities.

The increasingly dominant Republican Party was meanwhile being transformed by these developments and by others, all of which pushed the party further to the right. The incorporation of the white south into the Republican coalition brought in a constituency which was conservative, martial (it was the region most strongly supportive of war against Iraq in 2003)[23] and internationalist (thanks to its traditional reliance on agricultural exports and a growing dependence on defence industries)[24] but with a strong unilateralist streak.[25] Meanwhile, the Republican right's traditional western base became steadily less protectionist and more internationalist as its economy was transformed by the expansion of hi-tech, aerospace and defence industries.[26] By the 1980s, therefore, it became possible for the Republicans to forge a new internationalist but conservative coalition rooted in constituencies in the south and west.[27]

The dominance of conservatives within the party was further reinforced by the influx of evangelical Christians who became politically active in the 1970s, primarily in response to domestic developments including the Supreme Court's ban on school prayer and support for abortion rights.[28] Nevertheless, their increasing influence had foreign policy implications as well since, as a demographic group, they are amongst the most supportive of a hard-line foreign policy and deeply hostile to the UN.[29] Rather different in orientation, but also important, were the defectors from the Democrats known as the 'neoconservatives'. This group, whose leading figures included Irving Kristol, Norman Podhoretz and Jean Kirkpatrick, were distinguished by their status as former leftists who had moved rightwards. Their leftism, however, was of the type, whether Trotskyite or Social Democrat, that was as viscerally anti-Soviet as that of any conservative.[30] Their defection from the Democratic Party in the 1970s was driven by the latter's declining enthusiasm for the vigorous prosecution of the Cold War and embrace of arms control and détente.[31] By 1980, most of this group had switched their support to the Republicans, the elision between them and the Republican right made relatively easy by their preference for 'rollback' over containment,[32] contempt for the UN, and inclination toward 'nationalist unilateralism'.[33]

As the Republican right grew in strength so the power of the moderate and liberal Republicans who had dominated the party in the 1950s and 1960s went into terminal decline. Their strength fell both absolutely, as the Democrats increasingly picked off their seats in the north-east, and relatively, as they were progressively outnumbered within their own party by conservative westerners and southerners. Having constituted more than half of all Republicans in some congresses in the 1960s, liberals and moderates were less than 10 per cent of the Republican congressional party by the 1990s.[34] The growing conservative dominance of the party was clearly manifested in its selection, and the subsequent election, of Ronald Reagan in 1980. It would not be fully achieved, however, until the election of George W. Bush, 'the first president fully to embody the Republican right's foreign policy views', in 2000.[35]

## THE UNITED STATES AND THE PERSIAN GULF REGIONAL SUBSYSTEM, 1945–79

The argument, thus far, is that American policy towards Iraq since 1979 is best explained by a theoretical framework which emphasises the primary objective of hegemonic maintenance, the particular dynamics of the Persian Gulf regional subsystem within which Iraq is located, and the rise of the Republican right resulting from changes within the US socio-economic system. What now needs to be addressed is the relationship of the Gulf regional subsystem to the broader operation of the WCS and the maintenance of American hegemony.

In September 1978 the United States Joint Chiefs of Staff identified three primary goals of American policy in the Middle East. The third was to assure the survival of Israel, but the first two were to assure continuous access to oil and to prevent a hostile power or combination of powers from establishing regional hegemony.[36] Two decades later, the United States Central Command's (CENTCOM) Strategic Plan stated that the number one American interest in the Gulf was 'maintaining the free flow of oil and assuring freedom of navigation and access to commercial markets'.[37] If the basic factor driving American foreign policy since 1945 has been the maintenance of the WCS and its own global hegemony, then the role of the Persian Gulf subsystem in that policy has been the provision of a reliable flow of oil.

Oil is a commodity unlike any other in its centrality to modern life and the functioning of the WCS. As a result, it is treated by states as a strategic commodity rather than one whose supply can be left purely to the operation of the market. Governments seek to ensure their ability to influence the international oil system in terms both of access to oil and of prices,[38] and no state is more preoccupied with this effort than the global hegemon. After 1945, just as it did in the wider WCS, the United States sought to secure and maintain the position of hegemonic state in the international oil system. It succeeded in this objective through a combination of deepened ties to the most important oil-producing state of Saudi Arabia, the control of production and marketing of Gulf oil by the major American oil companies, and American military predominance in the Middle East (albeit largely exercised through proxies such as Turkey, Israel, Iran and the UK).[39] Successive administrations maintained this hegemonic role not primarily in order to ensure America's own oil supplies (until the 1970s its imports from the region represented only a small fraction of its consumption), so much as those of the WCS as a whole:

> As a superpower and an economic giant possessing both a far-flung system of alliances and a host of trading partners whose economic well-being is critical for US exports, the United States has a vital interest in ensuring the unimpeded supply of petroleum not just to the United States but to world markets as well.[40]

America's leaders also understood that the consent of the other core states to American hegemony was sustained in part by Washington's ability to manage the oil system to their benefit, and by their awareness that they were dependent on the United States for the continued flow of oil.[41] American hegemony in the international oil system was thus a vital part of maintaining both the WCS and America's wider global hegemony.[42]

From 1945 until the 1970s, American hegemony in the international oil system remained fairly stable, thanks to the military predominance of the United States and its allies and the dominance of the oil system by the American oil majors. The main threats in this period came from the combination of Soviet expansionism and radical Arab nationalism, with the Soviets exploiting the latter to develop close relationships with Egypt, Iraq, Libya, Syria and South Yemen. The American position remained secure nevertheless, thanks to its relationships with the more militarily powerful non-Arab states of Israel, Turkey and Iran and the fact that the main oil-producing states remained firmly pro-Western.[43] In the 1970s, however, American hegemony was threatened by rising political and economic nationalism in the Third World, which led to the nationalisation of oil production in all of the main oil-producing states.[44] This development, along with the oil embargo and price rises imposed in 1973 by the Organization of Arab Petroleum Exporting Countries (OAPEC), led some observers to conclude that the era of American hegemony in the international oil system was over.[45]

In practice, American hegemony was 'refashioned rather than simply undermined'.[46] In response to nationalisation the United States simply changed partners, with Saudi Arabia now taking on the role of managing the oil supply in place of the major oil companies who had been ousted from their position of dominance. Despite its role in the 1973–4 embargo, from the mid-1970s onwards, Saudi Arabia re-inforced its ties to the United States and used its position as the swing producer in OPEC to moderate oil prices,[47] actions that reflected the Saudi regime's continued dependence on, and congruence of interests with, the United States. The enormous wealth generated by the rise in oil prices produced a huge surplus of 'petrodollars' most of which the Saudis invested in the United States, giving them a vested interest in the continued prosperity of the latter and the overall health of the global economy.[48] The key to continued American hegemony, never-theless, was its ability to provide security guarantees. The Saudi regime was rich but militarily weak and politically vulnerable. It had good reason to fear both internal opposition and the ambitions of more powerful Gulf neighbours like Iraq and Iran. That, and the fact that the Saudis knew that their security continued to depend on the willingness of the United States to protect them, was the key to continued American hegemony.[49]

While the Saudis could be depended on to manage OPEC on America's behalf, therefore, they were not capable of providing military security for the region. Before the 1970s the United States had been able to rely on a combination of its own overall global military predominance plus regional proxies to maintain security in the Middle East. In the Gulf the United Kingdom had performed the latter role. By the early 1970s, however, British forces had withdrawn from 'East of Suez', creating a potential power vacuum in the region. The Shah of Iran then offered his services as 'regional policeman' to Washington, an offer that was readily embraced by the Nixon administration in the face of a domestic reaction to the Vietnam War which made new American overseas commitments politically untenable. Nixon allowed the Shah to buy any conventional American weapons system he could afford and Iran's 'military strength ensured Western access to Gulf oil and served as a barrier to Soviet expansion'. Its influence within OPEC, moreover, further reinforced the pro-Western core of that organisation.[50]

The United States thus adapted to the changes of the 1970s by adopting the 'twin pillar' policy. The Saudi pillar kept the oil flowing at reasonable prices, whilst the Iranian pillar policed the Gulf and protected Saudi Arabia and the other pro-Western Gulf oil states against both Soviet influence and radical Arab regimes. The basis of American hegemony was transformed but maintained.

## IRAQ

One of the radical Arab states that Iran was supposed to contain was Iraq. Carved out of the defeated Ottoman empire after the First World War, Iraq was administered by Britain under a League of Nations mandate until 1932, when it formally gained independence. The resulting state was an artificial creation without any ethnic, religious or historical unity. Its borders were arbitrary, with the northern part of the country, populated mainly by Kurds, incorporated simply because of its known oil reserves and the determination of the British government to ensure that the British-owned Iraq Petroleum Company controlled the concession. The result was a country with an inbuilt Kurdish secessionist movement constituting some 15 to 20 per cent of its population.[51]

The rest of the population hardly constituted a meaningful Iraqi 'nation' either. The territory arbitrarily enclosed encompassed diverse peoples without a common identity, whose political and economic activities were localised. In religious terms, the country was divided between a Shia majority and a Sunni minority who 'seldom mixed, and as a rule did not intermarry. In mixed cities they lived in separate quarters and led their own separate lives.'[52] For the most part, however, immediate loyalties were to family and tribe rather than any higher or broader form of authority, whether secular or religious: 'the community is not one of citizens, but of family and clan members, fellow tribesmen or conspirators'.[53] The fragmented character of the Iraqi nation was further exacerbated by the actions of external powers. The Ottomans had exploited the Sunnis' minority status in order to create a loyal administrative class which dominated the political and military establishments, a practice that continued under British colonial rule. Iraq thus became a country in which a predominantly Sunni elite ruled over an oppressed Shia majority constituting some 60 per cent of the population.[54]

'Of all the major states in the Middle East', therefore, 'Iraq faced the most formidable obstacles to state formation'.[55] The creation of an artificial state fragmented along ethnic, religious and tribal lines meant that Iraqi politics became characterised by:

> the deployment of extreme levels of violence by the state to dominate and shape society; second, the use of state resources . . . to buy the loyalty of sections of society; third, the use of oil revenue by the state to increase its autonomy from society; and, finally, the exacerbation and re-creation by the state of communal and ethnic divisions as a strategy of rule.[56]

On top of this divided 'nation' the British installed a constitutional monarchy ruled by a non-Iraqi Hashemite dynasty. Most of the senior administrative and military elite was also made up of non-Iraqi Sunnis who had served with the new King, Faisal, in the First World War. The Iraqi parliament, meanwhile, was dominated by an agrarian elite of tribal leaders promoted by the British. The political structure was thus designed to present a facade of independence whilst ensuring indirect British control. The price of continued British influence, however, was a regime with an extremely narrow base of support and little or no legitimacy.[57] Rebellions against the regime began within months of its creation and would become a permanent feature of its existence. There were seven military coups between 1936 and 1941 alone.

The monarchy, and with it British influence, was ended by the 1958 'revolution' which brought to power a younger generation of Iraqi military officers, inspired by the Arab nationalism of Egyptian president Gamel Abdel Nasser.[58] The coup plotters soon fell out amongst themselves, however, and General Abd al-Karim Qasim established himself as Iraq's dictator, with the backing of the Iraqi Communist Party (ICP). Qasim survived until February 1963, when he in turn was overthrown by those he had fallen out with in 1958, namely Colonel Abd al-Salam Aref and the Baath Party.[59] The Baathists then formed a regime which lasted just nine months before its internal faction fighting created the opportunity for Aref to seize power for himself. His rule would prove short as well, however, dying in a helicopter crash in 1966 and being replaced by his brother, Abd al-Rahman Aref, who proved to be a weak and ineffective leader. He voluntarily went into exile in 1968 and the Baathists seized power again in what would prove to be the last change of regime until 2003.

The so-called 'July revolution' of 1968 brought to power a party with as few as 2,500 members and an exclusively Sunni leadership dominated by a handful of Tikritis, including both the new president, Brigadier Ahmad Hassan al-Bakr, and his second in command, Deputy Chairman of the Revolutionary Command Council (RCC), Saddam Hussein.[60] In the absence of any kind of popular base whatsoever, the only way for them to secure their rule was through the elimination of potential rivals, a task at which they proved significantly more adept than their predecessors. They quickly eliminated their military collaborators in the 1968 coup and then proceeded to purge the army as a whole of non-Baathist elements whilst putting in place a system of commissars to ensure loyalty. All rival politicians, starting with pro-Western factions and concluding with the more dangerous ICP, were ruthlessly suppressed.[61] To ensure control, a massive security apparatus was created which by 1978 employed 125,000 people, representing 20 per cent of all public sector employees.[62]

Alongside coercion went measures designed to secure more willing consent to Baathist rule. Baathist ideology, with its opaque blend of Arab nationalism and vague commitment to socialism, was one dimension of this effort.[63] More important, however, was the massive surge in oil revenues after 1973, which enabled the regime to buy a degree of acquiescence from the Iraqi population. The wealth generated was used to instigate a process of modernisation and secularisation, including free education and a massive campaign to eliminate illiteracy and sexual inequality in pay and work. Land was expropriated from the upper classes and given to peasants, while basic foodstuffs were subsidised and ambitious development schemes launched in housing and health.[64] Violence and oil revenue thus became the twin pillars upon which Baathist rule rested.[65]

The nature of the Iraqi state and Iraqi political culture are crucial to an understanding of Iraqi foreign policy. Whilst all states conduct foreign policy with an eye to legitimating the regime with domestic constituencies, the Sunni elite's minority status within an artificial state with no national identity made this need for legitimation all the more compelling in the case of Iraq.[66] The championing of Arab nationalism by all Iraqi regimes after 1958 was as much an attempt to subsume the divisions in Iraqi society within a larger pan-Arab identity as it was an expression of a genuine ideological commitment. Baathist support for the Palestinian cause should also be understood primarily as an effort to legitimise the regime through the backing of a cause that cut across sectarian lines,[67] whilst Saddam Hussein's response to the emergence of a radical Shiite regime in Iran in 1979 is incomprehensible without an understanding of the way that it impacted upon Iraq's own sectarian divide.

A second key characteristic of the Iraqi state with major impli-cations for its foreign relations is the arbitrary nature of its borders. Charles Tripp has argued that Iraq suffers from existential doubt as a result of its being no more than a bunch of artificial lines on a map created by imperialists. There is a sense of fear that what was so arbitrarily created can equally readily be eliminated, lending an extra dimension to border disputes.[68] Certainly it is the case that all of Iraq's major conflicts before 2003 stemmed from the drawing of its borders. The on-off conflict with the Kurds was rooted in their undesired incorporation into the Iraqi state. Repeated Iraqi threats (one fulfilled) to invade Kuwait derived from the fact that the British deliberately limited Iraqi access to the Persian Gulf when drawing its borders and in doing so entrenched conflict between Iraq and Kuwait.[69] Conflict between Iran and Iraq has been fuelled by the same problem and the disputed border along the Shatt al-Arab waterway.

A final aspect of the Iraqi state which has had a major impact on its foreign policy is the highly personalised nature of its rule, an aspect that reached its apotheosis under Saddam Hussein. The centrality of a single individual makes it difficult to determine what exactly is driving foreign policy at times, since the objectives of state and personal ambitions became blurred and interchangeable. Saddam's stated objectives certainly indicated grand ambitions. In January 1980 he declared that 'we want Iraq to possess a weight like that of China, a weight like the Soviet Union, a weight like the United States'.[70] At a minimum, he wanted to make Iraq the hegemon of the Gulf region, as indicated by his development of Iraqi military power, attempt to cow Iran, and eventual effort to push the United States out of the Gulf. His ultimate goal was to make Iraq the leading Arab state and in so doing secure for himself the position of leading Arab statesmen.

In addition to making the ambitions of the individual those of the state, personalised leadership also makes the flaws of that individual those of the state. In the case of Iraq this meant that, after 1979, its foreign policy was determined by a man of violence with little sense of limits who rose to power through conspiracy and the extermination of his enemies, and who saw the world through lenses shaped by that domestic experience. Saddam's understanding of international relations was that it was a ruthless power struggle in which any means was acceptable and the recourse to violence an everyday occurrence. When added to Iraq's weak sense of identity, need for legitimation, and artificial borders, this led to a 'tendency to embark on military adventurism beyond its borders'.[71] Unfortunately for Iraqis however, Saddam was also a man with little experience or knowledge of the outside world, and in particular, of the United States and the West, one result of which was that he repeatedly miscalculated the likely response to his military adventures.[72]

Immediately on seizing power, the Baathist regime found itself confronting a foreign policy problem deriving from the combination of its non-existent national identity and artificial borders, in the form of a full-scale Kurdish rebellion. The new government was forced to send fully two-thirds of its army into the Kurdish region to repress the rebellion, which they managed to do successfully. The Kurdish problem, however, was soon reinforced by a growing conflict with Iran. Iraqi–Iranian relations had been peaceful throughout most of the twentieth century, but the Shah's desire to make Iran the leading Gulf power and regional policeman altered this situation. Iraq was the only possible obstacle to the Shah's ambitions and he therefore decided to compel Baghdad to acknowledge Iran's regional predominance. On April 19 1969 he unilaterally abrogated a 1937 agreement which had placed most of the Shatt al-Arab inside Iraqi territory and required all ships sailing it to pay tolls to Iraq and have Iraqi pilots.[73] Simultaneously, the Shah began to provide assistance to the Kurds, which meant, given the US–Iranian relationship, that Washington was also supporting the Kurdish insurgency. Arms and other assistance flowed from Washington to Tehran and on to the Kurds, who soon returned to outright rebellion.[74]

In response, the Baathist regime moved to secure its own super-power backer, signing a Treaty of Friendship and Cooperation with the Soviet Union in 1972. By thus allying with Iran's principal security concern and securing a source of arms to counter those Iran was receiving from the United States, Baghdad sought to redress an unfavourable balance of power. Equally importantly, the treaty provided Iraq with cover for the nationalisation of the Iraqi oil industry, which duly followed in June of the same year.[75] When combined with the new regime's aggressively Arab nationalist rhetoric and rejectionist stance on the Arab–Israeli conflict, these developments placed Iraq firmly in the camp of radical, pro-Soviet Arab regimes. The Shah and the United States responded by increasing their support for the Kurds as the Cold War conflict fuelled the regional one in characteristic fashion.

The effectiveness of that support was clearly evident when a renewed Iraqi campaign against the Kurds rapidly ground to a halt in the face of the now well-armed Kurdish peshmerga fighters. Unable to defeat the Iranian–Kurdish alliance, the Baathists decided to make concessions to the former in order to secure victory over the latter. In the Algiers Agreement of 6 March 1975, Baghdad renounced its claim to the Iranian region of Khuzestan and accepted a demarcation of the Shatt al-Arab favouring Iran. In addition, the two sides pledged non-intervention in each other's internal affairs. Iraq thus gave up half of its only access to the Gulf in order to buy-off the Shah and free itself to deal with the Kurds, who now found their Iranian and American support suddenly cut off. In the absence of that support the Kurdish rebellion was swiftly crushed by Iraqi forces.[76]

Humiliated by the Algiers Agreement, and with its radical foreign policy having gained it little but enemies, Iraq turned in a more pragmatic direction in the second half of the 1970s. Arab nationalist rhetoric was toned down and aggression towards the pro-Western Gulf states replaced by diplomatic engagement. A number of agreements were signed with the Saudis, diplomatic relations were established with Oman, and support for the Soviet-backed regime in South Yemen was ended. Iraq also abandoned its support for Palestinian armed resistance in favour of the 'phased strategy', recently adopted by the Palestinian Liberation Organization (PLO), which called for the establishment of a state in the West Bank and Gaza as a step towards the ultimate liberation of Palestine. In March 1978 Iraq restored diplomatic relations with Egypt despite the latter's moves toward peace with Israel.

Growing Iraqi engagement with the West and its allies was also fuelled by a reassessment of its relationship with the USSR. The Iraqi alliance with Moscow had only ever been opportunistic, and by the late 1970s its continued utility was increasingly questionable. Oil nationalisation had been successfully achieved and the Kurds had been crushed, whilst Soviet goods were of poor quality compared to the Western ones that Iraq could now afford to buy. Moreover, the Baathists were fearful of possible subversion, a fear fuelled by the Soviet-backed coup in Afghanistan in April 1978, which led the Iraqis to repress the ICP, a move that significantly worsened relations between Moscow and Baghdad. Iraq therefore began to look to reduce its dependence on Moscow and to expand its relations with the West, and by 1981 83 per cent of Iraqi civilian imports came from outside the Soviet bloc whilst the Soviet share of Iraq's military purchases fell from 95 per cent in 1972 to 63 per cent in 1980.[77]

By the end of the 1970s, therefore, there were indications that Iraq was moving away from its former status as a radical, pro-Soviet Arab state towards a more 'moderate' and 'pragmatic' position.

## THE UNITED STATES AND IRAQ SINCE 1979

Before 1979, Iraq did not play a central role in American Gulf policy. In the 1950s it had played a limited role as one of the conservative pro-Western states that the United States tried to form into an anti-Soviet barrier in the shape of the Baghdad Pact. After the 1958 revolution, Iraq became one of the radical nationalist regimes to be contained, but not one which caused Washington any great alarm. By and large it existed on the margins of America's foreign policy vision. After 1979, however, Iraq moved centre stage. In that year the Iranian revolution undermined the twin pillar strategy on which the United States had come to rely to maintain its hegemonic position in the Gulf, transforming Iran from America's regional proxy and protector of the Gulf oil states into the primary threat to American hegemony. That development forced the Carter and Reagan administrations to seek a new strategy for the preservation of American hegemony through the containment of Iran and the maintenance of a regional balance of power. After Saddam Hussein sought to exploit the turmoil created by the Iranian revolution to attack Iran, only to find, not for the last time, his plans going awry, the survival of the Iraqi regime became an urgent American priority. These developments are discussed in the next chapter.

Chapter 2 analyses the period between 1984 and 1989. After initial bureaucratic struggles between 'pro-Iraqi' and 'pro-Iranian' factions within the Reagan administration were resolved in favour of the former, American policy evolved from an effort to maintain a balance of power between Iran and Iraq into an effort to co-opt Iraq into an informal alliance. That policy reached its apotheosis under the first Bush administration but was dramatically halted by Saddam Hussein's decision to invade Kuwait. By thus making Iraq an imminent threat to America's Gulf allies and regional hegemony, however, Saddam ensured American military intervention and his decisive defeat, as described in Chapter 3.

The 1991 Gulf War seemingly cemented American regional and global hegemony by crushing the Iraqi military threat and demonstrating both the reliance of the Gulf oil producers on American security guarantees and the dependence of the core states on Washington's ability to secure their oil lifelines from the Gulf. However, the decision not to eliminate Saddam Hussein, in part because of continued American fears of Iran, left the incoming Clinton administration facing two hostile states in the Gulf. The administration accordingly adopted a policy of 'dual containment'. The fourth chapter demonstrates that during the 1990s American hegemony in the Gulf nevertheless became increasingly unstable. Saddam Hussein remained in power and the regime of sanctions, weapons inspections and air strikes which had been put in place to contain Iraq and to eliminate its weapons of mass destruction (WMD) steadily weakened as international support for it crumbled. Meanwhile, the punitive effect of sanctions on Iraqi civilians, as well as the failure to secure an equitable solution to the Palestinian problem, fuelled anti-American sentiment in the Arab world, a resentment also driven by Washington's status as the ally and protector not of Arab nations so much as of autocratic, corrupt and self-serving Arab regimes. A significant cause of the vulnerability of American hegemony was thus due to its ongoing one-dimensionality. The consensual dimension of American hegemony which had resulted from economic integration and the development of political pluralism in other parts of the globe did not apply in the Gulf, which remained relatively autonomous from the WCS and resistant to the spread of American culture and values.

With America's regional hegemony looking increasingly unstable, and Saddam Hussein's survival a central source of that instability, the year 2000 brought a crucial change at the level of the American political system. With the election of George W. Bush a new conservative coalition, much less willing to be constrained in its use of American power and openly advocating the unilateral use of military force to assert American hegemony, came to office. The events of 11 September 2001 subsequently created an opportunity to reassert American hegemony in the Persian Gulf. By forcibly removing Saddam Hussein and seeking to create a new democratic Iraq aligned with the United States, the second Bush administration hoped to eliminate an immediate obstacle to the preservation of American regional hegemony and to resolve America's wider regional problems with one blow. Whilst Saddam was seen as the principal threat to American hegemony, however, the George W. Bush administration also saw regime change in Iraq as an opportunity to simultaneously address the wider range of obstacles to continued American hegemony. The elimination of Saddam would also serve to intimidate and contain Iran, contribute to an Israeli–Palestinian peace agreement and allow the United States to draw down its military presence in the region. Most importantly of all, the successful creation of a market-democracy in Iraq was to serve as a catalyst for the spread of democracy and free markets in the wider region. That, in turn, would lay the basis for the deeper integration of the Middle East into the WCS and the creation of the conditions in which American regional hegemony could be rooted in consensus rather than coercion. This ambitious effort to reconstruct American hegemony is discussed in Chapter 5.

The final chapter discusses how and why those ambitions failed. Taking no account of the absence of the preconditions for democracy in Iraq, and utterly failing to prepare for the post-war situation, the American invasion in 2003 precipitated the collapse of the Iraqi state and the descent of the country into sectarian warfare. After three years of failing American policies, a change of course in 2007–8 at last produced an improvement in security, but Iraq remained a state perched on the brink of a return to violence and sectarian warfare. The conclusion discusses the implications of these developments for the future of American hegemony.

American policy towards Iraq since 1979 has been driven, ultimately, by the need to maintain a dominant position in the international oil system, a position which allows it to guarantee a reliable flow of oil to the WCS and thus helps secure the consent to its hegemony of the other core powers. Maintenance of the American position in the international oil system in turn requires the United States to maintain a hegemonic position in the Persian Gulf and it is that which has been the fundamental consideration underpinning American policy toward Iraq. The American effort to maintain its position as the dominant power in the Gulf has in turn been determined by the two other levels of structure which constrain the American state. The dynamic of the regional subsystem, in the shape of the Iranian revolution, the Iran–Iraq War, the Iraqi invasion of Kuwait in 1990, the Arab–Israeli conflict and the nature of Arab societies and states, including their limited integration into the WCS, have all shaped the precise course of American policy. Finally, economic, social and political change within the United States itself, and the nature of its dominant ruling coalition, have produced different approaches to dealing with the problem of how to maintain hegemony. Above all, the emergence of a new, dominant, conservative coalition and its seizure of power in 2000 is a critical factor in explaining the decision to pursue regime change in Iraq.

## NOTES

1. Lind, 'The weird men behind George Bush's war'.
2. Halper and Clarke, *American Alone*, is the most comprehensive version of this argument.
3. Cumings, *Origins of the Korean War*, vol. II, pp. 4–22.
4. For a more detailed discussion, see Hurst, *Cold War US Foreign Policy*, pp. 124–35. On structure and agency, see Thompson, 'The theory of structuration'.
5. The individual most closely associated with the development of WST is Immanuel Wallerstein (*The Capitalist World Economy*), though Wallerstein's version is significantly more determinist than that employed here and gives no role to the domestic socio-economic level of explanation.
6. R. Cox, 'Social forces, states and world orders'; McCormick, 'Every system needs a center sometimes'.

7. Hinnebusch, *International Politics of the Middle East*, p. 216.
8. R. Cox, 'Social forces, states and world orders'.
9. McCormick, *America's Half Century*.
10. For more extensive discussions, see Bromley, *Rethinking Middle East Politics*; Hinnebusch, *International Politics of the Middle East*, pp. 3–21.
11. Henry, 'The clash of globalisations in the Middle East'; Mohdavy, 'Patterns and problems of economic development'.
12. Halliday, *Middle East in International Relations*, pp. 98–9.
13. The Republican Party was divided between a free-trade, multilateralist, Atlanticist wing rooted in internationally oriented sectors of business and banking in the north-east of the United States, which had significant interests in common with the New Deal internationalists and the economically protectionist, expansionist, unilateralist western wing. See Caridi, *The Korean War*; Himmelstein, *To the Right*; Miles, *Odyssey of the American Right*.
14. Cumings, *Origins of the Korean War*, pp. 4–22; see also Schurmann, *Logic of World Power*, pp. 48–65.
15. J. Burnham, *Containment or Liberation?*, pp. 36–7, 69–70, 138. Burnham was arguably the most important intellectual representative of the 'new nationalism' of the Republican right when it came to foreign policy.
16. McGirr, *Suburban Warriors*, p. 173.
17. Ikenberry, 'Power and liberal order'.
18. 'The magazine's credenda', *National Review*, 19 November 1955, p. 6.
19. J. Burnham, *The War We Are In*, pp. 219, 153, 170.
20. Critchlow, *The Conservative Ascendancy*.
21. Carmines and Stimson, *Issue Evolution*; Shafer and Johnston, *The End of Southern Exceptionalism*.
22. Ansell, 'Business mobilization and the New Right'; Ferguson and Rogers, 'The Reagan victory', pp. 17–18.
23. Judis, 'War resisters', p. 11.
24. Markusen *et al.*, *The Rise of the Gunbelt*, pp. 11, 231.
25. Fischer, *Albion's Seed*, p. 843; Fry, *Dixie Looks Abroad*; Miles, *Odyssey*, p. 265.
26. Nash, *The American West Transformed*.
27. Trubowitz, *Defining the National Interest*.
28. Bruce, *The Rise and Fall of the New Christian Right*; Wilcox, *Onward Christian Soldiers?*
29. S. Diamond, *Roads to Dominion*, pp. 95–101; Mead, 'God's country'.
30. Dorrien, *The Neoconservative Mind*, p. 9.
31. Podhoretz, *The Present Danger*.
32. Ibid. pp. 17–24.
33. Kristol, 'Foreign policy in an age of ideology'.

34. Fleisher and Bond, 'Congress and the President in a partisan era'. See also Rae, *The Decline and Fall of the Liberal Republicans*.
35. Cumings, 'Is America an Imperial power?', p. 360.
36. Palmer, *Guardians of the Gulf*, pp. 102–3.
37. US CENTCOM, *Strategic Plan, 1995–1997*, p. 5.
38. Bromley, *American Hegemony*, p. 53; Wilson, 'World politics and international energy markets', p. 143.
39. Bromley, *American Hegemony*, pp. 89–108; Randall, *United States Foreign Oil Policy*; Shaffer, *The United States and the Control of World Oil*; Vitalis, 'Black gold'; Yergin, *The Prize*, pp. 409–30.
40. Barnes and Myers Jaffe, 'The Persian Gulf and the geopolitics of oil', p. 145.
41. Ibid. p. 145; Bromley, *American Hegemony*; Keohane, *After Hegemony*, pp. 140–1; Painter, 'Explaining US relations', p. 532.
42. Bromley, *American Hegemony*, p. 247.
43. Halliday, *Middle East in International Relations*, p. 99; Hinnebusch, *International Politics of the Middle East*, pp. 24–34.
44. Yergin, *The Prize*, pp. 577–612.
45. Pelletiere, *Iraq and the International Oil System*, pp. 141–2; Shaffer, *The United States and the Control of World Oil*, pp. 175–6.
46. Bromley, *American Hegemony*, p. 243.
47. The fact that the Saudis had the largest oil reserves of any oil producer, large financial reserves and significant spare production capacity gave them an ability to both increase and decrease production possessed by no other OPEC member. This in turn allowed them to discipline OPEC and force the other members into line. Alnasrawi, *Arab Nationalism*, pp. 109–13; Mitchell *et al.*, *New Geopolitics of Energy*, pp. 45–7; Odell, *Oil and World Power*, p. 100.
48. Bronson, *Thicker than Oil*, pp. 126–7; Vasiliev, *History of Saudi Arabia*, pp. 398–404.
49. Halliday, *Middle East in International Relations*, pp. 274–5; Hinnebusch, *International Politics of the Middle East*, pp. 41–2.
50. Vance, *Hard Choices*, p. 314.
51. The best discussion of this earlier period is in Batatu, *The Old Social Classes*.
52. Batutu, *The Old Social Classes*, p. 17.
53. Tripp, *History of Iraq*, p. 2.
54. Marr, *Modern History of Iraq*, pp. 9, 36–7.
55. Bromley, *Rethinking Middle East Politics*, p. 135.
56. Dodge, *Inventing Iraq*, pp. 169–70.
57. Marr, *Modern History of Iraq*, pp. 37–9.
58. Bromley, *Rethinking Middle East Politics*, p. 137.

59. This coup was reportedly aided by the CIA because of Qasim's relationship with the ICP. Mufti, *Sovereign Creations*, pp. 144–6.
60. Karsh and Rautsi, *Saddam Hussein*, pp. 37–8; Marr, *Modern History of Iraq*, p. 212.
61. Karsh and Rautsi, *Saddam Hussein*, pp. 37–54; Marr, *Modern History of Iraq*, pp. 206–18.
62. Farouk-Sluglett, '"Socialist" Iraq'.
63. Bromley, *Rethinking Middle East Politics*, pp. 139–40; Farouk-Sluglett and Slugglet, 'Iraqi Ba'thism'.
64. Anderson and Stansfield, *Future of Iraq*, pp. 54–8; Karsh and Rautsi, *Saddam Hussein*, pp. 90–1.
65. Bromley, *Rethinking Middle East Politics*, pp. 138–9.
66. Halliday, *The Middle East in International Relations*, p. 61.
67. Tripp, 'Foreign policy of Iraq', pp. 174–5.
68. Ibid. p. 170.
69. Hinnebusch, *International Politics of the Middle East*, p. 154.
70. Benigo, *Saddam's Word*, p. 146.
71. Dodge, *Inventing Iraq*, p. 170.
72. Hinnebusch, *International Politics of the Middle East*, pp. 112, 119; Tripp, 'Foreign policy of Iraq', pp. 172, 181–2.
73. Karsh and Rautsi, *Saddam Hussein*, p. 68.
74. Sluglett, 'The Kurds', pp. 195–7.
75. Marr, *Modern History of Iraq*, p. 225.
76. Karsh and Rautsi, *Saddam Hussein*, pp. 82–4.
77. Marr, *Modern History of Iraq*, p. 238; Coughlin, *Saddam*, p. 126.

## Chapter 1

# TOWARDS A NEW RELATIONSHIP, 1979–1984

### THE IMPORTANCE OF 1979

'1979 constitutes a major watershed, if not *the* major watershed, in modern Middle East history.'[1] The events of that year fundamentally transformed the Middle East and undercut the 'twin pillar' strategy on which US regional hegemony had rested since the early 1970s. Since 1979 the fundamental objective of American policy toward the Persian Gulf has been to re-establish a stable hegemonic position. The US relationship with Iraq has been at the heart of that effort.

Not everything that happened in 1979 was a disaster for the United States. The signing of a peace treaty between Israel and Egypt represented a significant gain. By removing Egyptian armed forces from the potential anti-Israeli military balance, the Treaty effectively precluded a successful Arab military attack on Israel and thus strengthened the strategic position of the United States and its ally in that particular arena of Middle-Eastern conflict.[2] It also secured the role of the United States as the external honest broker in the peace process, to the exclusion of the Soviet Union. There was, nevertheless, a price to be paid for this gain. The agreement led to the expulsion of Egypt from the Arab League with the result that the one major Arab state with which America had good relations was no longer a powerful influence in the Arab world. This meant that there was an opening for a new leader of that world, an opportunity that Saddam Hussein was keen to exploit.

That he was in a position to do so was due to the fact that, on 16 July 1979, he formally assumed the presidency of Iraq after forcing Ahmad Hassan al-Bakr into retirement. Although he had been the dominant figure in the Iraqi leadership for several years, Saddam now had total control. On assuming the leadership he proceeded further to consolidate his position with a violent and bloody purge of the Baath Party. In total, some sixty-six alleged plotters against his leadership were denounced, including five members of the Revolutionary Command Council. Twenty-two were executed.[3] That done, Saddam moved to improve Iraq's regional position, and it was at his instigation that the summit at which Egypt was expelled from the Arab League met in Baghdad. Simultaneously, he sought to bolster Iraq's position by moving to restore cordial relations with the PLO, the Gulf states and Jordan. On 8 February 1980 Saddam issued an eight-point Pan-Arab Charter which, amongst other things, condemned the superpower presence in the Middle East and called for the rejection of any foreign presence on Arab soil. In so doing he sought further to reassert Iraq's Arab nationalist credentials and claims to Arab leadership.

By far the most significant development of 1979, however, was the Iranian revolution. The upheaval, which began in 1978, and led to the overthrow of the Shah and the installation of a theocratic regime led by Ayatollah Ruhollah Khomeini in February 1979, was primarily a product of widespread discontent resulting from the Shah's domestic policies. His pursuit of modernisation at any cost had caused massive economic and social dislocation, and the subsequent unrest had been ruthlessly repressed by his security forces. There was also, however, an important foreign policy dimension to the revolution which had major implications for the United States. The United States had engineered a coup in 1953 to overthrow the nationalist government of Prime Minister Mohammed Mossadeq and imposed the Shah on the Iranian people. The latter had then reciprocated by denationalising Iranian oil and giving American companies a 40 per cent share in its production. The Shah was thus widely viewed as an American proxy and, under those circumstances, any revolution was bound to be nationalist and aggressively anti-American.[4]

The Iranian revolution therefore undermined US strategy in the Gulf in one fell swoop. The fall of the Shah transformed the most powerful state in the region from America's principal ally into its implacable enemy. The revolutionary regime led by Khomeini demonised the United States and preached the duty of Muslims to fight imperialism and to end foreign control of Middle-Eastern oil. In practical terms this meant challenging and seeking to undermine America's regional client states through the mobilisation of the Arab masses. Khomeini denied the legitimacy of the Gulf regimes and denounced their 'American Islam'. He sought to exploit the same grievances that had mobilised pan-Arabism amongst the Arab masses – Israel, imperialism, client regimes and corruption – to give Iran's revolutionary ideology a pan-Muslim appeal; with significant success, stimulating opposition movements in virtually every Arab country.[5]

The threat thus posed to America's Gulf allies by Khomeini's revolution was significant. These were autocratic Sunni regimes with limited popular legitimacy and, in many cases, large, oppressed Shia populations (Iran was overwhelmingly Shiite, as well as non-Arab, introducing a sectarian element into the conflict between Iran and the oil states of the Gulf). There were Shiite protests and demonstrations inspired by Iranian revolutionary broadcasts in Kuwait in September and November 1979, in Saudi Arabia in February 1980 and in Bahrain in April 1980. A CIA report evaluating the situation warned that the survival of the Saudi regime 'could not be assured beyond the next two years'.[6]

Just as the administration of President Jimmy Carter was doubtless reflecting that things could get no worse, in December 1979 the Soviet Union invaded Afghanistan. This action, whilst essentially defensive in orientation, was nevertheless a shock. It was the first time the USSR had intervened militarily outside its Eastern European sphere of influence since 1948, and it put Soviet forces closer to the Persian Gulf than they had been since the Second World War. Moreover, it placed them on the borders of a politically unstable Iran where the pro-Communist Tudeh party remained a significant force. The invasion thus generated fears amongst some American observers of the growth of Soviet influence in Iran.[7]

Overall, the events of 1979 posed a clear threat to the US position in the Persian Gulf and the international oil system and thus to its overall global hegemony. The new Iranian regime threatened to foment a region-wide Islamic revolution which would overthrow America's allies in Saudi Arabia and drive American influence from the Gulf. The Soviet invasion of Afghanistan simply made an already bad situation worse by raising the possibility of increased Soviet influence in Iran and the wider region.

## THE AMERICAN RESPONSE

The Carter administration reacted to the events of 1979 with a public declaration of its intention to maintain America's regional hegemony. In his 1980 State of the Union address, Carter asserted that 'the denial of these oil supplies – to us or to others – would threaten our security and provoke an economic crisis greater than that of the Great Depression'. Accordingly, he declared that an

> attempt by any outside force to gain control of the Persian Gulf region will be regarded as an assault on the vital interests of the United States of America and such an assault will be repelled by any means necessary, including military force.[8]

This statement of intent became known as the 'Carter Doctrine', the concrete manifestation of which was the Rapid Deployment Joint Task Force (RDJTF, usually abbreviated to RDF). Designed to give the United States the capability to project military force into the Gulf region, the creation of the RDF was announced shortly after Carter's address.

The implication of the Carter Doctrine and the RDF was that the USA was going to play a more direct role in Gulf security than previously. The proxies who had previously shouldered the security burden in the Gulf, first Britain and then the Shah's Iran, had fallen by the wayside. Now there was no obvious candidate for the role. Saudi Arabia did not have the military capability or the will and nor did the smaller oil monarchies. The two regional Arab states with the potential to contain Iran – Iraq and Syria – were Soviet allies with which America had no diplomatic relations and both of whom were on the administration's list of state sponsors of terrorism. This lack of an effective regional proxy would draw the United States into ever more direct military intervention in the region over the next quarter of a century.

Carter's State of the Union address was made in the immediate aftermath of the Soviet invasion of Afghanistan, and the reference to 'outside force' implied that it was, in fact, the USSR which was its principal target. Whilst concerns about Soviet advances in the region were real, however, the central development driving American policy was the Iranian revolution and its potential ramifications. All the major policy decisions which led to the Carter Doctrine and the RDF were taken before the Soviet invasion of Afghanistan. The idea for the RDF had actually been approved by Carter in 1977 in Presidential Directive 18, though it had languished ever since. Planning was accelerated in response to the Iranian revolution and by the time the Soviet invasion occurred was already in an advanced state, with force assignments decided and headquarters identified.[9] A more direct US military role in the Persian Gulf would also require regional bases, and the Carter administration began seeking access rights in 1979, leading to the announcement in February 1980 of agreements for access to the air and naval bases at Berbera in Somalia, the port at Mombassa in Kenya and the air base at Marisa and the port at Muscat in Oman.[10]

For all Carter's rhetoric, the administration's actions were more symbolic than substantive.[11] The RDF lacked adequate forces, the strategic lift capability to transport them to the Gulf and, despite the February 1980 agreements, access to bases in the Gulf itself.[12] The latter problem, in particular, highlighted a fundamental dilemma confronting the administration. Without an obvious regional proxy, the Carter administration saw little choice but to increase the direct American role in Gulf security. However, whilst America's friends in the region continued to seek American security guarantees, they also found themselves caught between their fear of the threat from Iran and a concern that closer and more visible ties to the United States would only exacerbate their security problems by fuelling the allegation that they were imperialist lackeys. The tenuous legitimacy of America's autocratic allies thus continued to undermine its regional strategy. In addition, many regional states did not want to tie themselves too closely to the United States because they feared its commitments lacked credibility given its inability to save the Shah.[13] None of the Gulf states responded positively to American requests for new basing rights.

The Carter administration thus faced a conundrum. On the one hand, it needed to deter any possible expansion of Soviet influence and to bolster the position of its regional allies against Iranian subversion. On the other, an overt increase in the American military presence was likely to fuel anti-American radicalism in the Arab world, destabilise America's allies, and rebound to the advantage of both the USSR and Iran.[14] Given those dangers, and the fact that America's ability to project military power in the Gulf was, in any event, extremely limited, and would remain so for some time, other ways of containing Iranian and Soviet influence needed to be found.

It was in this context that Iraq began to assume a new place in American strategic thinking. Shortly after the fall of the Shah, National Security Adviser Zbigniew Brzezinski began floating the idea that the US should reconsider its 'nonrelationship' with Iraq, an idea that found echoes in other parts of the administration.[15] There was also significant opposition, however. A 1979 Department of Defense (DOD) study led by Paul Wolfowitz concluded that Iraq represented a threat to Kuwait and Saudi Arabia and thus to US oil interests. It argued that it was only a matter of time before Iraq attacked Kuwait.[16] When Howard Teicher made a similar argument in a paper for Secretary of Defense Harold Brown, however, Brown sent it back with the comment 'I disagree. Iraq has changed. It has moderated its behaviour.'[17]

The Brown–Brzezinski argument was given added weight by the clear evidence of a breakdown in the Iraqi–Soviet relationship. From Baghdad's point of view, the alliance had largely served its purpose by the late 1970s, having provided cover for oil nationalisation and the arms to enable Iraq to deal with the Kurds. Iraq accordingly began to pursue a more independent line, threatening to cut off diplomatic relations if Moscow continued to support Ethiopia in its conflict with its Eritrean rebels, vigorously condemning the Soviet invasion of Afghanistan and repressing the Iraqi Communist Party despite strong Soviet protests.[18] Thus encouraged, in April 1980 Brzezinski told an interviewer that he saw no fundamental clash of interests between the United States and Iraq. Both sought a secure Persian Gulf and the administration did not wish to continue the anomalous state of having no diplomatic relations with Baghdad.[19] Further evidence of a shift in US policy was seen when the Department of Commerce approved the sale of turbines for Italian frigates destined for the Iraqi navy. In July 1980, Carter approved the sale of five Boeing airliners to Iraq.[20]

## THE IRAN–IRAQ WAR BEGINS

Any further rapprochement was put on hold, along with the sales of turbines and airliners, when, on 22 September 1980, the Iraqi air force struck targets inside Iran and, the following day, Iraqi ground forces invaded Iran.[21] Saddam's reasons for attacking Iran have been hotly debated, with some seeing his motives as essentially defensive[22] and others regarding the invasion as proof of his overweening ambition to make Iraq the hegemonic power in the Gulf.[23] In reality, the invasion is best understood as the result of a combination of both sets of motives.

The fall of the Shah was as great a disaster for Saddam as it was for the United States. Having paid a high price for peace with Iran in 1975, the Baathist regime did all that it could to keep him in power, up to and including expelling Khomeini from his place of exile in Iraq at the Shah's request. Only when it became clear that the Shah's overthrow was a foregone conclusion did Iraq shift course and seek to conciliate the new Iranian regime, sending 'good wishes' and expressing desires for 'close ties of fruitful cooperation'.[24] Khomeini, however, was not so easily appeased, condemning the 'heretic' Baathist regime whose secular ideology he regarded as anathema and which, moreover, represented the principal obstacle to his ambition to spread the Iranian revolution to the rest of the region. He now called on Iraqi Shiites to overthrow Saddam.[25] The *al-Dawa al-Islamiyyah* (Dawa) party, founded in the 1960s and fuelled by increasing Baathist repression of the Shiite clerical establishment during the 1970s, responded to Khomeini's appeal. February 1979 saw widespread demonstrations in support of Khomeini amongst the Iraqi Shia and in June riots erupted in Karbala and Najaf when Baghdad refused to allow Ayatollah Muhammad Baqir al-Sadr to lead a delegation to Tehran to congratulate Khomeini. Martial law was imposed and membership of Dawa made punishable by death. Suspected members were rounded up and al-Sadr, its spiritual leader, placed under house arrest.[26]

When al-Sadr was transferred to Baghdad in order better to isolate him from his followers, further demonstrations broke out in the south and Baghdad, only to be brutally repressed by the Iraqi security forces with thousands of arrests. Despite the brutality of the regime's response, in April 1980 Dawa made an unsuccessful attempt on the life of Iraqi Deputy Prime Minister Tariq Aziz. Saddam now had al-Sadr and hundreds of other prisoners executed whilst expelling 100,000 Iraqi Shiites into exile in Iran. Undeterred, on 9 June 1980 Khomeini called on Iraqis to 'wake up and topple this corrupt regime in your Islamic country before it is too late'.[27]

In part, therefore, Saddam's motivation for attacking Iran was indeed defensive. In the face of a genuine challenge to his regime, he sought to deliver a blow that would compel Iran to desist in its efforts to overthrow him and cow his domestic opponents.[28] As Defence Minister Adnan Khayrallah explained it, 'we decided to lay our hands on points vital to Iran's interests inside Iranian territory to deter Iran from striking our national sovereignty'.[29] But though Saddam's decision to attack Iran was a result of Iranian provocation, this did not mean that he did not see opportunities beyond that of simply eliminating the Iranian threat to his regime. If Iran was now directly threatening Iraq, it was also a country in revolutionary turmoil. The Iranian military was both disorganised and in poor morale. Many of its officers had been killed or exiled. Iraq, for its part, had spent the 1970s using the massive increase in its oil revenue to build up its armed forces, which were now superior in virtually every measurable way to those of Iran.[30] The international situation also appeared to be favourable, with the fact that Iran was at loggerheads with the United States encouraging Saddam to believe that there would be no retaliation from that quarter.

Saddam thus undoubtedly saw an opportunity to inflict a decisive military defeat on Iran and in so doing achieve a number of objectives beyond eliminating the immediate threat to his regime. In the first place, he would reverse the humiliating Algiers agreement. Iraqi First Deputy Prime Minister Taha Yasin Ramadan declared that Iraq's war aim was to 'force Iran to recognize our rights and respect them' and that this meant acknowledging full Iraqi sovereignty over the Shatt al-Arab and a redefinition of the Iran–Iraq border.[31] Moreover, by defeating Iran, Saddam would establish Iraq as the dominant power in the Persian Gulf and the champion of the Arab world against Iranian subversion.[32] At the outer reaches of his expectations, Saddam may have hoped that his invasion would lead to the overthrow of the new Iranian regime and its replacement by one more quiescent. A war forced on Iraq by Iranian subversion was thus also an opportunity to assert Iraq's claim to regional power.

## THE AMERICAN RESPONSE TO THE IRAN–IRAQ WAR

A decisive victory for either side in the Iran–Iraq War looked undesirable from the American point of view. An Iranian victory would clearly be a disaster, with nothing then standing between it and the militarily weak Gulf monarchies. An Iraqi victory was less obviously threatening but, whilst the Iraqi regime had shown sufficient signs of foreign policy 'moderation' to encourage thoughts of a US–Iraqi rapprochement, it remained allied to Moscow. Potential Iraqi dominance of the Persian Gulf could not, therefore, be regarded with equanimity. The primary American objective therefore became to ensure that neither side was able to secure a decisive victory and thus to dominate the Gulf. Other important objectives were to ensure that the Soviets were not able to exploit the conflict to secure a predominant influence in either country, to protect the oil monarchies, and to ensure that Gulf oil kept flowing.[33]

The American position was somewhat eased by the fact that the USSR faced a very similar set of problems to its own. Whilst it was formally allied to Iraq, that relationship was troubled and Saddam was proving to be wholly his own man in foreign and domestic affairs. In response, the Soviets had taken advantage of the Iranian revolution to make overtures to Tehran. The outbreak of war thus posed a dilemma for Moscow. If it sent aid to its established ally it risked losing the opportunity to extend its influence with Iran. But if it decided to help Iran in order to woo the new regime there, it risked the loss of an established ally without any guarantee of gaining a new one. Formal neutrality was thus the default option for the USSR, though it also continued to try and woo Tehran, apparently informing it of the impending Iraqi attack via the Tudeh Party.[34] When the Carter administration broached the issue with Moscow, they found ready agreement to their proposal of declaring neutrality and imposing an arms embargo on both sides.[35]

Having thus secured tacit Soviet agreement to its strategy of maintaining the existing balance of power in the Gulf, the Carter administration's next goal was to reassure its regional allies of the continued credibility of its security guarantees. The Gulf oil monarchies primary concern was to prevent an Iranian victory at all costs, and they therefore began to provide assistance to Iraq. Saudi Arabia allowed Iraqi aircraft access to its airspace and even to its airfields. In so doing, however, they made themselves potential targets for Iranian attack. They therefore abandoned their earlier caution about being seen as too close to the United States and requested American military assistance. The Carter administration responded by beginning to move American forces into the Gulf, including deployment of a squadron of airborne warning and control planes (AWACs) to Saudi Arabia, and increasing naval deployments in the Indian Ocean.[36]

## REAGAN'S VICTORY

Within less than two months of the Iraqi invasion of Iran, Jimmy Carter lost the American presidential election to Ronald Reagan, with both the Iranian revolution and the Soviet invasion of Afghanistan having contributed to the sense of American powerlessness which led voters to reject him.

The 1980 election was the first major harbinger of the conservative ascendancy that would culminate in the election of George W. Bush twenty years later, putting an openly conservative Republican in the White House for the first time since Herbert Hoover. It also saw the emergence of the southern and western 'sunbelt' coalition that would come to underpin conservative dominance; the defeat of the party's eastern wing in the shape of John Anderson and George H. W. Bush; the mobilisation of white evangelicals as a bloc for the first time; and the transfer of the support of large sections of internationally oriented capital from the Democrats to the Republicans.[37] On the basis of the National Election Survey conducted by the University of Michigan, on seven of nine key issues the voters wanted a policy more conservative than the status quo.[38]

Reagan won by taking from the New Deal coalition white southerners and the financial backing of much internationally oriented big business, with the former brought into the Republican coalition by growing affluence and the Democrats support for civil rights and the latter by fears of declining global competitiveness.[39] But there was also a significant foreign policy dimension to the shift. Many ordinary Americans were fearful and angry at the perceived decline of American global power, as manifested by defeat in Vietnam, the 1973–4 oil embargo, a succession of Third World revolutions, cul-minating in that in Iran, and the Soviet invasion of Afghanistan. Much of the multinational business sector was equally concerned that such developments threatened its investment in the Third World.[40] Developments in the Persian Gulf, in particular, were critical in turning key sectors of business towards support for a defence build-up and a more aggressive foreign policy. Corporate America had massive investments in Iran, and stood to make major losses as a result.[41] When the Iranian revolution was soon followed by the shock of the Soviet invasion of Afghanistan, the demand for a more assertive American posture grew even stronger.

The concrete manifestation of this rising support for a more assertive, conservative foreign policy was the rise to public prominence of the Committee on the Present Danger (CPD). Formed in 1977 as a vehicle to attack the Carter administration's liberal 'world order' policies, the CPD brought together the right of the Republican Party with first generation neoconservatives. According to the CPD, under Carter, the United States had been unilaterally disarming whilst the Soviets continued to seek military superiority. Combined with incompetent economic policies at home and abroad, this had undermined America's global standing and facilitated the advance of the USSR and its radical allies around the world. The only way to reverse this trend was through a sustained rebuilding of American military power and aggressive confrontation of the USSR and other radical regimes which threatened American interests.[42]

The right was clearly on the rise in 1980, therefore, but conservative dominance of American politics was nowhere near complete. Reagan had managed to dealign voters from the Democratic Party, but they voted for him because they were fed up with Carter and wanted a change rather than because they had fully embraced conservatism.[43] The Republican lock on the south was also not yet in place. Reagan won most of the region, but did so by very small margins, winning no state by more than 2.1 per cent and not breaking the 50 per cent barrier in any of them.[44] There also remained a significant residue of liberal Republicans within Congress which would act as a brake on conservatism.[45]

The incomplete nature of the Conservative triumph clearly manifested itself in the foreign policy sphere. Whilst the liberal, eastern wing of the party was in decline, it was still sufficiently strong to exert significant influence, as was indicated most clearly by Reagan's choice of its representative, George H. W. Bush, as his vice-presidential candidate, despite vigorous protests from the right of the party.[46] The eastern wing's continued influence also manifested itself in the selection of Reagan's foreign policy appointees. Whilst the CPD saw a large number of its leading members join the administration, they did so largely in second and third rank positions, with the most prominent, Jeanne Kirkpatrick, in the fairly marginal position of Ambassador to the United Nations. The top positions, in contrast, went to mainstream figures, many of whom were associated with the eastern wing of the party and the détente policies of Henry Kissinger so despised by conservatives. Secretary of State Alexander Haig and his key deputies had all been part of Kissinger's State Department, whilst Secretary of Defence Caspar Weinberger was appointed because of his renown as a budget-cutter rather than as a 'Cold Warrior'. Haig's eventual replacement as Secretary of State, George Shultz, was cut from similarly pragmatic cloth.[47] When Reagan's foreign policies consequently failed to conform to the hard-line prescriptions of the CPD, some leading conservatives started to complain that he was little better than Carter.[48]

Whilst the election of Ronald Reagan was a significant moment in America's shift to the right, therefore, that shift was far from complete, and the liberal, eastern wing of the Republican Party continued to hold considerable sway over foreign policy.[49] The incomplete nature of the conservative takeover, and the existence within the administration of different factions with inconsistent interests and world views, would make foreign policy a sphere of considerable contention during the Reagan administration, resulting in extensive bureaucratic conflict, which was further fuelled by Reagan's hands-off leadership style.[50]

## THE REAGAN ADMINISTRATION'S FACTIONS

Those disagreements were quite evident when it came to policy toward the Persian Gulf, with the most obvious division being that between 'pro-Israeli' and 'pro-Arab' factions. Generally speaking, the pro-Israeli camp was rooted in the conservative wing of the administration, reflecting the neoconservatives' commitment to Israel as an outpost of democracy and the wider belief amongst conservatives that Israel was a key strategic ally in the effort to contain the USSR and its radical Arab allies. The attitude of this faction towards America's 'moderate' Arab friends was one of either general distrust or an assumption that their antipathy towards the USSR and need for US security guarantees left them with nowhere else to go regardless of their unhappiness with American support for Israel.

The pro-Arab camp was rooted in the eastern wing of the party, which was much more sensitive to the concerns of the Arab oil-producing states, reflecting its roots in internationally oriented big business and connections to the major US oil companies. This group of policy-makers was rather less preoccupied with the Soviet threat and rather more concerned about that posed to the Gulf states by Iran and by their own internal opposition. Conscious of how the Arab–Israeli and Palestinian conflicts exacerbated those problems, they wanted even-handed American support for the peace process in order to shore up the American position in the Arab world and to ease America's Arab allies' domestic positions.[51]

This simple binary division, however, does not fully capture the complexity of the Reagan administration's internal conflicts. In addition to the two factions described above, there was a third, 'pro-Iranian' camp within the administration. Overlapping to some extent with the pro-Israeli faction, members of this group argued that the Reagan administration should seek to explore opportunities to restore good relations with Tehran. Underpinning that proposition was the argument that Iran remained the most powerful state in the Gulf and that its new leadership was implacably anti-communist. Despite its fierce anti-Americanism, therefore, the United States should attempt to cultivate improved relations with it as a means to containing the USSR.[52]

American policy toward the Persian Gulf would thus be contested by three factions, all anti-Soviet, but in disagreement about the priority to be given to containing the USSR as compared to other concerns, and differing in their views as to the other priorities of US Gulf policy. The pro-Israeli camp thought the alliance with Israel represented the best means of containing the USSR whilst the pro-Arab camp felt this ignored the importance of oil and also helped to destabilise moderate Arab regimes and inflame Arab radicalism. The pro-Iranian camp wanted to pursue the cultivation of Iran in order to contain the USSR and tended to side with the pro-Israeli camp because of a shared preoccupation with the Soviet threat. The pro-Israeli faction would dominate Reagan's initial policy towards the Gulf, with the support on most issues of the pro-Iranian faction, an alliance reflecting the strong relationship between the Shah's Iran and Israel based on their mutual interest in containing radical Arab states. In the early 1980s, Israel began to explore the possibility of establishing a similar modus vivendi with the new Iranian regime, a development that forged a common interest between the pro-Iranian and pro-Israeli camps in the Reagan administration; both supported the effort to explore the possibility of an improvement in both Iranian–Israeli and US–Iranian relations.

Over time, however, the balance within the administration would tilt towards the pro-Arab camp for a variety of reasons. In the first place, the anti-Soviet preoccupation of the other two factions became increasingly anachronistic as the absence of any Soviet threat in the Middle East became apparent and US–Soviet relations gradually improved. The pro-Israeli faction was also weakened by a range of other developments, including the replacement of the pro-Israeli Haig by the more even-handed Shultz, Israel's self-serving exploitation of US–Israeli strategic cooperation, and the comprehensive failure of the strategic consensus strategy. The pro-Iranian faction, for its part, was utterly discredited by the arms to Iran episode as well as by a growing perception that radical Islam of the Iranian type was a far greater threat to American interests than a declining radical Arab nationalism. As the other two factions found their positions undermined, so the pro-Arab faction would become increasingly dominant, with significant implications for US–Iraqi relations.

## THE STRATEGIC CONSENSUS POLICY, 1981–2

Reagan's initial policy toward the Persian Gulf confirmed the increased strategic importance accorded to the region and the focus of conservative hardliners on the Soviet threat. Under Reagan, the Carter administration's focus on the Arab–Israeli peace process was initially sidelined in favour of an effort to forge an anti-Soviet 'strategic consensus' incorporating both Israel and the moderate Arab states.[53] Iraq was largely irrelevant to this strategy, and with the Iran–Iraq War stalemated, the administration continued the Carter policy of neutrality and support for restoration of the status quo, stating that victory for either side was 'neither militarily achievable nor strategically desirable because of its destabilizing effect on the region'.[54]

The influence of the pro-Israeli faction within the Reagan administration did not mean that the Gulf oil producers could be ignored. Saudi Arabia, in particular, was simply too important for that to happen. Reagan himself made this clear when he declared that 'Saudi Arabia we will not allow to be another Iran'.[55] Moreover, in addition to its role as America's proxy in OPEC, the Reagan administration saw

Saudi Arabia, as the leading moderate Arab state, as vital to forging the new strategic consensus between Israel and America's Arab allies.

The importance the administration thus attached to Saudi Arabia was indicated by the political resources it expended on one of the most controversial issues of its first year in power. Concerned about the ongoing threat posed by Iran, and anxious to test the reliability of American promises, Riyadh sought to purchase a number of AWAC planes. The administration readily agreed, since the AWACs would serve US strategic interests as much as those of the Saudis, and represented a prepositioning of equipment vital to any future American intervention in the region. It was also clear that a failure to deliver would undermine a key bilateral tie and strangle the strategic consensus policy in the cradle.[56] However, the administration's decision set off a storm of protest led by the Israeli lobby, which claimed that the administration was endangering America's most reliable ally by providing technology that could be used against Israel. The administration was forced to invest vast amounts of time and effort to overcome this opposition, and it took eight months of negotiations and repeated personal interventions on the part of the president to finally secure approval of the sale by a margin of fifty two to forty eight votes in the Senate.

The administration's decision to sell AWACs to the Saudis was not well received by Israel, but Reagan continued to push the strategic consensus concept nevertheless. In April 1981, Haig visited Israel to outline the strategy and the basic tenets of US–Israeli strategic cooperation premised on a mutual interest in containing the USSR. The initial objective of cooperation would be to develop military–military coordination in order to enhance the American ability to project power in the region. The policy was almost derailed before it had begun, however, when Israeli jets attacked and destroyed the Iraqi nuclear reactor at Tuwaitha on 7 June 1981. The Reagan administration joined in the widespread condemnation of the attack and the pro-Arab camp inside the administration, in the shape of Weinberger, seized the opportunity to argue that the administration needed to reconsider the policy of strategic cooperation with Israel. Reagan nevertheless ordered that an agreement be drawn up and a Memorandum of Strategic Understanding was signed in November 1981.[57]

That was about as far as the strategic consensus policy got, however. The belief that the moderate Arab states could somehow be persuaded to join an anti-Soviet alliance with Israel was a fantasy from the start. The Saudi regime had neither the ability nor the inclination to act as a regional leader and even less to join any kind of consensus with Israel, given its domestic problems of legitimacy and the Iranian threat. Haig's assertion that the Arab states had come to feel 'equally – and perhaps as grievously – threatened' by the Soviets and their proxies as by Israel, and that the 'strategic consensus' in effect already existed, was the purest nonsense.[58] Virtually every Arab state was far more concerned about the threats posed by Iran and/or Israel than it was by that posed by the USSR. This was reflected in the continued rejection of American requests for new base rights and access agreements in the Gulf. The most the Saudis would agree to do was to deliberately overbuild their bases to make them capable of accommodating large US deployments and to increase their purchases of US weaponry (which effectively doubled as pre-positioned equipment for US forces).[59]

The Israelis were hardly more enthusiastic about the strategic consensus concept. Whilst Reagan and Haig wanted to forge an Arab–Israeli alliance to contain Soviet influence, the Israelis wanted an American–Israeli alliance that would enhance their ability to pursue their strategic interests vis-à-vis the Arab states. This much should have been clear to Washington when, having signed the memorandum on strategic cooperation, the Begin government proceeded to annex the Golan heights. The point was then forcibly driven home by the Israeli invasion of Lebanon in June 1982. Having sought, and received, American approval for the action on the grounds that it would be a temporary incursion into southern Lebanon, the Israeli army proceeded to drive all the way to Beirut, setting in motion a process which would ensnare US forces in Lebanon and lead to the killing of over two hundred American marines.[60] The Israeli deception of the administration, and exploitation of American support, led Bush and Weinberger to advocate an embargo on military supplies to Israel and the cancelling of an upcoming visit to Washington by Israeli Prime Minister Menachem Begin. Conservatives, led by Haig, Kirkpatrick and CIA Director Bill Casey, argued that Israel was advancing US strategic interests by striking a blow against the PLO and Syria.[61]

Despite the protests of its partisans inside the administration, the Israeli invasion of Lebanon effectively killed off the strategic consensus policy, a demise made certain when Haig was replaced as

Secretary of State by George Shultz in June 1982. Shultz came to the administration from Bechtel, a company with major Arab contracts, and proved far more in tune with the pro-Arab camp's concerns than Haig had been.[62] Immediately on taking up his post, he began pressing for a revival of the peace process, leading to the announcement in September 1982 of a new peace proposal based on 'land for peace'. Israel's blunt rejection of the proposal did little to improve its relations with the administration.

As the strategic consensus policy thus fell apart, American interest in Iraq would revive, as the administration began searching for an alternative strategy to stabilise American hegemony in the Gulf and to contain the Soviet and Iranian threats. That search was made all the more urgent when, in 1982, after two years of military deadlock, Iranian forces began to get the upper hand in the Iran–Iraq War, advancing into Iraqi territory for the first time.

## TOWARDS RAPPROCHEMENT WITH IRAQ, 1982–4

When he went to war in September 1980, Saddam Hussein had expected to strike a swift and decisive blow against a weak Iranian regime which would immediately capitulate. Accordingly, Iraqi forces crossed the border into Iran, advanced for a week and then halted whilst Saddam offered to negotiate in the clear expectation that the Iranians agree to his terms. Khomeini, however, rejected them outright. Moreover, Iranian forces, bloodied but not decisively defeated thanks to the Iraqi failure to press home their advantage, were thus given the chance to regroup, and the new regime in Tehran was able to use the Iraqi invasion as a means to rally popular support and consolidate its own position. Saddam's decision to halt the Iraqi offensive thus ensured a prolonged conflict, and by May 1981 Iranian offensives were beginning to drive Iraqi forces back towards the border. Saddam again tried to sue for peace, claiming that Iraqi objectives had been met and that Iraqi forces would withdraw if an acceptable settlement could be reached. The Iranian response was a further series of offensives in March 1982 which virtually drove Iraqi forces out of Iranian territory. In July 1982 Saddam withdrew his forces to a defensive line along the border.[63]

By early 1982 Iraq had come firmly back into the Reagan administration's focus. Fears of an Iranian victory were growing rapidly amongst America's allies in the Gulf and, along with Egypt, they now called on the Reagan administration to act to prevent that outcome, warning of disaster if the Iraqi regime were to collapse.[64] With Iranian forces massing for an offensive, a briefing memorandum for Haig outlined the possibility that a successful Iranian advance into Iraq could lead to the fall of Saddam Hussein. Such an outcome, it warned, 'would increase tremendously the concern of Gulf Arab governments about Iranian intentions and capabilities for further destabilization in the region'.[65]

The administration's concerns were reinforced by a shift in its own threat perceptions. By 1982 it was increasingly clear that the fear of expanding Soviet influence in the Persian Gulf, following the invasion of Afghanistan, had been greatly exaggerated. The Soviets were now bogged-down in a prolonged guerrilla conflict whilst their efforts to cultivate better relations with the new Iranian regime had come to nothing. Tehran had brutally repressed the Tudeh Party in late 1981 and demonstrated almost as much hostility toward Moscow (the 'Little Satan') as it did towards Washington (the 'Great Satan'). Whilst the Soviet threat was declining, however, that from Iran was increasing as Tehran became bolder in its efforts to export the revolution. In the last four months of 1981 it had fomented riots in Mecca by incorporating militants amongst Iranian pilgrims going on the *hajj*, attacked Kuwait in retaliation for the latter's support for Iraq, and sponsored an attempted coup in Bahrain. Most significant however, was Iran's support for the radical Shiite forces in Lebanon, who were engaged both in that country's civil war and in using it as a base to launch attacks against Israel. Iran's role in the bombing of the US embassy and marine barracks in Beirut in 1983, and the kidnappings of US hostages that followed, would further reinforce American hostility toward Iran.

Whilst Iran was thus continuing to alienate the Reagan administration, Saddam Hussein was doing his best to cultivate it. With the war going badly, and the Soviets having cut off arms deliveries when fighting began, Iraq needed friends wherever it could find them. Having initiated the expulsion of Egypt from the Arab League in 1979 Saddam now sought to restore good relations with Cairo, his primary objective in so doing being to get access to military supplies and spare parts for his Soviet-made equipment.[66] He also further moderated his position on the Israeli–Palestinian question, participating in the

1982 Fez Summit which implicitly accepted a two-state solution and publicly expressing support for peace negotiations between the Arab states and Israel.[67] Meanwhile, the Iraqi charge d'affaires in the United States, Nizar Hamdoun, began a charm offensive, touring the United States visiting schools, factories and interest groups in an effort to improve the image of Iraq.[68] Rapprochement was also being urged on the Reagan administration by its friends in the Arab world, and there were the first signs of the emergence of an Iraq lobby, as domestic commercial interests and the farm lobby and their representatives in Congress began pressing for a loosening of restrictions on trade with Iraq.[69]

None of these developments was crucial, since the threat posed to America's regional hegemony by Iran, and the need to contain it by whatever means necessary, was the fundamental consideration underpinning Reagan's policies. Iraq's perceived 'moderation' and the emergence of potential commercial interests in Iraq nevertheless made it easier to rationalise any improvement in US–Iraqi relations to a sceptical public and Congressional audience. The decision to tilt US policy in favour of Iraq was also made easier by the lack of alternatives, the most obvious of which was for the administration to maintain the balance of power in the Gulf directly as implied by the Carter Doctrine and the RDF. That option remained stymied, however, by the unwillingness of the Gulf states to accept a more high-profile American role in the region. Despite urging the Reagan administration to do whatever it could to stave off an Iraqi defeat, America's regional allies continued to refuse the United States base and access rights, insisting it keep its forces 'over-the-horizon'.

Whilst thus refusing to contemplate a larger direct American role in the Gulf, America's friends in the region were in no position to provide for their own security. In May 1981, in response to the outbreak of the Iran–Iraq War, the six peninsular oil kingdoms (Saudi Arabia, Kuwait, Bahrain, the United Arab Emirates (UAE), Oman and Qatar) had formed the Gulf Cooperation Council (GCC), announcing plans for intelligence sharing, joint manoeuvres and cooperation in air defence. In practice, however, even if they were able to develop effective coordination, the GCC militaries would still lack the capability to balance those of Iraq or Iran. Whilst they certainly had the oil wealth to purchase hi-tech weaponry (and did so), they lacked all the other necessary resources. Saudi Arabia could stand as an example for all of the GCC states in this regard. Its population was small, the educated population with the necessary technical skills for modern warfare was even smaller, and those with the education had more attractive employment opportunities available. In addition, armies require a great deal of unskilled manual labour which most Saudis did not want to do, and the Saudi military was therefore dependent on expatriates – Jordanians, Pakistanis and Americans primarily. Nor did the GCC states really want strong militaries, since they regarded them as potential sources of opposition. Indeed they actively sought to limit the capability of their armed forces, by practising policies of divide and rule such as not putting air defence and air forces under unified command and limiting communications between air and ground forces.[70]

All in all, therefore, the Reagan administration perceived little option but to prop up the Iraqi regime in its war against Iran. Even officials like Howard Teicher, who saw Iraq as a long-term threat to American interests in the Gulf, conceded that 'given the alternatives, neither the United States nor its Arab allies wanted to see Saddam Hussein swept away by Islamic fundamentalists answering Tehran's call'.[71] By no means, however, did this mean that the administration was ready to embrace the Iraqi regime. The US objective at this point was simply to re-establish stability in the Gulf and to 'return the parties [to the conflict] substantially to the *status quo ante*'. Policy-makers remained cautious about 'tilting' too far towards an Iraqi regime whose future was 'uncertain' and which might want more from the administration than it was prepared to deliver.[72]

The first concrete manifestation of the new policy was seen on 26 February 1982, when the administration removed Iraq from the State Department's list of state sponsors of terrorism. Ostensibly, this was a response to, and an attempt to further encourage, the recent foreign policy moderation of the Iraqi regime. In practice, the primary objective was to eliminate an obstacle to aiding the Iraqi war effort. By removing Iraq from the list, the administration made it a candidate for the extension of US government credit guarantees and loosened controls on the export of US goods to Iraq. The move also acted as a signal to America's friends that they were free to do business with Baghdad.

In the short-term, however, the move would not provide any material succour to the Iraqi regime, and in mid-1982, with Iran poised to strike a potentially decisive blow against Iraq, a worried White House convened a meeting of senior policy-makers to discuss what could be done to prevent that outcome. They concluded that the United States would have to intervene more directly in order to bolster the Iraqi war effort, and it was therefore decided that the administration would supply Iraq with US satellite intelligence on Iranian troop positions and movements.[73] In addition, the administration became more active diplomatically. Having had little interest in working to end the war whilst it was deadlocked, the administration now backed passage of UN Security Council Resolution 514, calling for a ceasefire and a withdrawal to established borders, in July 1982.[74] The Iranians, now with the upper hand, and feeling that the resolution failed adequately to reflect the fact that Iraq was the aggressor, rejected it.

One of principal ways that the Reagan administration came to support the Iraqi war effort was by facilitating its ability to trade with American corporations and buy American goods. The removal of Iraq from the list of state sponsors of terrorism was a crucial development in this regard and came at a critical time for Iraq. Saddam had initially been able to pay for his war with a combination of the financial reserves built up during the oil price boom of the 1970s and financial transfers from the Gulf oil monarchies. After that point, however, the transfers declined as global oil demand, and prices, fell, whilst Iraqi oil revenues had fallen from $29 billion in 1980 to $9 billion in 1982 as a result of the war.[75] In March 1983, Shultz was therefore informed that the Iraqi financial situation was nearing crisis. His advisers reviewed a number of possible options for US action, including pressing the US Export–Import (Exim) Bank to extend credit guarantees to Iraq in order to facilitate American exports. Their preferred option, however, was to extend credits through the Department of Agriculture's Commodity Credit Corporation (CCC) which guaranteed exports of agricultural rather than industrial goods. The Department of Agriculture had already proposed the extension of CCC credits in December 1982 (whereas the Exim Bank was reluctant to extend credit guarantees to Iraq), and in February 1983 the first tranche of $230 million in CCC credits was approved. American credits were thus extended at a key moment, and whilst they were only designed to support the import of agricultural products, they would free Iraqi financial resources to be spent on the war effort.[76]

The administration was barred by law from the simplest course of action to aid the Iraqi war effort – selling it military equipment. America's friends and allies, however, were generally not so constrained, and the administration duly encouraged them to extend assistance to Saddam, though in many cases no such encouragement was required. France was Iraq's main non-Soviet arms supplier, and had been for several years. When the Iran–Iraq War started France had taken the opportunity to increase its defence sales to Iraq, and soon began supplying its most advanced equipment, including Mirage fighter jets, Roland 2 air defence missiles and the CGT Self-Propelled Gun. In 1983 France delivered five Super-Etendard fighter-bombers to Iraq on loan. Armed with Exocet anti-ship missiles, these gave Iraq a greatly increased capacity to attack Iranian shipping.[77] Other states given the green light to arm Iraq included Italy. According to Prime Minister Giulio Andreotti, Reagan personally asked him to sell arms to Iraq during a meeting at the White House.[78] And this Italy happily did, selling Saddam helicopters, nuclear reprocessing laboratories and a navy that was never actually delivered. Egypt was likewise encouraged to supply Iraq with the spare parts it needed for its Soviet-built equipment until the Soviets restored supplies in 1982.[79] More controversially, though largely unnoticed at the time, the administration allowed third parties to sell on US-supplied arms to Iraq, in contravention of America's formal neutrality and the Arms Export Control Act (AECA), which required that Congress be notified of any such transfers.[80]

Although the Reagan administration began aiding the Iraqi war effort directly in 1982, it would be another two years before diplomatic relations were formally restored. Both sides were now keen to move in that direction, but they also had their preconditions. In the case of the US, these were largely matters of presentation. In order to minimise any domestic backlash, they needed the Iraqis publicly to distance themselves from support for terrorism and to continue to express support for a peaceful resolution of the Arab–Israeli conflict.[81] The Iraqis, for their part, desperately wanted US assistance but were also sceptical of US intentions and, in particular, fearful that Washington was more interested in restoring relations with Iran than developing a new relationship with Iraq. That belief was fuelled by the fact that ammunition and spare parts for Iran's American-made military equipment was being supplied to Iran by Israel, Turkey and other

NATO countries with, the Israelis claimed, the Reagan administration's active cooperation.[82]

In January 1983, Shultz extended an invitation to Iraqi Minister of
State for Foreign Affairs Saddoun Hammadi to meet him the next
time the latter was in the United States. A meeting was duly held on
14 February and was followed in May by one between Shultz and Aziz
(now Iraq's Foreign Minister) in Paris on 10 May. The latter meeting
took place shortly after the bombing of the US embassy and marine
barracks in Beirut, developments which the Iraqis sought to exploit,
with Aziz offering to provide information on Iranian-backed terrorist
groups. In fact, events in Lebanon were important in the evolving
American tilt towards Baghdad in more ways than one. After Iran, the
Reagan administration's main concern in the Middle East was Syria,
and in particular its efforts to establish predominant influence in
Lebanon. Cultivating Baghdad could thus serve a double purpose,
containing Iran in the Gulf and isolating Syria in the Arab–Israeli
context.[83] In light of the recent terrorist attacks, however, Shultz
demanded that Iraq expel the Palestinian terrorist Abu Nidal, who was
then living in Baghdad, before any further progress could be made.[84]
Shortly thereafter Baghdad announced Abu Nidal had died of a heart
attack, though he soon turned up in Libya.

In October 1983 Shultz and Aziz met again in New York, where the
Iraqis were seeking passage of a UN resolution condemning Iran for
the continuation of the war. The US supported the resolution but Aziz
nevertheless expressed Iraqi doubts about American intentions and
objectives, complaining that Israel and other US allies were continuing
to arm Iran. At least partly in response to this, as well as simply in
order to bring the war to a satisfactory conclusion as quickly as
possible, the Reagan administration launched Operation Staunch. In
December 1983 the administration sent a message to its ambassadors
warning that 'for those in the Gulf, Iraq's defeat would constitute an
immediate security threat'. Accordingly, they were to press their host
governments to block the flow of arms to Iran in order to bring an
early end to the Iran–Iraq conflict and protect the flow of Gulf oil.[85]

Following indications from Iraq that they would welcome such a
visit, on 17 December 1983 US Special Envoy for the Middle East
Donald Rumsfeld flew to Baghdad with a letter from Reagan offering
to restore diplomatic relations and to expand military and business
ties. Rumsfeld told his Iraqi interlocutors that the US and Iraq had

'common interests in preventing Iranian and Syrian expansion' and expressed the administration's desire that the Iran–Iraq War be ended in a way that 'did not expand Iran's interest and preserved the sovereignty of Iraq'. He also emphasised American efforts to halt the flow of Western arms to Iran. Saddam and Tariq Aziz, for their part, stated that Iraq did not want to be dependent on the USSR, desired regional and international stability, opposed Syrian and Iranian interference in Lebanon and, as an oil exporter, sought stable long-term relationships with its customers. They also expressed their desire for American help to end the war. Saddam expressed the hope that relations would now move towards the establishment of full diplomatic relations.[86]

Rumsfeld returned to Washington from a further visit to the Middle East in spring 1984 with a stark warning that there was a 'disaster on the horizon'. He told Shultz that 'Iran's forces were now pushing the Iraqi army back inside Iraq, and soon they could threaten Kuwait and Saudi Arabia'.[87] Fears such as these, and desperation to prevent an Iranian victory, led the administration to downplay growing evidence of Iraqi use of chemical weapons (CW) against Iranian forces. The administration sought 'to maintain the credibility of US policy on CW' by privately seeking to dissuade the Iraqis from their use, and on 7 March 1984 it publicly condemned Iraqi actions and subsequently banned the export to Iraq of a number of chemical precursors that could be used in the production of CW. The American fear of an Iranian victory nevertheless ensured that no other substantive action was taken and that movement towards the restoration of diplomatic relations was unaffected.[88] In fact the US tilt towards Iraq became ever more obvious. In June 1984 the administration publicly blamed Iran for the continuation of the war, with Reagan declaring that Iraq was 'playing by the rules of the game' whilst Iran was 'the one who seems to resist any effort' to end the conflict.[89] This was then backed by American votes in the UN Security Council in favour of resolutions condemning Iran's refusal to negotiate a ceasefire and, on 26 November 1984, US–Iraqi diplomatic relations were formally restored.

## NOTES

1. Lesch, *1979*, p. 2.
2. Quandt, 'The Middle-East crises', p. 549.

3. Karsh and Rautsi, *Saddam Hussein*, pp. 114–15.
4. Bill, *The Eagle and the Lion*; Cottam, *Nationalism in Iran*; Ramazani, *Revolutionary Iran*; Sick, *All Fall Down*.
5. Hunter, 'Islam in power', pp. 265–80; Hinnebusch, *The International Politics of the Middle East*, p. 194.
6. Stork, 'Saudi Arabia and the US', p. 29.
7. Bowker and Williams, *Superpower Detente*, pp. 234–53; Halliday, *Threat from the East*.
8. President Jimmy Carter, 'The State of the Union', 23 January 1980, *Weekly Compilation of Presidential Documents*, vol. 16, 28 Jan 1980, p. 197.
9. Wooten, *Rapid Deployment Force*, p. l; Klare, 'Have RDF, will travel', p. 266.
10. Gordon, *Conflict in the Persian Gulf*, p. 141.
11. Brzezinski, *Power and Principle*, p. 446.
12. Acharya, *US Military Strategy*, pp. 80–4.
13. Teicher and Teicher, *Twin Pillars*, p. 79.
14. Jabber, 'US interests and regional security', p. 80.
15. Teicher and Teicher, *Twin Pillars*, p. 61.
16. Gordon and Trainor, *The Generals' War*, pp. 8–10.
17. Teicher and Teicher, *Twin Pillars*, pp. 69–70.
18. Karsh and Rautsi, *Saddam Hussein*, p. 130.
19. 'An open eye on Baghdad', *New York Times*, 5 May 1980, p. A18.
20. Timmerman, *The Death Lobby*, pp. 77–8.
21. It has been claimed that Saddam attacked Iran with the knowledge and approval of the Carter administration (Sluglett, 'The Cold War in the Middle East', p. 53), but there is no concrete evidence available to support the claim.
22. Karsh and Rautsi, *Saddam Hussein*, pp. 136–8; Marr, *Modern History of Iraq*, pp. 292–5; Freedman and Karsh, *The Gulf Conflict*, pp. 19–22; Gause, 'Iraq's decisions to go to war'.
23. Cordesman, *The Gulf and the Search for Strategic Stability*, pp. 645–6; Cottam, 'Levels of conflict in the Middle East', pp. 30–6.
24. BBC, *Summary of World Broadcasts* (SWB), *Middle East* (ME), 15 February 1979.
25. Karsh and Rautsi, *Saddam Hussein*, pp. 138–9.
26. Bengio, 'Shi'is and politics'.
27. O'Ballance, *The Gulf War*, pp. 11–12.
28. Chubin and Tripp, *Iran and Iraq*, pp. 27–9.
29. BBC, *SWB, ME*, 27 September 1980, pp. A4–6.
30. Tripp, *History of Iraq*, p. 232.
31. Gordon, *Conflict in the Persian Gulf*, p. 157.
32. Tripp, 'The foreign policy of Iraq', p. 180.
33. *Department of State Bulletin*, December 1980, pp. 2–3.

34. Chubin, 'The USSR and Southwest Asia', p. 159.
35. Brzezinski, *Power and Principle*, p. 452. The Carter administration's position was complicated by the ongoing hostage crisis, which was a further reason to declare a position of neutrality.
36. Acharya, *US Military Strategy in the Gulf*, pp. 128–9; Gordon, *Conflict in the Persian Gulf*, pp. 160–1.
37. Busch, *Reagan's Victory*, pp. 179–80.
38. Abramson *et al.*, *Change and Continuity in the 1980 Elections*, p. 155.
39. Cox and Skidmore-Hess, *US Politics and the Global Economy*, pp. 161–2.
40. Ibid. pp. 164–5.
41. Ferguson and Rogers, 'The Reagan victory', pp. 28–9.
42. Taylor (ed.), *Alerting America*.
43. Burnham, 'The 1980 earthquake', p. 109.
44. Busch, *Reagan's Victory*, p. 127.
45. Rae, *The Decline and Fall of the Liberal Republicans*, pp. 176–80.
46. Ferguson and Rogers, 'The Reagan victory', pp. 51–2.
47. Cumings, 'Chinatown', pp. 222–5.
48. Podhoretz, 'Appeasement by any other name'.
49. Halper and Clarke, *America Alone*, pp. 162–75.
50. Haig, *Caveat*.
51. Rubin, 'The Reagan administration and the Middle East', pp. 377–8; Teicher and Teicher, *Twin Pillars*, p. 194.
52. Hooglund, 'Reagan's Iran'.
53. Teicher and Teicher, *Twin Pillars*, p. 112.
54. US Congress, *Developments in the Persian Gulf, June 1984*, p. 5.
55. *New York Times*, 2 October 1981.
56. Kupchan, *The Persian Gulf and the West*, pp. 146–7.
57. Israel MFA, 'Memorandum of understanding'; Acharya, *US Military Strategy*, p. 108; Rubin, 'The Reagan administration and the Middle East', pp. 380–1.
58. US Department of State, 'Secretary Haig: News Conference', p. 3.
59. Acharya, *US Military Strategy*, pp. 112–4; Kupchan, *The Persian Gulf and the West*, pp. 143; Rubin, 'The Reagan administration and the Middle East', pp. 383–4.
60. Kelly, 'Lebanon: 1982–1984'.
61. Teicher and Teicher, *Twin Pillars*, pp. 199–204.
62. Rubin, 'The Reagan administration and the Middle East', pp. 377–8.
63. Chubin and Tripp, *Iran and Iraq at War*, pp. 54–7; Robins, 'Iraq in the Gulf War: objectives, strategies and problems', p. 50.
64. Teicher and Teicher, *Twin Pillars*, pp. 177–9.
65. *Iraqgate*, 'Your meeting with Israeli Defense Minister Ariel Sharon, 4–5 pm Tuesday May 25', 21 May 1982.

66. Chubin and Tripp, *Iran and Iraq at War*, pp. 145–6; Karsh and Rautsi, *Saddam Hussein*, pp. 161–2.
67. *International Herald Tribune*, 27 November, 5 December 1984.
68. Bhatya and McGrory, *Brighter than the Baghdad Sun*, pp. 142–5.
69. Teicher and Teicher, *Twin Pillars*, p. 276.
70. McNaugher, *Arms and Oil*, pp. 134–48.
71. Teicher and Teicher, *Twin Pillars*, p. 271.
72. *Iraqgate*, 'Iran–Iraq War: analysis of possible shift from position of strict neutrality', 7 October 1983.
73. Friedman, *Spider's Web*, p. 27. This decision effectively put US and the USSR on same side in the conflict, since Moscow had restored arms supplies to Iraq in 1982. Both superpowers were seeking to maintain the status quo by preventing an Iranian victory.
74. UNSCR 514, www.daccessdds.un.org/RESOLUTION/GEN/NRO/435/38/IMG/NRO43548.pdf?OpenElement.
75. Nonneman, *Iraq*, pp. 96–7; Farouk-Sluglett, 'After the war'.
76. *Iraqgate*, 'US credit possibilities for Iraq', 16 March 1983; 'CCC GSM-102 credit guarantees for Iraq', 18 December 1982; 'CCC-proposed $230 million blended credit program', 1 February 1983; Friedman, *Spider's Web*, pp. 93–4. The CCC guaranteed payments to US exporters of agricultural goods on credit sales to foreign countries.
77. Timmerman, *The Death Lobby*, pp. 91–5, 136–8.
78. Friedman, *Spider's Web*, p. 82.
79. *Iraqgate*, 'Reports of alleged US arms supplies to Iraq via Egypt: possible items on the agenda for MINDEF [Ministry of Defense]', 24 May 1982.
80. Seymour M. Hersh, 'US secretly gave aid to Iraq early in its war against Iran', *New York Times*, 26 January 1992, pp. A1, 12.
81. *Iraqgate*, 'Visit of Iraqi Foreign Minister', 15 January 1982.
82. *Iraqgate*, 'Arens public remarks on alleged US–Israeli arms supply to Iran', 22 October 1982. This would later be revealed to be true; see Chapter 2.
83. Coughlin, *Saddam*, p. 214.
84. *Iraqgate*, 'Visit of Iraqi Foreign Minister', 15 January 1983; 'Your meeting with Iraqi Minister of State Dr Saddoun Hammadi, February 14 1983 at 2.30–3.00 pm', 7 February 1983; Timmerman, *The Death Lobby*, pp. 129–30.
85. *Iraqgate*, 'Staunching Iran's import of Western arms and urging restraint on Iraq', 14 December 1983.
86. *Iraqgate*, 'Rumsfeld's larger meeting with Iraqi Deputy Prime Minister and Foreign Minister Tariq Aziz', 20 December 1983; 'Rumsfeld's mission: December 20 meeting with Iraqi President Saddam Hussein', 21 December 1983.

87. Shultz, *Turmoil and Triumph*, p. 235.
88. *Iraqgate*, 'Iraq use of chemical weapons', 1 November 1983; 'Iraqi use of chemical weapons', 21 November 1983; 'Iraq's use of chemical weapons: control on US ingredients', 14 March 1983; Shultz, *Turmoil and Triumph*, pp. 239–40.
89. *Middle East International*, 29 June 1984, p. 13.

*Chapter 2*

# FROM A TILT TO AN EMBRACE, 1984–1989

═══════════

## FINANCIAL CREDITS, THE COMMODITY CREDIT CORPORATION, THE EXIM BANK AND *BANCA NAZIONALE DEL LAVORO*

Between 1984 and 1990, American policy towards Iraq evolved from a 'tilt' designed to maintain the balance of power in the Gulf into a more ambitious attempt to draw Iraq permanently into the camp of America's Gulf allies. That it did so was, in large part, due to the continued lack of any obvious alternative strategy for securing American regional hegemony. The development of US trade with Iraq, however, also fostered a powerful Iraq lobby which actively supported the deepening of US–Iraqi relations.

Even before it re-established diplomatic ties with Baghdad, the Reagan administration had developed an extensive inter-agency programme to support the Iraqi war effort. The first CCC credit guarantees had been extended in early 1983, and by 1984 the first tranche of $230 million had been increased to $680 million. By 1988, the CCC would be offering to guarantee $1.1 billion worth of agricultural exports a year.[1] CCC guarantees, however, whilst enabling Iraq to divert revenue away from paying for food, were otherwise of little assistance to the Iraqi war effort. In order to provide greater support, the administration needed to extend credit guarantees for non-agricultural products, but the Exim Bank was unwilling to do so because it considered Iraq credit unworthy in light of its financial difficulties. In December 1983, Under-Secretary of State Lawrence Eagleburger had written to the chairman of the Exim Bank, William Draper, in an effort to change his mind. He pointed out that extending credits would demonstrate American support for Iraq, benefit US businesses and workers and 'secure a foothold in a potentially large export market'.[2] The Exim Bank, however, stuck to its guns, refusing a request for export financing in April 1984 on the grounds that repayment could not be assured. In response, the State Department decided to increase the pressure. In June 1984 the Department sent a memo to Vice-President Bush's national security adviser, Donald Gregg, outlining the need to extend Exim credits and stating that 'a call by the Vice President [to Draper] would be particularly useful in confirming the administration's support'. Attached was a paper outlining the talking points Bush should use in his call, including the key point that the US needed 'to bolster Iraq's ability and resolve to withstand Iranian attacks'.[3] Bush duly made the call and on 25 June the Exim Bank reversed itself, authorising $484 million in credits for Iraq.[4]

Christopher Drogoul, the manager of the Atlanta Branch of the Italian *Banca Nazionale del Lavoro* (BNL), would become an important actor in the process of extending credit guarantees to Iraq. BNL Atlanta became involved when grain companies began to ask it to take on their rights to sale proceeds and the CCC guarantees.[5] Drogoul was authorised to proceed by BNL headquarters in Rome and in early 1985 he established a $100 million line of credit for Iraq under the CCC programme. By the end of that year, however, Drogoul had unilaterally expanded the line of credit to $556 million. When he then asked for retrospective authorisation to extend the credits, Rome refused. Drogoul's response was to conceal the extent of the credits he had authorised from his own bank and everyone else and to keep on extending them in secret. He also made BNL Atlanta an important credit source for industrial exporters to Iraq once the Exim Bank was persuaded to start guaranteeing exports to Iraq. By the end of the 1980s, the American government would have issued a total of $5 billion in CCC loan guarantees for Iraq and BNL Atlanta would have a $1.89 billion share of that total.[6]

## SALES OF ARMS AND DUAL-USE TECHNOLOGY

The direct arming of Iraq by the United States was never seriously contemplated by either the Reagan or George H. W. Bush administrations. It would have been legally and politically difficult for them to have pursued such a course given Iraq's human rights record, use of chemical weapons and potential threat to Israel, as well as legislation such as the AECA. The United States would therefore remain formally neutral in regard to the Iran–Iraq War, and the arms embargo imposed by the Carter administration would remain in place.

The direct sale of arms apart, however, the Reagan and Bush administrations would consistently err on the side of generosity in their granting of licences for the export of dual-use and militarily sensitive technologies to Iraq, frequently bending and sometimes breaking the law in the process. Such behaviour was clear from early on in the Iran–Iraq War, when the administration approved the sale of sixty Hughes 500 MD Defender helicopters. In what would become a familiar pattern, the DOD objected to the sale on the grounds that the helicopters had potential military applications, but State and Commerce insisted that they were for civilian purposes and that they had assurances from the Iraqi government to that effect. In June 1983, however, the State Department was informed by the US interests section in Iraq that the Iraqi government had approached an unidentified country to upgrade the helicopters for military use.[7] Nevertheless, when the Italian subsidiary of Bell-Textron, Augusta Bell, sold eight AB-212 military helicopters to Iraq in February 1984, the administration made no objection. The ACEA required the administration to seek congressional approval for such transfers of US-made equipment by third-parties, but the administration ignored the requirement, as well as the continued opposition of the DOD.[8]

## THE IRAQI WEAPONS OF MASS DESTRUCTION PROGRAMME

One of the reasons the DOD objected to the sale of dual-use technologies to Iraq was the risk that they would assist in the latter's efforts to develop WMD. Those efforts dated back to late 1974, when Saddam had established a three-man Strategic Planning Committee composed of himself, Defence Minister Adnan Khayrallah and Adnan Hamdani, to draw up plans for the development of an indigenous arms industry. In their initial five-year plan they aimed to create six laboratories for chemical, biological and physiological analysis and to train 5,000 technicians to work in them. In addition, Iraq's chemical and biological infrastructure would be adapted to dual-use.[9] Between 1974 and 1977 more than 4,000 technical personnel had been recruited from around the world to construct CW and biological weapons (BW) plants.[10]

Saddam also intended to develop nuclear weapons. The Soviet Union had supplied Iraq with an experimental research reactor in the late 1960s, but when Saddam sought more advanced technology he was rebuffed and forced to look elsewhere.[11] In 1974 Iraq entered into negotiations with France to buy a seventy megawatt experimental nuclear reactor for the declared purpose of civilian nuclear development, and on 18 November 1975 a Franco–Iraqi nuclear cooperation treaty was signed, incorporating both the sale of a French Osiris Reactor (renamed Osirak) and the training of Iraqi nuclear technicians. The Osiris reactor used weapons-grade uranium which could be readily converted for use in nuclear weapons. However, in response to Iraq's efforts to obtain nuclear weapons, Israeli Prime Minister Begin ordered a campaign of sabotage and assassination. In April 1979, Mossad agents broke into a warehouse at La Seyne sur-Mer and blew up the Osirak reactor cores before they could be shipped to Iraq. Then, in April 1980, they assassinated Dr Yehiya El Meshed, an Egyptian nuclear scientist working for Iraq, and later that year they bombed the headquarters of the Italian SNIA Techint company which was supplying Iraq with nuclear reprocessing technology. Finally, when all else had failed to halt Iraqi nuclear efforts, in June 1981 Israeli planes bombed the Osirak reactor at Tuwaitha before it could become operational.[12]

With its efforts to acquire nuclear weapons thus set back, Iraq concentrated more of its immediate efforts on developing CW and BW. Procurement teams were despatched to Western countries in the guise of employees of civilian companies in an effort to obtain the necessary technology. Sometimes they failed – both the British ICI and the US Pfaulder companies rejected an invitation to build a large chemical plant supposedly for pesticide production – but mostly they succeeded. Iraq's first bacteriological lab was built in the late 1970s by the French Institut Merieux, ostensibly for the purpose of creating vaccines.[13] The primary source of technology for the Iraqi CW programme, meanwhile, was West Germany. In late 1981, Thyssen Rheinstahl Technology signed a contract to build a chemical laboratory at Salman Pak, and another West German firm, Karl Kolb GmbH, became the main contractor for another 'pesticides' plant at Samarra. Between 1983 and 1986, Karl Kolb completed six separate CW manufacturing lines at Samarra, and Iraq thus acquired substantial CW production capability.[14]

Along with the development of WMD, Saddam also put considerable resources into developing their means of delivery in the form of an indigenous ballistic missile production programme. In order to acquire missiles with sufficient range to reach Tehran and Israel, Iraq pursued two strategies. In the short term, it helped fund an Argentinean missile project – Condor – run by German engineers from the MBB firm. Meanwhile, Iraq also began an effort to procure the technology necessary for an Iraqi missile programme, known as Project 395. As a first step, in early 1984, Iraq signed a contact with Gildemeister Projecta of West Germany to design and construct a missile testing centre near Mosul (Saad 16).[15]

## STATE TAKES CHARGE

By the time of the American tilt towards Iraq in the early 1980s, therefore, Iraq already had an extensive WMD programme, and the Reagan administration was well aware of it. In September 1983, Reagan ordered the CIA to produce a National Intelligence Estimate on the spread of CW in the Third World which noted Iraq's steady accumulation of technology, production facilities and precursor agents for CW.[16] Proof of just how much progress Iraq had made was provided in early 1984 when, after initial attacks failed to dislodge Iranian forces from the recently captured Majnun islands north of Basra, CW were used to do so.[17] Whilst the Reagan administration made a formal protest and tightened controls on chemical exports, as noted in the previous chapter, the tilt towards Iraq pressed ahead because 'the fact remained that a radical Iran now posed an immediate threat to the strategic Gulf area, and Iraq was the only military machine that could block the path of Khomeini's forces'.[18]

Nevertheless, what precisely was required to prevent an Iranian victory, and what should, and should not, therefore be allowed to be sold to Iraq, remained a bone of contention. Much of the technology for which the Reagan and Bush administration ultimately granted licences, particularly from 1986 onwards, had clear military uses and did, in fact, end up being used for purposes such as the upgrading of missile systems. According to one report, some $94 million worth of US computer equipment was sold directly to Iraqi weapons plants.

Some of the technology also had potential applications in the development of chemical, biological and nuclear weapons.[19]

The Pentagon objected to many of those sales precisely because it saw what it regarded as strategic technology being sold to the Iraqi military. The leading objector was Assistant Secretary of Defense Richard Perle, who was profoundly sceptical of the whole policy of tilting toward Iraq, regarding it as 'foolish to think that a pro-Marxist, pro-Soviet Ba'th regime, the leader of Arab radicalism and rejectionism, is about to become an American ally or even a tacit partner without exacting an enormous price'.[20] He was even more deeply opposed to the transfer of dual-use technology to Iraq, claiming both that Baghdad could transfer the technology to the USSR, and that it might contribute to nuclear proliferation. As he wrote in a letter to Weinberger in July 1985, 'there is a body of evidence indicating that Iraq continues to actively pursue an interest in nuclear weapons' and that it had been 'somewhat less than honest in regard to the intended end-use of hi-technology equipment'.[21]

Perle continued to make his case throughout 1985, arguing that a tightening of export controls was necessary, but the weight of power in the bureaucratic battle was against him. State was now pressing the Department of Commerce to reconsider licences for hi-tech goods that it had previously refused to authorise. It derided Perle's objections, claiming that there was no evidence whatsoever of technology diversion to the Soviets and that Iraq had legitimate civilian uses for all the technology in question. In an effort to force Perle back into line, Shultz wrote directly to Weinberger to reiterate these points and to remind him that the US objective was to 'draw Iraq further away from the Soviets and help restrain its behaviour'. He also reassured him that 'we will continue to scrutinize advanced technology exports to assure that they do not provide Iraq the ability to develop nuclear weapons'.[22]

Iraq policy had thus developed into a bureaucratic struggle between State and Commerce, on the one hand, and the DOD, with some support from the Treasury and the Exim Bank, on the other. In part, this reflected the factional divisions of the administration, with the pro-Arab faction dominant at State and the pro-Israeli Perle at Defense. But it also reflected narrower bureaucratic interests, with the pro-Arab Weinberger nevertheless concerned about US military technology getting into the wrong hands and Commerce, Treasury and the Exim Bank all driven by bureaucratic imperatives rather than geopolitical considerations.

The driving force behind Iraq policy was the State Department, where there was a growing belief that Iraq could be encouraged down the path of moderation. Washington was repeatedly informed by its diplomats in Baghdad that Iraq had changed and that, in the words of US ambassador to Iraq David Newton, 'would prefer to act as a member of the club'. Expanded trade was seen as the key to encouraging this trend.[23] This view soon percolated all the way to the top of the State Department. Shultz, writing with the benefit of hindsight, claimed that, while sceptical, he 'was nevertheless willing to work to move Iraq toward a more responsible position'.[24] In June 1985 he therefore wrote to Representative Howard Berman to ask him to withdraw a proposed bill which would return Iraq to the list of state sponsors of terrorism, asserting that Iraq 'has effectively disassociated itself from international terrorism'. Putting it back on the list would, he argued, undermine the administration's dialogue with Iraq on a range of important issues. Berman subsequently agreed to drop the bill.[25]

With the Exim Bank and the CCC now guaranteeing exports, and controls on doing business with Iraq loosened, Iraq rapidly became big business for many US industries and agricultural interests, a fact reflected in the establishment in May 1985 of the US–Iraq Business Forum. Members of the Forum included Amoco, Exxon, Hunt Oil, Mobil, Occidental and Texaco; At&T, Bechtel, Brown and Root, Caterpillar, Bankers Trust, GM, BMY, Bell Textron, Lockheed and other defence companies. It soon became a powerful lobby for the expansion of business with Iraq.[26]

The political and bureaucratic forces thus arrayed against the opponents of looser export controls were extremely powerful, and the factor which lent greatest weight to their arguments was the overriding imperative of preventing an Iranian victory. Even with the ever-expanding assistance of the West and its Gulf allies, Iraq remained unable to turn the tide of the war. By 1985 Saddam sought no more than a return to the status quo ante as the price of peace, but Tehran refused to abandon its pursuit of outright victory. The Iraqi war effort was now directed toward repelling repeated Iranian ground offensives and in so doing imposing a sufficiently high cost on Iran to force it to the negotiating table. Saddam also tried to impose those costs in other ways. Having largely withdrawn the Iraqi air force from combat after the initial invasion, he now began to use it to attack Iranian cities, including Tehran. However, this only brought retaliation against Basra and Baghdad by Iranian missiles. This 'war of the cities' broke out sporadically and then was halted by both sides on several occasions. Overall, Iraqi attacks on Iranian civilian targets did not weaken the resolve of the Iranian leadership or stir significant domestic opposition in Iran.[27]

In February 1986 the Iranians succeeded in seizing the strategically significant Fao peninsula, bringing them within artillery range of both Basra and Kuwait. Saddam once more sued for peace, but Tehran ignored the plea and continued to attack, making further significant advances in June. In Washington there were growing fears about 'Iraq's ability to sustain its defenses' and the possibility of an Iranian victory. The State Department therefore began pressing ever more strongly for active steps to broaden America's relationship with Iraq in order to ensure the latter's survival. In July 1986, State demanded a National Security Council (NSC) inter-agency meeting to make a final decision on export licences and, in effect, to end the bureaucratic dispute over Iraq policy.[28] The result was complete victory for State and its allies at Commerce and Agriculture, with National Security Adviser John Poindexter issuing a National Security Decision Directive (NSDD) calling on all government agencies to be 'more forthcoming' with regard to licence requests for exports to Iraq.[29] The effect was clear: in 1987–8 241 licences for exports to Iraq would be approved and only six denied.[30]

By the late 1980s all this technology transfer from the United States and other Western states would begin to bear fruit for Saddam, with the most striking and public progress being made in the missile programme. On 5 August 1987, Iraq announced the successful test of an al-Hossein missile which, it claimed, had flown 615 kilometres, double the range of the Soviet-supplied Scud B which had been assumed to be the most powerful missile Iraq possessed. Iraq then proved its claim was no idle boast when, on 29 February 1988, it launched missile attacks on Tehran – 550 kilometres from the border. The following year Iraq announced the successful test of the al-Abbas missile, which reportedly flew 860 kilometres. Iraq had its desired indigenous missile production capacity.[31]

The Iraqi nuclear programme was also making progress. After the destruction of the Osirak reactor, Iraqi nuclear scientists had chosen to go down the technologically more primitive, but less easily detectable, route of using centrifuges, known as Calutrons, to enrich the uranium needed for nuclear weapons. Rather than openly buy the centrifuges, they had instead purchased the technology and sought to develop the technical capacity to manufacture their own, which they had achieved by 1987. By 1989, Iraq had full scale production of enriched uranium up and running at its plant at Taji as well as an experimental cascade at Tuwaitha. It was about two to three years away from having sufficient enriched uranium for a bomb.[32]

## ARMS TO IRAN

In November 1986, the American media picked up a story in a Lebanese paper which reported that the Reagan administration had been selling arms to Iran in return for the release of American hostages held in Lebanon. This revelation, and the subsequent public unravelling of the whole unhappy affair,[33] exposed the extent to which some members of the administration still hoped that US–Iranian relations could be restored, as well as the depth of the continued divisions over America's Gulf policy. It would also have significant implications for the future of that policy, tipping the balance decisively in favour of the pro-Arab camp within the administration.

To some extent, it was now revealed, the Reagan administration had been playing a double-game in the Gulf right from the start. When the administration first came to office, Alexander Haig had declared 'categorically' that there would be no arms sales to Iran. But it was later testified to at the congressional hearings into the Iran–Contra affair that Haig had authorised Israel to sell Iran arms, including US equipment, soon after coming to office.[34] In addition, it now emerged that the administration had maintained a secret dialogue with Tehran, largely related to the USSR. It had passed on information from KGB defector Vladimir Kuzichkin about Soviet spy networks in Iran and had also supplied Iran with intelligence on the disposition of Soviet forces close to the Iranian border.[35]

Reagan sought to justify his actions on the grounds that arms had been sold to Iran in the hope of securing the release of the American hostages in Lebanon,[36] but for those who were actually behind the scheme, the primary reason for the sales was geopolitical rather than humanitarian. The policy-makers involved, mainly from the NSC staff, felt that if the United States was to seek a partner in the Gulf, then Iran was a better bet than Iraq since it was by far the more powerful of the two states. In addition, they reasoned, Iran ultimately had little choice but to seek a rapprochement with the United States, because it was an 'unavoidable geostrategic fact' that '*any* Iranian government that wants to stay free of Soviet influence *has* to turn to the US'.[37]

The pro-Iran camp was thus motivated primarily by the fear of Soviet expansion. A draft NSDD, written in mid-1985, warned that economic deterioration and internal conflict within the Iranian regime were creating instability that the USSR was better-positioned than the US to exploit. Without a 'major change in US policy', it warned, this situation would get worse. The US should therefore encourage its allies to do business with Iran, including providing selected military equipment, in order to reduce Soviet influence. In addition, the United States should seek opportunities to influence the direction of change inside Iran and provide support to moderate factions of the regime.[38] This strategic logic was happily complemented, from the point of view of those in favour of an opening to Iran, by the possibility of also securing the release of the US hostages held in Lebanon.

The draft NSDD never became formal US policy thanks to the opposition of both Weinberger and Shultz. Having read the draft, Shultz wrote to National Security Adviser Robert MacFarlane to express his more or less complete disagreement with its arguments. In his opinion it exaggerated both the degree of anti-regime sentiment within Iran (the 'moderates' the Iranian camp hoped to do business with) and the extent of Soviet influence. He was particularly critical of the idea of supporting arms sales to Iran, pointing out that this could lead to an Iranian victory over Iraq and do huge damage to US relations with Saudi Arabia and the other Gulf oil states.[39]

Despite the opposition of both of his most senior national security officials (and without their knowledge), in August 1985 Reagan auth-orised the delivery of a shipment of American TOW anti-tank missiles to Iran via Israel, in the expectation that this would lead to the release of most of the hostages. Despite the fact that none were in fact freed, a further shipment was authorised the following month. This time the Reverend Benjamin Weir was released. In November 1985 the United States shipped more arms, including HAWK anti-aircraft missiles, but no further hostages were released. In January 1986, despite the strongly stated opposition of Shultz and Weinberger, Reagan signed a secret finding authorising direct US arms sales to Iran. Several shipments of arms in 1986, however, resulted in the release of just one more hostage, Father Lawrence Jenco, in July.[40] All things considered, the policy of selling arms to Iran in the hope of encouraging Iranian 'moderates', rekindling US–Iranian relations, and securing the release of US hostages in Lebanon, was a fiasco. Just two hostages were released whilst Iran remained unremittingly hostile to the United States.

Moreover, the eventual exposure of 'arms to Iran' in November 1986 was not only deeply embarrassing for the Reagan administration, but also had major implications for American Gulf policy. In late 1986 and early 1987 Iran launched a series of offensives towards Basra, the Fish Lake and areas to the north which met with great success. The Iranian air force demonstrated a hugely increased capability, whilst the HAWK missiles enabled the Iranians to shoot down Iraq's most advanced fighters and the TOW anti-tank missiles destroyed Iraq's Soviet-supplied armour.[41] Saddam was, unsurprisingly, furious at the revelation that the US had been arming Iran and at the clear evidence of the military edge this had supplied to Iranian forces. This only served to reinforce his doubts about the untrustworthy nature of the United States and its preference for a relationship with his Iranian enemies. Hardly less angry were the oil monarchies of the Gulf, who were similarly shocked to discover that the US had been arming the state they regarded as the primary threat to their own survival.

The ultimate effect of the whole 'arms to Iran' episode was nevertheless to reinforce the American tilt towards Iraq. The Iranian option was off the table for the foreseeable future, and the pro-Iranian faction was now discredited and effectively eliminated as a political force. The cultivation of Iraq was thus the only game in town and its advocates now dominated American policy-making. Moreover, given the reaction of Iraq and the Arab states to the exposure of Washington's duplicity, the administration would now have to be more assiduous than ever in its courting of Saddam in order to reassure him and them of American intentions. In the immediate aftermath of the first reports of the arms sales, the State Department warned that 'US–Iraqi relations are in crisis' and that the US needed to be more forthcoming with export licences and credit guarantees if it was to 'retrieve our influence in Iraq'.[42]

## THE TANKER WAR AND KUWAITI RE-FLAGGING

In 1987, the United States became directly involved in the war in the Persian Gulf through the policy of reflagging Kuwaiti oil tankers.[43] It felt compelled to do so in part by the need to restore credibility with its Gulf allies but mainly by the fact that, for the first time, the war threatened to have a significant impact on the oil flow from the region. Unable to force Iran to the negotiating table through victory on the battlefield, Saddam had sought alternative means of compelling it to negotiate, including attacks on Iranian shipping,[44] a tactic that had the added advantage of threatening the oil supply to the world market and thus increasing the motivation of the oil-consuming states of the West to seek an end to the war.

Iraqi attacks on Iranian shipping began as early as 1981, but escalated from 1984 onwards, with Iran responding in kind. In 1984 some thirty tankers were hit, mostly by Iraq, increasing to fifty in 1985 and 102 in 1986.[45] Iraq further escalated the conflict with a raid on Iran's Kharg Island oil terminal in August 1985, and Saddam warned that 'worse is yet to come'. With large tankers no longer able to call at Kharg Island, the Iranians tried to shift operations to Sirri Island, further down the Gulf, but in August 1986 Iraqi planes bombed that facility as well. The Iranians then shifted to facilities at Larak Island but, with in-flight refuelling, the Iraqis hit that in November 1986.[46]

In response to this escalation and the damage to its oil exports, Iran responded by threatening to take the battle not just to Iraq but to its Saudi and Kuwaiti backers and to close the Straits of Hormuz, and thus the Gulf, to shipping. By late 1986, American intelligence concluded, Iran had decided to increase the pressure on Kuwait in particular, increasing both attacks on Kuwaiti shipping and efforts to foment unrest among the Shia community in Kuwait. In February 1987, the Americans also identified the development of sites along the Iranian coast which appeared to be for Chinese-supplied Silkworm anti-ship missiles.[47] The Reagan administration was now becoming seriously concerned about the threat to the oil lanes, and it was Iran which was deemed to be responsible for 'threatening to close the Gulf and strangle the states of the Arabian Peninsula'.[48]

In the face of Iranian attacks, the Kuwaiti government sought assistance from both the Soviet Union and the United States in protecting its shipping. To some extent, therefore, the Reagan administration was forced into the policy of re-flagging Kuwaiti tankers by Kuwait's playing off of the superpowers against each other. In addition, the administration acted to try and restore American credibility with the Gulf monarchies in the aftermath of the 'arms to Iran' imbroglio. Weinberger, for one, argued that the United States should not only be 'supportive of Iraq but should be seen to be supportive' in order to reassure America's friends in the Gulf.[49] Above all, however, the re-flagging operation was an exercise in hegemonic management. The Reagan administration re-flagged Kuwaiti tankers and sent ships to patrol the Gulf in order to guarantee the continued flow of oil to its industrialised allies and the global economy, as well as to reassure its regional allies amongst the oil producers. In so doing, moreover, the Reagan administration used the leverage its ability to provide security conferred to extract some quid pro quos. Having struggled for years to get better access to bases in the region, the administration now extracted agreement to American use of Kuwaiti ports and improved access to Saudi bases in return for its protection.[50] The re-flagging was also evidence of the increased power of the pro-Arab faction within the administration, with the opposition of the Israeli lobby and unrepentant Cold Warriors being overridden by the imperative of protecting the Gulf monarchies and their Iraqi shield.[51]

The increased threat to the oil supply lines also gave added impetus to the Reagan administration's desire to see an end to the conflict as soon as possible. Since Iran was the party which was refusing to negotiate, that meant finding ways to persuade Tehran to change its mind. The re-flagging itself was a first step along this path, since by agreeing to re-flag Kuwaiti tankers and to patrol the Gulf to protect neutral shipping, the United States had, in effect, joined the war on Iraq's side. The presence of US, Soviet and NATO warships not only served to deter Iranian attacks on shipping, but also left Iraq free to continue its attacks on Iranian tankers and oil platforms behind a shield provided by the US navy.

Moreover, American involvement soon went beyond the ostensibly neutral role of protecting shipping. The Reagan administration used the cover provided by the re-flagging, and the American presence in the Gulf that it legitimised, to initiate a covert military operation aimed at compelling Iran to accept a ceasefire. US–Iraqi intelligence cooperation was increased and the US navy began supplying the Iraqi air force with details of Iranian shipping. US Special Operations helicopters began to conduct reconnaissance operations to gather intelligence for Iraq. The accidental attack by an Iraqi fighter on the *USS Stark* in May 1987, which killed thirty-seven American personnel, could have had serious ramifications for this burgeoning relationship, but Baghdad immediately apologised and offered to pay compensation, largely containing any negative fallout.[52] Indeed, if anything the event made US–Iraqi military cooperation closer in an effort to ensure such errors did not happen again. The American readiness to overlook the *Stark* incident was also reinforced by clear evidence of the continued Iranian threat. At the end of July, thousands of Iranian 'pilgrims' fought with Saudi police in Mecca. In response, the Saudi and Kuwaiti embassies in Tehran were ransacked and the Iranian government called for the overthrow of the Saudi regime and conducted naval manoeuvres in Saudi territorial waters.[53]

The tanker war and the threat posed to the shipping lanes of the Gulf also produced a new urgency on the diplomatic front, leading to the passage on 20 July 1987 of UNSCR 598, demanding an immediate ceasefire in the Iran–Iraq conflict.[54] Iraq accepted the resolution two days later but Iran continued to refuse to negotiate (perhaps unsurprisingly since the resolution demanded a return to pre-war borders as a precondition for negotiations, thus requiring Iran to surrender its principal bargaining chip before negotiations began). The Reagan administration tried to secure agreement that non-compliance with the resolution (assuming that Iran would reject it) should lead to the imposition of sanctions, but it could not rally sufficient support in the Security Council.[55]

With diplomatic pressure thus unavailing, the Reagan administration stepped up its military action against Iran. On 1 September 1987 American forces boarded an Iranian landing craft which had been laying mines in the Gulf, and on 8 October US helicopters sank three Iranian gunboats. A week after that Iran retaliated by firing a Silkworm missile at the re-flagged tanker *Sea Isle City*. In retaliation, American forces destroyed two Iranian oil rigs used as a base for gunboats. Then, in April 1988, after an Iranian mine damaged the *USS Samuel Roberts*, the United States responded by sinking six Iranian ships and destroying two oil rigs.[56] Asked later if the Reagan administration had in effect been fighting an undeclared war against Iran, Secretary of Defense Frank Carlucci responded, 'Oh yes, I don't think there's any question' about that.[57]

US military action was part of a wider set of pressures that, in the first half of 1988, began to force Iran toward the negotiating table. In particular, and in large part as a result of the technology freely exported to it by the US and other Western states, Iraq was beginning to turn the tide of the war. In addition to its ongoing assault on Iranian shipping and oil facilities in the Gulf, in February 1988 Iraq launched a ferocious missile assault on Iranian cities. Then, in March, after Iraqi forces were pushed out of the town of Halabja, they responded with a devastating use of CW which killed thousands and saw Iranian forces flee in panic. With Iranian military and public morale becoming severely undermined, in April Iraq went on the offensive for the first time in six years and retook the Fao peninsula, following this with a further string of victories. Possibly the last straw for the Iranians was the shooting down, on 3 July, of an Iranian civilian airliner by the *USS Vincennes*. Although accidental, coming as it did on top of American naval actions against Iranian targets, Tehran apparently saw this as proof that the United States was moving towards full-blown war against Iran. On 18 July, Tehran therefore reluctantly accepted UNSCR 598.[58]

## THE ANFAL CAMPAIGN

Iraq's use of CW against Iranian forces at Halabja in March 1988 marked the beginning of a sustained campaign, codenamed *al-Anfal*, aimed at breaking the Iranian–Kurdish alliance. The Kurds, isolated and crushed after the Algiers Agreement of 1975, had taken the opportunity presented by the outbreak of the Iran–Iraq War to once again exploit the conflict between the two countries to their own advantage and the Iranians began once again to arm the Iraqi Kurds. By 1986 they had formed an effective alliance against Saddam's regime, with the Kurds constituting the northern front of the Iranian war effort.[59] The Iranian decision to sign the ceasefire in July 1988, however, once again left the Kurds without friends or supporters, and Saddam intended to make full use of the opportunity to wreak his revenge. Within two months of the end of the war some sixty-five Kurdish villages were subject to CW attack, resulting in at least 5,000 deaths and tens of thousands of Kurds fleeing their homes toward Turkey or Iran. Within twelve months there would be over 250,000

Kurdish refugees living in those two countries and a similar number displaced within Iraq itself.[60]

The scale of the Iraqi atrocities drew the attention of the world, and the US Senate Foreign Relations Committee (SFRC) sent a team to investigate. With the assistance of the American embassy in Baghdad, they were able to get into Kurdistan and, in October 1988, the SFRC issued a staff report detailing the atrocities and use of CW by Iraqi forces against the Kurds which generated considerable support in Congress for some kind of punitive action.[61] That sentiment was reinforced by revelations about the extent of Iraq's WMD and missile programmes. In June 1988, the US Customs Service had intercepted missile technology and related illegal exports destined for Iraq. The missile for which the parts were destined, the Argentinean-built Condor, was in violation of the Missile Technology Control Regime and easily capable of striking Israel.[62]

Whilst this evidence of Iraqi weapons programmes and the campaign against the Kurds generated considerable concern in Congress, it had little or no discernible impact on the Reagan administration. As it had in previous instances of Iraqi CW use, the administration sponsored a UN resolution condemning the attacks and tightened some export controls on materials related to CW production, but no more. The business as usual attitude was reflected in a symposium held by the US–Iraq Business Forum for business leaders interested in trade with Iraq in May 1988 with State Department support. Nor was there any alteration in the Commerce Department's attitude towards licences for hi-tech exports. Indeed, with the war now over, Commerce took the view that Iraq was fully open for US business and that there would be lucrative opportunities to be made from Iraqi reconstruction.[63]

There were still those within the administration who continued to distrust Saddam and his regional ambitions, and they now argued that, with Iran defeated and the threat to the Gulf oil states neutralised, the United States needed to adjust its policies in order to ensure the maintenance of the regional balance of power. NSC staffer Zalmay Khalilzad even went so far as to suggest that the US should now contemplate a tilt towards Iran in order to prevent Iraq from becoming too dominant.[64] The State Department, however, was arguing that the United States should seek to cement its regional hegemony through the co-optation of Iraq, and its Bureau of Near

Eastern Affairs was convinced that Baghdad was well on its way to becoming a reliable American ally. In a March 1988 memo it argued that Iraq's shift towards moderation seemed to be permanent, that it had re-established good relations with Kuwait and no longer threatened it, and that fears of Iraqi aggression were 'exaggerated'.[65] The escalation of the Anfal campaign did little to shake this perception, with a paper in September emphasising that 'in many respects our political and economic interests run in parallel with those of Iraq'. The Iraqi market offered great opportunities for US business and it was in the US interest to draw Iraq into alignment with Egypt, Jordan and Saudi Arabia in order to isolate Syria and Iran.[66] Moreover, it argued, Saddam too recognised that he had a 'long-term interest in developing relations with the US to take advantage of our technology and to counter-balance his relationship with the Soviets'. Iraqi use of CW was a potential obstacle to the further deepening of relations and as such was to be discouraged, but through diplomacy and persuasion rather than punitive actions which would have a 'sharp negative impact on our ability to influence the Iraqi regime'.[67]

On 9 September the Senate passed the Prevention of Genocide Act of 1988, which would have barred the provision of all US military and financial assistance to Iraq as well as the export of any products subject to export controls. It would also have led to the cut off of CCC and Exim Bank credits and banned US imports of Iraqi oil.[68] Similar legislation was then introduced in the House. The Reagan administration immediately announced that it would oppose the legislation. In a letter to the Chairman of the House Foreign Relations Committee, Dante Fascell, the State Department argued that the administration was working to 'persuade Iraq to stop using chemical agents' and that 'sweeping sanctions' were premature.[69]

The administration feared that the imposition of sanctions 'will undermine relations and reduce US influence in a country that has emerged . . . as one of the most powerful Arab nations'[70] and one which was 'important to our long-term political and economic objectives in the Gulf and beyond'.[71] That concern was reinforced by warnings from the US embassy in Baghdad that Saddam would allow the relationship to collapse rather than be seen to cave in to American pressure and that he still suspected that the US wanted to rekindle its relationship with Tehran.[72] In addition, policy-makers argued that sanctions would be 'useless or counter-productive' since the Iraqis would simply look to Western Europe or Japan to supply their economic and military needs.[73] Sanctions would thus lead to the 'unravelling of the US–Iraqi economic relationship' and US businesses would be excluded from Iraq to the benefit of their competitors. Finally, they argued, sanctions were unnecessary because American diplomatic efforts had 'begun to pay off' and the Iraqis were now pledging not to use CW.[74] If Iraq violated that assurance, Assistant Secretary of State Richard Murphy promised Congress, the administration would impose sanctions.[75]

The administration was given considerable assistance by the Iraq lobby, which had grown considerably as US export guarantees had expanded over the previous five years. The US–Iraq Business Forum mobilised its resources to oppose the House bill, as did the farm lobby, which stood to lose a major export market if CCC credits were banned. Democrats from agricultural districts joined with Republicans in the House to block the bill, forcing its sponsor, Representative Howard Berman, to delete the CCC sanctions element. The Senate then passed a compromise bill that would have immediately banned the sale or licensing for export of arms and any item on the Export Administration Act control list, as well as any chemicals that might be used for CW. The bill also required the president to impose additional sanctions unless he was able to certify that Iraq was not using CW and had guaranteed that it would not do so.[76] The House of Representatives also rejected this bill. On 7 October, the Senate offered a further compromise with a specific exemption for agricultural goods in the hope of getting the farm lobby back onside. However, with time running out in the Congressional session and continued strong opposition, the legislation died.[77]

The Reagan administration's response to the Prevention of Genocide Act of 1988 was indicative of the extent to which the pro-Arab, pro-Iraqi faction had come to dominate policy towards the Persian Gulf. The pro-Iranians had been discredited by Iran–Contra, whilst many of those most concerned with Israel now saw Iran, rather than Iraq, as the primary threat, and very few were focused on the Soviet 'threat' any more. As a result, those within the administration whose primary focus was on Gulf oil, and the stability and security of America's Gulf allies, were in the ascendancy. Even with the Iranian threat to the Gulf states effectively contained, the Reagan administration did not change course. American policy had now gone beyond

power balancing to a fully fledged attempt to co-opt Iraq as a US
partner in Gulf security.

## FROM REAGAN TO BUSH

In January 1989, Reagan was succeeded as president by his former
vice-president, George H. W. Bush, who had defeated the Democratic
candidate, Michael Dukakis, in the election the previous November.
Bush's victory ensured continuity in American policy towards Iraq,
since he himself was one of the leading figures in the pro-Arab/pro-
Iraq lobby and had personally intervened to press for the extension of
credit guarantees to Iraq when the Exim Bank was being resistant.
Indeed, Bush was probably the most pro-Arab president since
Eisenhower. Being both an Eastern internationalist attuned to the
interests of the US oil majors and the rest of multinational capital,
and an oilman himself, he was very focused on the Gulf and the
international oil system in general. Under Bush, therefore, the US
effort to woo Iraq would continue until it was decisively ended by the
Iraqi invasion of Kuwait on 2 August 1990.

Bush's victory in the 1988 presidential election was further evidence
of the growing dominance of the Republican Party. Bush defeated
Dukakis by overwhelming margins, winning 53 per cent of the
popular vote and 426 Electoral College votes. The geographic source of
those votes also confirmed the emerging Republican lock on the states
of the south and the west, with Bush sweeping both regions. On the
other hand, there was a noticeable retreat from New England and the
west coast, confirming the decline of Republicanism in those areas.[78]
The 1988 election thus reflects the ongoing transformation of the
Republican Party and the emergence of a dominant southern and
western conservative coalition. That transformation, nevertheless,
remained unfinished and half-formed at this point. Democrats still
held fifteen of the twenty-two Senate seats in the old confederacy,
while there remained a significant minority of liberal and moderate
Republicans in the north-east.[79]

Moreover, whilst at the electoral level the 1988 election unquestionably demonstrates the ongoing trend in both US politics and
the Republican Party itself towards the right, in electing George H. W.
Bush as president it actually produced a temporary reversal of that
trend (at least in the executive branch) and four years of control for

the dying eastern wing of the Republican Party. This anomalous outcome was a residual effect of the influence of the eastern wing on Reagan's choice of vice-presidential candidate in 1980. Eight years of loyal service and Reagan's own endorsement put Bush in prime position to secure the Republican nomination and enabled him to overcome the challenge of a number of candidates from the right of the Party.[80] For four years, as a result, the rightward drift of the Republican Party would be temporarily halted, at least at the level of the executive branch. In foreign affairs the pragmatic, realist, multi-lateralist outlook of the eastern wing of the Republican Party would hold sway over the more militaristic and unilateralist inclinations of the conservative south and west. That much was made clear as soon as Bush announced his appointees to the key national security portfolios. Secretary of State James Baker, National Security Adviser Brent Scowcroft and Chairman of the Joint Chiefs of Staff Colin Powell were all well-known moderates and pragmatists. The only representative of the conservative wing of the party was Secretary of Defense Dick Cheney, who was only chosen because Bush's initial nominee, John Tower, was refused confirmation by the Senate. Overall, only a third of Bush's appointees were holdovers from the Reagan administration, leading former Reagan adviser Martin Anderson to complain that there was a 'very systematic purge that went into effect of anyone with any association with the Reagan–Nixon–Goldwater wing of the party'.[81]

Bush's victory thus brought to office an eastern internationalist who believed in multilateralism and evinced a clear preference for order and stability over change. He was not opposed to the use of force, indeed as a member of the generation that came of age during the Second World War rather than Vietnam, his formative experiences had taught him that war was sometimes an unavoidable necessity.[82] If he was to use force, however, he would prefer to act with the support of others, wherever possible. Moreover, unlike his predecessor and his son, Bush was even prepared to argue that the UN 'still serves a valuable purpose'.[83] His multilateralism reflected his assessment of the limitations of the power of even the United States, which needed friends and allies to help it carry the burden of leadership. That assessment also, in part, shaped Bush's preference for stability and order over change, though it was more deep-rooted than that. In his campaign autobiography he wrote that 'if the experience of the last fifty years teaches anything, it's that a "new idea" on how to shape a coherent foreign policy or develop the economy isn't good just because it's new'.[84] Bush's default response in the face of a problem was therefore to 'not make things worse'.[85]

These basic characteristics of Bush and his administration would be clearly demonstrated in their conduct of policy towards the Persian Gulf, and nowhere more clearly than in the Gulf War of 1990–1. In that episode Bush would demonstrate a readiness to use force in order to preserve American hegemony but within a mutlilateralist framework of allied military and financial support and with the imprimatur of the UN. With victory secured he would then choose the option of a return to the status quo ante, rather than seek to radically overturn the existing regional order. In all of this he would stand in marked contrast to his son.

## NATIONAL SECURITY DIRECTIVE 26

The Bush administration's transition paper on Iraq policy, prepared by the Department of State, declared that it was time to 'decide whether to treat Iraq as a distasteful dictatorship to be shunned where possible, or to recognize Iraq's present and potential power in the region and to accord it relatively high priority. We strongly urge the latter view' because Iraq 'has the wherewithal to be a major player in regional affairs' and is currently aligned with America's moderate Arab allies. Moreover, 'the losses of war may have changed Iraq from a radical state challenging the system to a more responsible status-quo state working within the system and promoting stability in the region'. Given Iraq's political, economic and military strength, it went on, the isolation of Iraq in the manner of Syria was not possible and therefore engagement was the only realistic option. It did note that 'we may find ourselves opposed to Iraqi ambitions if they include hegemony in the Gulf', but at present the United States and Iraq agreed on the need for 'stability, which focuses on containing Iran'. With regard to how best to encourage Iraqi 'moderation' it stated that 'trade is the best key to political influence in Iraq' and that the administration should make a 'major effort to free up licensing requests' so as to facilitate trade and achieve the ultimate objective, which was to 'rope Iraq into a conservative and responsible alignment in foreign policy'.[86]

The Bush administration was encouraged to pursue the course of constructive engagement with Iraq by the latter's behaviour. Whilst he may have used CW against the Kurds and have an appalling human rights record, when it came to the issues that really concerned the administration, Saddam was taking the positions they wanted. Iraq had supported the PLO in its decision to recognise Israel and to pursue a two-state solution through negotiations (unlike Iran and Syria), and it continued to align itself with America's friends in the region. Saddam's support was a key factor in the return of Egypt to the Arab summit in May 1989, whilst three months earlier he had established the Arab Cooperation Council (ACC) with Jordan, Egypt and North Yemen and signed non-aggression pacts with Saudi Arabia and Bahrain.[87] In terms of the all-important strategic question of whether Iraq was contributing to, or threatening, the stability of the region and American regional hegemony, it seemed clearly at this point to be doing the former. Moreover, as the transition paper had noted, Iraq had just fought an eight-year war. It was widely assumed, therefore, and not just within the administration, that it was not likely to engage in further adventures any time soon.[88] There were also plenty of people outside the administration pressing it to continue the opening to Iraq, primarily for reasons of economic self-interest. The US–Iraq Business Forum, the farm lobby, and their representatives in Congress, were all pushing for the expansion of trade and, as James Baker admitted in his memoirs, the administration's policy toward Iraq was 'not immune from domestic economic considerations'.[89]

There were, on the other hand, relatively few people, inside or outside the administration, pushing in the other direction. Many of those who had feared Iraqi ambitions, like Teicher and Perle, were now out of office. There were still concerns about Iraq within certain agencies, albeit for different reasons (the Treasury and Exim Bank doubted Iraq's creditworthiness, some at the Department of Energy worried about Iraq's nuclear ambitions, and some at the DOD worried about the export of dual-use technology), and there were some, such as Deputy-Secretary of Defense Paul Wolfowitz, who continued to be concerned about Iraq's regional ambitions.[90] But their collective bureaucratic weight was insignificant compared to that of the forces arrayed against them.

Even the clear evidence that Iraq continued actively to pursue all forms of WMD did not strengthen their hand. The transition paper simply stated that there was 'nothing we can say that will stop' Iraq developing WMD and that all the United States could do was to ask its allies not to sell Iraq material that might contribute to WMD programmes. Whilst some within the administration were concerned about Iraq's nuclear weapons programme, the analysis of the Department of Energy was that whilst Iraq was acquiring nuclear technology, no such programme had actually been identified and that, at best, Iraq might have nuclear weapons capability in ten years.[91] As with Iraqi human rights abuses, Congress expressed greater concern, and on 25 January 1989 the Senate passed the Chemical and Biological Control Act, which would have cut off the export of sensitive technologies and barred government-supported loans to Iraq. Bush vetoed the act within days of coming to office.[92]

The Bush administration's attitude towards the export of dual-use technology was made clear in the spring of 1989 when Dennis Kloske, Bush's nominee to head the Bureau of Export Administration at Commerce, informed the DOD that Commerce would no longer refer licences for exports to Iraq to them because of their obstructive behaviour.[93] Even when the suppliers of dual-use technology were themselves concerned, the Bush administration was not. In spring 1989, the Consarc Corporation of New Jersey wrote to the Department of Commerce with regard to an Iraqi order for four specialised furnaces with potential military applications, including nuclear ones. Commerce told them they did not need a licence for the furnaces, just end-user certification from the Iraqis that they were for civilian use.[94] This relaxed attitude to the export of dual-use technology would continue despite the growing evidence, detailed in reports by US intelligence agencies, that Iraq was using a web of front companies in order to acquire Western technologies for use in its WMD programmes.[95]

After a formal review of Iraq policy, Bush signed NSD-26, outlining US strategy for the Persian Gulf, on 2 October 1989. After the standard repetition of the self-evident fact that 'access to Persian Gulf oil and the security of key friendly states in the area are vital to US national security', it went on to outline a policy which conformed to the reasoning of the January transition paper and the actions of the last few months. It asserted that 'normal relations between the United States and Iraq would serve our longer-term interests and promote stability in both the Gulf and the Middle East' and that the United States should therefore 'propose economic and political incentives for

Iraq to moderate its behaviour and to increase our influence with Iraq'.[96]

## BANCA NAZIONALE DEL LAVORO AND COMMODITY CREDIT CORPORATION CREDITS

In accordance with this policy, the Bush administration was about to extend an extra $1 billion in CCC guarantees when the BNL scandal broke. On 4 August 1989, having been tipped off by two of its employees about Christopher Drogoul's secret and illegal loans to Iraq, the FBI raided the Atlanta Branch of BNL. The subsequent investigation revealed that whilst BNL had officially guaranteed $720 million in loans to Iraq, Drogoul had unofficially lent a further $4 billion in largely unsecured loans. More importantly, from the administration's point of view, the investigations revealed a range of potential violations of US laws with regard to the use of CCC credits, including the solicitation of bribes and after-sales services and the imposition of illicit taxes.[97] On 12 October, officials from the Department of Agriculture met the prosecutor in the BNL case and, after what she told them, suspended discussions with Iraq with regard to further CCC credits.[98]

The exposure of the BNL deception and the diversion of agricultural credits for illicit purposes threatened to derail Iraq policy. Both the Treasury and the Exim Bank had been expressing their concerns about Iraq's creditworthiness for several years,[99] and there was now powerful additional evidence to support their arguments for opposing the extension of further credits and guarantees to Iraq. In addition, the CCC itself now called for the National Advisory Council (NAC) to reconsider the proposed $1 billion in new credit guarantees.[100] The State Department, however, had little or no interest in Iraqi creditworthiness, concerned as it was with the bigger geopolitical picture. Its determination to extend further credits was further reinforced when the Iraqis made clear that they considered it to be a test of whether or not the United States was sincere about its desire for improved bilateral relations. When the two met in Washington in early October, Foreign Minister Aziz complained to Baker that US–Iraqi relations had not moved forward quickly enough since the end of the Iran–Iraq War and that there was a campaign inside the United States to smear and discredit Iraq. The Iraqis warned that if new credits were not extended they would look elsewhere and rethink their relationship with the United States.[101]

With the administration's Gulf policy about to collapse about its ears, Baker decided to do whatever was necessary to ensure that the new loan guarantees were extended. Accordingly, he pressed Secretary of Agriculture Clayton Yeutter to put his department's full weight behind extension of the $1 billion, providing that the Department's review of the Iraqi CCC programme found no evidence of wrong-doing.[102] Nevertheless, at the next NAC meeting, State and Agriculture found themselves in the minority as the representatives of the Treasury, the Federal Reserve and the Office of Management and Budget all opposed extension of further CCC credits. In order to overcome these objections, State called for another NAC meeting involving more senior departmental representatives on 8 November. Before the meeting they also leaned heavily on the reluctant Treasury to get in line. Deputy Secretary of State Lawrence Eagleburger wrote to his counterpart at the Treasury, John Robson, to emphasise that the credits were vital 'on foreign policy grounds'. Specifically, they were 'important to our efforts to improve and expand our relationship with Iraq' as 'ordered by the President in NSD-26'.[103] Under-Secretary of State Robert Kimmit then drove home the message at the meeting itself: The credits were 'crucial to the US bilateral relationship with Iraq', which was 'key to the achievement of our objectives in the Middle East, the Gulf and Lebanon'. Refusing to extend the credits would 'clearly run counter to the president's intention and would, furthermore, cause a deterioration in our relationship with the Iraqis . . . Overwhelming foreign policy considerations' therefore called for extension of the guarantees. In the face of this argument and the extensive bureaucratic pressures that had been brought to bear, the meeting duly approved the new credit guarantees in two tranches of $500 million.[104]

In addition to the extension of further CCC credits, the Bush administration was determined to restore Exim Bank guarantees. The Exim Bank itself was not so inclined, and indeed had never been, because of Iraq's debt problems and difficulties in paying back loans. In fact the bank had actually suspended Iraq from the list of countries eligible for loans. In so doing it simply anticipated the attitude of Congress which, evidently more concerned about the evidence of the diversion of dual-use technology by Iraq than the administration, in late 1989 began to consider legislation barring the extension of Exim Bank loans and guarantees to Iraq. Congress and the Bank both now came under severe pressure from State and Commerce as well as from the business lobby. Indeed, given Iraqi financial problems and the threat they posed to US exporters, the US–Iraq Business Forum now began demanding that the Exim Bank extend not just loan guarantees but the actual loans themselves.[105] In the face of this pressure, Congress included in its legislation a provision which would allow the president to waive the ban.[106] The State Department duly prepared a memorandum for Bush setting out the rationale for a waiver of the congressionally imposed restrictions: 'It is in the national interest of the United States to maintain existing political and economic incentives . . . to encourage Iraq to moderate its behaviour and increase our ability to deal effectively with Iraq on issues of importance to the United States'.[107] Two weeks later, Bush waived the ban on new loan guarantees for Iraq.

## THE APOTHEOSIS OF CONSTRUCTIVE ENGAGEMENT

By early 1990, the Bush administration was pressing full steam ahead to try and co-opt Iraq into the fold of moderate Arab states through political and, above all, economic engagement. This policy was driven primarily by hegemonic considerations but was strongly reinforced by growing American commercial interests in Iraq. Evidence of Iraq's ongoing efforts to acquire nuclear weapons and of possible violations of CCC programme rules were not deemed of sufficient importance to alter this policy. Part of the reason for this was the almost total dominance of the pro-Arab faction within the administration. The exposure of the 'arms to Iran' farrago had led to the eclipse of those who wanted to restore the US–Iranian relationship and compelled the Reagan administration to tilt even more overtly towards Iraq in order to reassure both Baghdad and America's Gulf allies. That consideration, plus the threat to the oil flow from the Gulf posed by the escalating 'tanker war', led to the re-flagging of Kuwaiti tankers and America's covert military intervention against Iran in order to force it to the negotiating table. It also meant that when, with the Iran–Iraq War now finished and the *Anfal* campaign demonstrating Saddam's brutality, the Reagan and Bush administrations might have reconsidered policy toward Iraq, there was hardly anyone within the ranks of senior policy-makers who was inclined to do so. Congressional efforts to punish Iraq through sanctions were accordingly opposed and defeated in the name of the larger strategic objective of coaxing Iraq toward the path of moderation.

## NOTES

1. *Iraqgate*, 'Report on the Commodity Credit Corporation's GSM 102/103 export credit guarantee programs and Iraq's participation in the programs', 16 October 1990.
2. *Iraqgate*, 'Eximbank financing for Iraq', 22 December 1983.
3. *Iraqgate*, 'Eximbank financing for Iraqi export pipeline', 12 June 1984.
4. *Iraqgate*, 'Eximbank offers to help Iraq–Jordan pipeline', 25 June 1984; Jentleson, *With Friends Like These*, pp. 43–4; Friedman, *Spider's Web*, pp. 29–30.
5. The CCC allowed exporters to receive immediate payment for their goods by assigning the account and the repayment guarantee to an American bank, which paid the exporter and then sought repayment from the country which had received the goods.
6. Friedman, *Spider's Web*, pp. 96–104.
7. *Iraqgate*, 'Sale of Hughes helicopters to Iraq', 16 December 1982; 'Sale of helicopters to Iraq', 29 December 1982; 'Hughes civilian helicopter sale to Iraq', 18 February 1983; 'Militarization of Hughes helicopters', 8 June 1983.
8. Timmerman, *The Death Lobby*, pp. 175–6. The ACEA requires State Department approval of any US exports with military potential as well as barring the selling on by third parties of arms supplied to them without notification of Congress.
9. Ibid. pp. 18–19, 35–6.
10. Karsh and Rautsi, *Saddam Hussein*, pp. 129–30.
11. Coughlin, *Saddam*, pp. 132–3.
12. Bhatya and McGrory, *Brighter than the Baghdad Sun*, pp. 94–108.
13. Coughlin, *Saddam*, pp. 129–30.
14. Timmerman, *The Death Lobby*, pp. 106–12.
15. Ibid. pp. 149–57.
16. Shultz, *Turmoil and Triumph*, pp. 238–9.
17. UN Security Council, 'Report of the specialists'.
18. Shultz, *Turmoil and Triumph*, pp. 240–1.
19. US Congress, Senate, 'Strengthening the export licensing system'; Jentleson, *With Friends Like These*, pp. 62–3.
20. *Wall Street Journal*, 29 April 1981.
21. *Iraqgate*, 'High technology dual-use exports to Iraq', 1 July 1985.

22. *Iraqgate*, 'Letter to Secretary Weinberger on US–Iraqi relations and advanced technology exports to Iraq', 29 April 1985.
23. Timmerman, *The Death Lobby*, p. 211.
24. Shultz, *Turmoil and Triumph*, p. 240.
25. US Congress, House, Committee on Foreign Affairs, *US Exports of Sensitive Technology to Iraq*, p. 22.
26. Timmerman, *The Death Lobby*, p. 220.
27. Chubin and Tripp, *Iran and Iraq at War*, pp. 61–2.
28. *Iraqgate*, 'Iraq crisis pre-planning group, meeting of Wednesday July 25', 23 July 1986.
29. Timmerman, *The Death Lobby*, p. 241.
30. Jentleson, *With Friends Like These*, p. 62.
31. Timmerman, *The Death Lobby*, pp. 267–8, 287–90.
32. UN, Security Council, 'Report on the 7th IAEA on-site inspection'.
33. *Tower Commission Report.*
34. Waas and Unger, 'In the loop', p. 67; *Iraqgate*, 'Arens public remarks on alleged US–Israeli arms supply to Iran', 22 October 1982.
35. *The Times*, 21 November 1986.
36. Reagan, *An American Life*, pp. 505–7.
37. Shultz, *Turmoil and Triumph*, p. 791. Shultz was opposed to the sale of arms to Iran, in part perhaps because he felt, given the logic expressed in this quote, that it was unnecessary.
38. *Iraqgate*, 'US policy toward Iran', 11 June 1985.
39. *Iraqgate*, 'US policy toward Iran: comment on draft NSDD', 29 June 1985; see also 'US policy toward Iran', 16 July 1985.
40. *Iraqgate*, 'Release of American hostages in Beirut', 4 April 1985; Jentleson, *With Friends Like These*, pp. 57–8.
41. Timmerman, *The Death Lobby*, pp. 244–5.
42. *Iraqgate*, 'US–Iraqi relations: picking up the pieces', 5 December 1986.
43. Re-flagging involved taking Kuwaiti tankers under temporary US sovereignty in order to deter Iran from attacking them.
44. Robins, 'Iraq in the Gulf War', p. 52.
45. *Iraqgate*, 'Persian Gulf tanker war: background', 18 May 1987.
46. *Khaleej Times*, 18 August 1985, quoted in Chubin and Tripp, *Iran and Iraq at War*, p. 63. Arguably this escalation can also be attributed to the 'arms to Iran' fiasco, in as much as the Iranian military success which resulted from the arms sales forced Iraq into a more aggressive strategy.
47. Weinberger, *Fighting for Peace*, p. 387.
48. Shultz, *Turmoil and Triumph*, p. 926.
49. *Iraqgate*, 'Iran–Iraq', 21 January 1987.
50. Bromley, *American Hegemony*, p. 227; Gause, 'International politics of the Gulf', pp. 275–7.

51. Pelletiere, *Iraq and the International Oil System*, p. 186.
52. *Iraqgate*, 'USS Stark: Iraq apologizes', 18 May 1987.
53. Shultz, *Turmoil and Triumph*, p. 933.
54. UNSCR 598, www.daccessdds.un.org//doc/RESOLUTION/GEN/NRO/524/70/IMG/NRO52470.pdf?OpenElement.
55. Malone, *International Struggle over Iraq*, p. 38.
56. Chubin and Tripp, *Iran and Iraq at War*, pp. 217–18; *Iraqgate*, 'SPOT intelligence report: the Iranian response thus far and what's ahead', 18 April 1988.
57. ABC News, *Nightline*, 1 June 1992. Carlucci replaced Weinberger as Secretary of Defense in November 1987.
58. Pollack, *Arabs at War*, p. 229.
59. Rabil, 'Operation "Termination of Traitors"'.
60. Karsh and Rautsi, *Saddam Hussein*, pp. 200–1.
61. US Congress, Senate, Committee on Foreign Relations, *Chemical Weapons use in Kurdistan*.
62. Jentleson, *With Friends Like These*, pp. 65–6.
63. Timmerman, *The Death Lobby*, p. 305.
64. Khalilzad, 'A geo-strategic overview'.
65. *Iraqgate*, 'Iraq's foreign policy: deeper into the mainstream?', 3 March 1988.
66. *Iraqgate*, 'Overview of US–Iraqi relations and potential pressure points', 9 September 1988.
67. *Iraqgate*, 'US policy towards Iraq and CW use', 19 September 1988.
68. *Iraqgate*, 'Background and summary of Iraqi sanctions legislation', 22 September 1988.
69. *Iraqgate*, 'State Department comments on the Prevention of Genocide Act of 1981 [sic]', 13 September 1988.
70. *Iraqgate*, 'US–Iraqi relations: implications of passage of economic sanctions bill', 18 October 1988.
71. *Iraqgate*, 'US policy toward Iraq and CW use', 19 September 1988.
72. *Iraqgate*, 'After US actions, Saddam changes his tone', 12 September 1988.
73. *Iraqgate*, 'US policy toward Iraq and CW use', 19 September 1988.
74. *Iraqgate*, 'Administration position on proposed Iraq sanctions', 18 November 1988.
75. *Iraqgate*, 'Statement by Richard W. Murphy, Assistant Secretary of State for Near Eastern, Eastern and South Asian Affairs, before the Subcommittee on Europe and the Middle East of the House Foreign Affairs Committee', 13 October 1988.
76. *Iraqgate*, 'Background and summary of Iraq sanctions legislation', 22 September 1988.

77. *Congressional Quarterly Almanac, 1988,* pp 510–11; Jentleson, *With Friends Like These,* pp. 77–9.
78. David Leip, 'Atlas of US presidential election results', www.uselection atalas.org/RESULTS/index.html.
79. For example, William V. Roth in Delaware, William Cohen in Maine, Warren Rudman and Robert C. Smith in New Hampshire, Henry John Heinz III and Arlen Specter in Pennsylvania, John Chafee in Rhode Island and James Jeffords in Vermont.
80. Critchlow, *The Conservative Ascendancy,* pp. 222–3; Ferguson, *Golden Rule,* pp. 255–6.
81. Parmet, *George Bush,* p. 361.
82. *Public Papers,* 'Remarks at the United State Military Academy, West Point, New York', 5 January 1993.
83. Bush, *Looking Forward,* p. 111.
84. Ibid. p. 205.
85. Duffy and Goodgame, *Marching in Place,* p. 65.
86. *Iraqgate,* 'Guidelines for US Iraq policy', 20 January 1989. According to Shultz, he and his advisers, in the transition book prepared for the Bush administration on the Gulf, argued that 'a new and tougher policy toward Saddam Hussein's Iraq was now appropriate' because the US no longer needed Iraq to balance Iran. Shultz, *Turmoil and Triumph,* p. 243.
87. Jentleson, *With Friends Like These,* pp. 99–100; *Iraqgate,* 'Meeting with Iraqi Under-Secretary Nizar Hamdoun', 23 March 1989.
88. Axelgard, *A New Iraq*; Helms, *Iraq: Eastern Flank of the Arab World*; Mylroie, 'The Bagdhad alternative'; Robins, 'Iraq in the Gulf War'.
89. Baker, *Politics of Diplomacy,* p. 263.
90. Jentleson, *With Friends Like These,* pp. 108–9; Pollack, *The Threatening Storm,* p. 29.
91. *Iraqgate,* 'Recommendations to strengthen nuclear non-proliferation policy', 17 April 1989; 'Comments on Iraq export control initiative', 17 April 1989.
92. Timmerman, *The Death Lobby,* p. 311.
93. Ibid. pp. 347–8.
94. Jentleson, *With Friends Like These,* p. 110.
95. *Iraqgate,* 'Iraq's European procurement network', 29 June 1989; Douglas Frantz and Murray Waas, 'CIA told White House of Iraqi arms efforts', *Los Angeles Times,* 6 August 1992, pp. A1, 3. In September 1989 the State Department did inform US embassies to make a demarche to foreign governments about Iran and Iraq's nuclear weapons programmes and the need to curb exports that might help them; *Iraqgate,* 'Nuclear cooperation with Iran and Iraq', 12 September 1989. There is no

evidence, however, of any tightening up on US exports of dual-use technology at this point.

96. *Iraqgate*, 'US policy toward the Persian Gulf', 2 October 1989.
97. *Iraqgate*, 'Iraq and CCC', 26 January 1990.
98. *Iraqgate*, 'CCC credits for Iraq', October 11 1989; Friedman, *Spider's Web*, p. 132; Jentleson, *With Friends Like These*, p. 132.
99. *Iraqgate*, 'National Advisory Council Staff Committee Minutes, Meeting 86-35', 4 September 1986; 'National Advisory Council Staff Committee Minutes, Meeting 88-14', 5 April 1988.
100. *Iraqgate*, 'Proposed agricultural credit guarantees to Iraq', 27 September 1989.
101. *Iraqgate*, 'Secretary's October 6 Meeting with Iraqi Foreign Minister Tariq Aziz', 13 October 1989; 'CCC negotiations', 9 October 1989.
102. *Iraqgate*, 'The Iraqi CCC program', 26 October 1989; 'Supporting export credits for Iraq', 27 October 1989.
103. *Congressional Record*, 28 April 1992, H2701.
104. *Iraqgate*, 'National Advisory Council deputies meeting, minutes meeting 89-1', 8 November 1989.
105. Timmerman, *The Death Lobby*, pp. 359–61; US–Iraq Business Forum, *Bulletin*, 2 May 1989.
106. *Iraqgate*, 'Legislation on Exim credit guarantees for Iraq', 14 December 1989.
107. *Iraqgate*, 'Memorandum of justification for a waiver of Export–Import Bank restrictions with respect to Iraq', 2 January 1990.

## Chapter 3

# THE PERSIAN GULF WAR, 1990–1991

## SADDAM'S DECISION TO INVADE KUWAIT

The first twelve months of the Bush administration had seen the United States' efforts to woo Iraq reach a peak. Despite the revelations accompanying the BNL scandal, the administration had ignored all objections to its pursuit of a deeper economic and political relationship and the holy grail of Iraqi foreign policy 'moderation'. In the first half of 1990, nevertheless, whatever moderation there may have been evaporated, as Saddam became increasingly hostile and bellicose towards the United States, Israel and, ultimately, Kuwait. Despite growing concern at Saddam's behaviour, the Bush administration did not abandon its policy, instead vacillating between occasional hints of a tougher line and continued efforts to court the Iraqi leader. Only when Iraq actually invaded Kuwait on 2 August 1990 did the administration finally abandon its attempt to co-opt Iraq. That invasion was like a repetition of the Iranian revolution, at one blow shattering the basis of the Bush administration's hegemonic strategy. As in 1979, the state that they had sought to make the centrepiece of their effort to maintain regional hegemony was transformed into the principal threat to American interests in the region. Faced with a direct military challenge to American hegemony, the Bush administration saw war as the only realistic course of action.

On one level, Iraq's invasion of Kuwait was the result of a long-held grievance, since Baghdad had claimed the territory of Kuwait ever since it was created. Saddam's primary motivation, nevertheless, was a concern for his own political survival, his 'victory' over Iran having turned out to be decidedly of the pyrrhic kind. Iraqi casualties were estimated at 200,000 dead and 400,000 wounded and Iraqi sources estimated the cost in terms of lost oil revenue and higher military expenditure at $208 billion, with war damage to Iraq's infrastructure a further $200 billion. Iraqi per capita income had halved as a result of the war, and when wartime subsidies ended inflation rose to 25–40 per cent.[1] Nor were the prospects for a rapid post-war recovery bright. Quota cheating and competition for market share within OPEC in the face of falling global demand for oil had produced a fall of 70 per cent in the oil price between November 1985 and mid-1986. Though the United States, Saudi Arabia and Kuwait then came to an informal agreement to keep the price at between $15 and $20 per barrel, this was still a half to a third cheaper than it had been in 1985.[2] Following the end of their war, both Iraq and Iran called on the other OPEC members to cut their quotas so they could increase theirs, but the demand was ignored and Kuwait and the UAE in particular continued to exceed their quotas.[3] Iraqi oil revenues (representing 97 per cent of Iraqi export earnings) in the year after the war stood at just $13 billion. Forty per cent of that revenue had to be used to service existing debts, estimated by different sources at between $50 and $80 billion,[4] and a majority of what remained was required to fund the Iraqi military machine.[5]

During the war, Iraq had borrowed heavily in order to cover the gap between income and expenditure, but credit was less easy to find now that the Iranian threat had been contained. 'By the end of 1988, Iraq's liquidity problems had become so severe that it was unable to meet principal and interest payment obligations to even favoured creditors like the United States',[6] and with Iraq unable to pay-off existing loans, Western lenders became increasingly reluctant to extend further credit. Saddam thus faced a growing crisis. Iraq's massive debts placed it at the mercy of its creditors, and with the oil price half what it had been five years earlier, his ability to buy the acquiescence of the Iraqi population had been seriously undermined, whilst the war had brought neither tangible nor intangible benefits to ordinary Iraqis. The result was both a loss of control over events on Saddam's part and increased dissatisfaction with his rule, developments which directly threatened his continued survival – as several attempts on his life in the two years following the end of the war demonstrated.[7]

First and foremost, therefore, the Iraqi invasion of Kuwait was an attempt to redress Iraq's parlous economic situation and in so doing to save Saddam's own skin. With the Gulf monarchies and the West refusing to provide the economic assistance he believed was due Iraq for its defence of their interests, Saddam decided to use the principal resource remaining under his control – armed might – to force them to do so.[8] Initially he issued rhetorical threats in an attempt to intimidate the Gulf monarchs into writing off his debts and cutting oil production. When that failed, he first planned to seize the islands of Warba and Bubiyan and the Kuwaiti oilfields. He could then demand that Iraq's debts be written off and, perhaps, that Kuwait cede the islands to Iraq as price of withdrawal. Finally, he would decide to take the ultimate option of simply annexing the whole country and its oil and bank reserves.[9] With Iraq's economic problems thus resolved, Saddam would be able to stabilise his regime.

Saddam was also motivated to act by a belief that the threat to Iraqi economic sovereignty and his regime was no accident. He told an interviewer in March 1990 that 'America is coordinating with Saudi Arabia, the UAE and Kuwait in a conspiracy against us. They are trying to reduce the price of oil to affect our military industries and our scientific research.'[10] His fears were inadvertently fuelled when, on 15 February 1990, the US government-funded *Voice of America* broadcast an editorial celebrating the recent fall of tyrannies in Eastern Europe and noting that, whilst dictators remained in place in countries such as Iraq, the tide of history was against them. The Iraqi government immediately called in US ambassador April Glaspie to express its outrage at this interference in its internal affairs.[11] Congressional resolutions condemning Iraqi human rights violations, continued limits on credits, the exposure of the BNL scandal and increasing media attention on Iraq's WMD programmes served further to fuel this perception of a conspiracy against Iraq.[12] On this assumption, if he did nothing, Saddam could only expect the stranglehold being exerted on the Iraqi economy and his regime to grow ever tighter.

Finally, Saddam may have perceived that the geopolitical balance was also moving against him. The collapse of communism in Eastern Europe and the advanced state of détente between the United States and the Soviet Union meant that he no longer had the option of playing the superpowers off against each other. Instead, he faced a situation where the United States was increasingly dominant, both regionally and globally. From Saddam's point of view, therefore, the United States posed an increasing threat to his own long-term ambitions for regional hegemony and leadership of the Arab world.

The invasion of Kuwait was thus also a pre-emptive strike against the cementing of America's regional hegemony. With Iran already weakened, if Saddam could seize Kuwait, mobilise the Arab masses through nationalist and anti-Israeli rhetoric, and in so doing deter the Gulf monarchies from siding with the US and Israel, he might be able to deter American retaliation and establish Iraq as the hegemon of the Persian Gulf.[13] It was this possibility, perhaps, that drove him to abandon his initial plan simply to seize the islands and the oilfields in favour of the annexation of the whole of Kuwait.

The final critical factor in Saddam's decision was the assumption that he would get away with it. His belief that the other Arab states would turn a blind eye, or at worst seek to buy him off,[14] and that the United States was unwilling to risk war and heavy casualties, demonstrated a deep parochialism and poor grasp of international politics. The mindset created by the experience of how to survive in the brutal world of Iraqi politics proved to be a poor basis for the successful conduct of international affairs.[15]

## PREPARING FOR WAR: JANUARY–JUNE 1990

In order to prepare the ground for a possible attack on Kuwait, Saddam sought to mobilise Arab nationalist sentiment behind Iraq and to portray it as the victim of a conspiracy involving the United States, Israel, and the Gulf oil monarchies. The first public signs of this strategy emerged at the ACC Summit in February 1990, where the Iraqi leader declared that the collapse of communist regimes in Eastern Europe and US–Soviet détente had left the United States 'in a superior position in international politics'. He further noted that the United States had stated its intention to keep its fleet in the Gulf and that this was driven by the American desire to control the oil of the region in order to perpetuate its superpower status. The consequence of this, he averred, was that 'if the Gulf people, along with all the Arabs, are not careful, the Arab Gulf region will be governed by the US will.'[16] He stepped up the rhetoric in April, when he declared that Iraq was besieged by the 'biggest conspiracy in modern history'. This outburst was fuelled by the outcry in the West over the discovery of 'nuclear triggers' destined for Iraq and the execution of Farzad Bazoft, an outcry, Saddam implied, that had been deliberately manufactured. Apparently fearing another pre-emptive Israeli strike like that of June

1981, he warned that 'by God, we will make fire eat up half of Israel if it tries [anything] against Iraq'.[17]

At the Arab summit in Baghdad on 28 May 1990, Saddam played a key rhetorical card: 'The United States has demonstrated that it is primarily responsible for the aggressive and expansionist policies of the Zionist entity against the Palestinian Arab people and the Arab nation'. It was the United States which armed Israel, whose money propped up the Israeli economy, and whose veto in the UN Security Council protected Israel from punishment for its violations of Palestinian rights. 'This is not a policy of friendship. It is a harmful policy that threatens the security and vital interests of the Arab nation'.[18] Such rhetoric was clearly calculated to whip up pro-Iraqi and anti-American sentiment in the Arab world, sentiment which would dissuade Arab regimes from opposing the invasion of Kuwait and thus make an American response impossible.

Alongside the attacks on the United States and Israel, Saddam also sought to put pressure on the oil monarchies. At the February ACC summit he demanded a moratorium on the $40 billion Iraq owed the other Arab states and called on them to provide $30 billion in new economic aid.[19] When that failed to have any effect, Baghdad reiterated its demands for an end to quota cheating and a higher oil quota for Iraq. Then, at the Baghdad Summit, Saddam ratcheted up the rhetoric a few notches. Once more accusing unspecified Gulf states of deliberately exceeding their OPEC oil quotas and thus reducing the price of oil, he declared that every dollar off the price of a barrel cost Iraq $1 billion a year and that, given Iraq's need for those revenues, this was 'an act of war'.[20]

The Bush administration's response to the change in Saddam's rhetoric was confused and uncertain. Every step toward a tougher line was compromised by the pervasive belief within the administration that Saddam's 'paranoia' about American intentions demanded ever greater efforts to provide reassurances of Washington's goodwill.[21] Continued efforts to engage Iraq also stemmed from a misunderstanding of Saddam's calculations. After meeting with Saddam in mid-February, Assistant Secretary of State John Kelly reported that 'Saddam's central message was that he wants regional peace and stability'.[22] Another State Department analysis concluded that whilst Iraqi 'ambitions are grandiose', a 'preoccupation with the threat from Iran' would 'restrain Saddam's freedom to pursue those ambitions', as would the fact that he 'must have the support of the Arab world' and needed 'strong ties to the West' in order to prevent a reversion to a situation 'in which Iran was the dominant regional power'.[23]

In response to Iraqi anger at the 15 February VOA broadcast, the State Department told Ambassador Glaspie to apologise and to reassure Baghdad that the US did not support regime change in Iraq.[24] The Department also continued to press for the extension of the second tranche of CCC credits, and to display a liberal attitude towards the licensing of dual-use exports.[25] Saddam's threat to make 'fire eat up half of Israel', however, produced a stronger response. This time Bush personally condemned the speech and the State Department told Glaspie to warn the Iraqis that Baghdad 'will be on a collision course with the US if it continues to engage in actions that threaten the stability of the region'.[26] On 16 April, it was decided that the second tranche of the $1 billion in CCC credits, which the administration had decided to extend to Iraq in late 1989, would now be placed under indefinite review and a decision on further Exim Bank loans be deferred. It was also agreed to impose more serious restrictions on exports of dual-use technology.[27]

These actions did not, however, represent a turning point in American policy. In fact, they were driven primarily by domestic political calculations. Iraqi actions had 'virtually eliminated political support for efforts to build useful relations with Iraq'. Consequently, 'in order to regain control of policy toward Iraq, we need to establish a political framework that provides a strong response to irresponsible Iraqi actions in the near term and lays down some longer term markers for gradually rebuilding the relationship'. The actions taken would, it was hoped, 'go a long way toward placating congressional critics and help head off sanctions legislation that would limit our flexibility'.[28] The administration's actions were designed to prevent the 'torpedoing of our relationship with an increasingly important state'.[29]

In mid-June, Kelly went before Congress to explain the administration's position. He began by reminding them of the importance of Iraq in the international oil system: 'Iraq not only produces a large quantity of oil, but also has great influence, for better or worse, over the stability of the entire Gulf and its oil'. He acknowledged Iraq's behaviour since January and the questions this raised about Saddam's intentions, as well as Iraq's continued pursuit of WMD. Despite this, he said that the administration opposed two sanctions bills currently being considered by Congress because 'we do not believe that legislating unilateral trade and economic sanctions would help us to achieve our goals in Iraq'. The Iraqi regime was 'well-aware' of American concerns, he averred, and the administration believed that 'it is important to give the government of Iraq an opportunity to demonstrate that it can act to reverse the deterioration in relations'.[30]

## DESCENT INTO WAR: JULY–AUGUST 1990

In his Revolution Day speech of 17 July 1990, Saddam once again accused unnamed Gulf states of plotting with the 'imperialist and Zionist forces'. This time, however, he also warned that they had better come 'back to their senses' and if they did not, 'we will have no choice but to resort to effective action to put things right'.[31] Glaspie nevertheless informed the State Department that Arab diplomats were 'optimistic' that Saddam was simply trying to extort money and a higher oil price and that the pressure on Kuwait would ease after a successful OPEC meeting on 25 July. She suggested that the 'limited deployment' of Iraqi troops toward the Kuwaiti border was for the 'political purpose of keeping the heat on Kuwait'.[32]

On the day of that OPEC meeting Glaspie was unexpectedly invited to meet with Saddam who told her that 'this is a message to President Bush'. He began by reiterating his claims about conspiracies by 'certain parties in the US' who had manipulated Kuwait and the UAE into deliberately forcing down the oil price in another 'war against Iraq'. He also emphasised that he would not stand idly by and that 'Iraq's rights . . . we will take one by one'. He nevertheless seemed to imply that a negotiated solution was possible – 'the solution must be found within an Arab framework and through direct bilateral relations' – and said that 'we don't want war because we know what war means. But do not push us to consider war as the only solution'. In an apparent attempt to deter American retaliation in the event of war, he offered both the carrot and the stick, seeking to reassure Glaspie that 'we clearly understand America's statement that it wants an easy flow of oil', but also warning that whilst the United States 'can harm us . . . we too can harm you . . . We cannot come all the way to you in the United States, but individual Arabs may reach you'.

In response, Glaspie reassured Saddam that Bush wanted better relations with Iraq. She replied to his complaints about conspiracies and criticism in the United States by condemning the American media and expressing sympathy for Iraq's desire for a higher oil price. Perhaps most importantly, she reiterated the State Department's guidance that 'we have no opinion on the Arab–Arab conflicts, like your border disagreement with Kuwait'. She did add, however, that given the deployment of Iraqi troops to its border with Kuwait and Iraq's recent statements, 'we are concerned and my government wishes to know your intentions'. Saddam then appeared to offer a glimmer of hope, assuring Glaspie that Iraq and Kuwait would be meeting for further talks. He ended, however, by stating that 'if we are unable to find a solution, then it will be natural that Iraq will not accept death'.[33]

Glaspie's report on the meeting to Washington encapsulated the Bush administration's failure to grasp Saddam's intentions. She wrote that Saddam's 'emphasis that he wants peaceful settlement [of the dispute with Kuwait] is surely sincere', and that he intended to begin negotiations to that end. She recommended that 'we ease off on public criticism of Iraq until we see how negotiations develop'.[34] That message was reinforced by the advice the administration was getting from its friends in the region – 'nobody in the Arab world thought he [Saddam] was going to do it [invade]'[35] – who were telling it to keep out and allow an 'Arab solution' to be negotiated.[36] The administration therefore drafted a personal message from Bush to Saddam emphasising that he was pleased to hear that Iraq sought a negotiated settlement and that 'my administration continues to desire better relations with Iraq'.[37]

No negotiated settlement was on the cards, however. Saddam had almost certainly already decided to invade Kuwait, and the Kuwaitis were not interested in talking either. Sharing the regional consensus that Saddam's threats were a bargaining tactic and military action very unlikely, they responded by asserting that Kuwait would not 'yield to threat and extortion'.[38] On 30 July, the senior US Defense Intelligence Agency analyst observing Iraqi troop movements e-mailed his agency director to warn that Saddam 'has created the capability to overrun all of Kuwait and all of Eastern Saudi Arabia', and that the only logical conclusion was that he was going to invade. His boss disagreed but forwarded the assessment. The CIA was similarly divided between those who did and did not believe an invasion to be imminent. More importantly none of the Bush administration principals believed it.

Some thought Saddam might make a small incursion as a negotiating tactic, but hardly anyone believed he would occupy the whole country.[39] A meeting between Iraqi and Kuwaiti officials did take place on 1 August, but its purpose was simply to lull the Kuwaitis into a false sense of security. The invasion began even before the talks had ended and Iraqi forces seized complete control of Kuwait within a matter of hours.

## THE BUSH ADMINISTRATION'S RESPONSE

The Iraqi invasion of Kuwait changed everything. National Security Adviser Brent Scowcroft opened an NSC meeting on 4 August with the blunt assertion that 'the stakes in this for the United States are such that to accommodate Iraq should not be a policy option'. Deputy Secretary of State Lawrence Eagleburger noted that this was 'the first test' of the post-Cold War international system and that if Saddam was allowed to get away with it 'others may try the same thing'. Cheney emphasised the threat to the American position in the international oil system: Saddam 'has clearly done what he has to do to dominate OPEC, the Gulf, and the Arab world. He is forty kilometers from Saudi Arabia and its oil production is only a couple of hundred kilometers away.'[40] If it succeeded, Iraq's invasion of Kuwait would give it control of 20.9 per cent of proven world oil reserves and 28.4 per cent of OPEC reserves.[41] That would make it as important an oil power as Saudi Arabia. If it was then able to dominate and coerce the Saudis and the UAE thanks to its position as the dominant military power in the Gulf, it would have effective control of 55 per cent of global oil reserves. As Cheney explained to Congress in September 1990: 'once he acquired Kuwait and deployed an army as large as the one he possesses, he was clearly in a position to dictate the future of world-wide energy policy'.[42]

Some observers have questioned whether the threat was really that great, advancing what might be called the 'he can't drink the oil' argument. According to this reasoning, Saddam's control of a larger share of Gulf oil reserves was an irrelevance because 'whoever owns the oil must sell it at the world-market price'.[43] This argument, however, ignores a number of important considerations. In the first place, Saddam could hardly have been deemed an acceptable replacement for the Saudis as the dominant actor within OPEC. They were pro-

Western, politically passive and, through the recycling of their oil profits, had a large stake in Western economic growth. Saddam was capricious, aggressive, bent on regional dominance and had no such stake in the health of the Western economies. The Gulf monarchies treated oil as a purely economic commodity, but there could be no assumption that Saddam would do the same. Indeed, given his ambitions, it was highly likely that he would seek to revive the oil weapon as a means of asserting his claim to Arab leadership.[44]

Above all, arguments which insist that Saddam would have continued to sell the oil at an acceptable price fail to grasp the centrality of America's ability to guarantee the oil flow to its wider hegemony. If Iraq dominated the Persian Gulf and OPEC, it would not be dependent on the United States for its security as Saudi Arabia and the other Gulf monarchies were. The United States would therefore lose its dominant position in the international oil system and become simply another consumer in the market. That, in turn, would mean a significant reduction in its leverage over the core states for which it had previously acted as guarantor of their oil supplies. America's global hegemony would be weakened. Moreover, with the end of the Cold War and the accelerating decline of Soviet power, American policy-makers were now seeking to cement the United States' position as the unchallenged global hegemon. Allowing Iraq to get away with such blatant defiance of the US-backed norms of the international system would be a significant blow to that project.[45] The Bush administration's determination to reverse the invasion of Kuwait, therefore 'was not about physically protecting oil or even seeking a specific price . . . it was rather about maintaining, indeed even projecting, US hegemony on a global scale'.[46]

The decision of the NSC meeting of 4 August was therefore to seek Saudi agreement to the deployment of US forces on its soil, initially to prevent any further Iraqi advance but ultimately to act as the basis for the eventual removal of Iraqi forces from Kuwait.[47] Riyadh had been resisting such a deployment for the best part of half a century, but this time Saudi room for manoeuvre was limited. Once Saddam had invaded Kuwait they had two options, either to try to buy him off or to fight. Once the Bush administration made clear its intentions, choosing to fight became the preferred option since they would otherwise face the probability that they would be buying off Saddam for ever. King Fahd accordingly agreed to the deployment of US troops, who began moving toward Saudi Arabia within days.

Saudi support alone, however, was insufficient. The administration also wanted the support of the wider Arab world in order to legitimate and facilitate its actions. Fortunately, Saddam's naked aggression and the other Arab states' own calculations of self-interest made this a relatively straightforward task. Besides the Saudis, the two most important Arab states were Egypt and Syria. Egypt's backing was assured by its economic dependency and its role as America's chosen interlocutor between the Arab world and Israel. Iraq's strategy of confrontation threatened to render that role redundant and with it the American need to prop up the Egyptian regime. Syria, for its part, saw Iraq as a rival and a military threat, and with the loss of Soviet support, it could not hope to regain the Golan Heights except through a US-brokered negotiation with Israel. It thus faced a diplomatic dependency on the United States and an opportunity to build up some credit with it.[48] With these three states setting the tone, twelve of twenty-one members of the Arab League backed UN sanctions on Iraq and agreed to supply troops to defend Saudi Arabia.

In addition to regional support, the Bush administration sought wider international legitimacy for its decision to expel Iraqi forces from Kuwait. America's core allies in Western Europe, Canada, Japan and Australasia readily backed the administration, cognisant, as they were, of their dependence on US military power for the security of their oil supplies. Not so dependent, however, was the USSR, whose support would prove critical to American policy. In this context, the end of the Cold War and Soviet decline became critical factors. Given the importance of US-Soviet rapprochement to his plans to revive the USSR, and consequent dependence upon the goodwill of the Bush administration, President Mikhail Gorbachev had little choice but to lend his support to American actions. Soviet support in turn enabled the US to legitimate its chosen policy at the UN. The Soviets voted with the United States for UNSCR 660 of 2 August 1990, which demanded an immediate and unconditional Iraqi withdrawal from Kuwait, and again on 6 August 1990 in support of UNSCR 661, which imposed a total economic embargo on Iraq and Kuwait.[49] In thus working through the UN, the Bush administration was able to achieve a number of important objectives, including the legitimation of the American goal of expelling Iraq from Kuwait, which in turn facilitated coalition-building and maintenance. It also ensured the economic and political isolation of Iraq, and the provision of important political cover to the Saudi government, making it easier for them to invite American troops onto their soil. Having widespread international support and the imprimatur of the UN would also be important in securing the backing of the US public for war.

## SADDAM'S GAMBLE

Saddam had invaded Kuwait because he deemed it necessary to his survival. When the United States and the international community confounded his expectations by responding as they did, he now had to calculate which course of action – withdrawal or defiance – was least likely to lead to his own demise. He decided on the latter, and on 8 August, Iraq announced the irrevocable merger of Iraq and Kuwait. Unconditional withdrawal from Kuwait as demanded by the international community would not have resolved any of the problems that had led Saddam to war in the first place, whilst adding a major humiliation. The likelihood of his being overthrown would thus only have increased. On the other hand, he stood a reasonable chance of surviving a conflict with the United States. UN resolutions called only for the restoration of Kuwaiti sovereignty, not Saddam's removal from power. And fighting the Americans, even if it led to defeat, would enhance his prestige in the Arab world. Nor did he think that such a defeat was inevitable, believing the Iraqi armed forces capable of inflicting sufficient damage on those of the United States to deter it from attacking.[50] Finally, whilst the international coalition ranged against him was exceptionally broad, he clearly held out hope that it could be fractured.

Accordingly, Saddam's principal strategy between August 1990 and January 1991 was to try to divide the coalition. In particular, he sought to 'Zionize' the conflict. If the annexation of Kuwait could somehow be made to seem designed to aid the cause of the Palestinians, then he could hope to unite the Arab masses behind him, making it more difficult for their governments to support American policy. On 12 August, an Iraqi statement therefore tied withdrawal from Kuwait to a preceding Israeli withdrawal from the occupied territories and Lebanon.[51] In an attempt to neutralise this threat, Bush subsequently announced his support for a Middle East peace conference, despite insisting that 'these issues [a conference and the Gulf Crisis] are not linked'.[52]

## WAR DELAYED

Within a week of the Iraqi invasion of Kuwait, the Bush administration had forged an international coalition, secured UN resolutions demanding Iraq's withdrawal and subjecting it to comprehensive economic sanctions, and begun moving the first of what would eventually be 400,000 American troops to the Saudi desert. It would be another five months, however, before those troops were actually used, even though, as early as August, Bush 'could not see how we were going to remove Saddam from Kuwait without using force'.[53] Indeed, Bush and most of his advisers soon concluded that the use of force was not only necessary but desirable. If Iraqi forces withdrew as UN resolutions required, the potential threat, including possible possession of nuclear weapons at some point in the not too distant future, would remain. With the coalition in place and the UN on board, it would be better to use the opportunity Saddam had presented to eliminate the threat he posed through decisive military action. As Cheney put it:

> it is far better for us to deal with him now . . . than it will be for us to deal with him five or ten years from now, when the members of the coalition have gone their disparate ways and when Saddam has become an even better armed and more threatening regional superpower.[54]

The principal reason for the time lag between the emergence of the conviction that force was the only option and its actual use was the time it would take to have the necessary forces in place. But the delay also reflected the difficulties involved in persuading both the American public and America's international partners of the necessity of war. Whilst readily persuaded that Saddam Hussein was a bad man, the American public did not perceive any immediate threat to the United States. Nor did they evince any great sympathy for the dethroned Kuwaiti autocrats. Consequently, they were deeply ambivalent as to whether the restoration of Kuwaiti sovereignty was worth the lives of American soldiers.[55] Similarly, whilst the Bush administration had had no difficulty in winning support for the demand that Iraq withdraw from Kuwait, persuading the international community to support military action was another matter entirely. Consequently, whilst it continued to make the case for the absolute necessity of Iraqi withdrawal, the administration also needed to convince both the American public and the international community that they had exhausted all options short of war before they could persuade them of the necessity of the latter. Even as he gave the orders to put in place the war machine necessary to defeat Iraq, therefore, Bush stated again and again that he hoped and expected that the economic sanctions imposed on Iraq in Resolution 661 would compel Iraqi withdrawal and that he was prepared to give them time to do so.[56]

The greatest threat to this strategy was that Saddam withdrew before that point was reached or accepted some compromise which was deemed acceptable by enough of the US public and/or the international community to make war impossible. Saddam had already outlined his terms for a diplomatic solution, and there were plenty of states that were interested in pursuing such a course. Various Arab leaders, and President Francois Mitterrand of France, put forward their own plans for a negotiated solution, each of which, in different ways, linked Iraqi withdrawal from Kuwait to the Palestinian question and/or the Arab–Israeli peace process.[57] That the proposals ultimately came to nothing and the coalition held together, was in large part down to Saddam, who chose to join the Bush administration in rejecting all of them. Throughout the pre-war period of the crisis he never shifted from the three conditions for withdrawal that he announced on 12 August: withdrawal of US forces from Saudi Arabia and their replacement by Arab forces under UN authority; the lifting of all sanctions; and 'the immediate and unconditional withdrawal of Israel from the Occupied Arab territories in Palestine, Syria and Lebanon', before an Iraqi withdrawal from Kuwait.[58] Since none of the various peace proposals came close to meeting these hopelessly ambitious demands, the Bush administration was saved. Why Saddam refused to deviate from these conditions is unknown, but we can surmise that he believed he needed a substantial reward, such as an Israeli withdrawal from the occupied territories, if the invasion of Kuwait was not to become a disaster and a threat to his own survival.[59]

## LAYING THE BASIS FOR WAR

On 30 October 1990, Bush and his senior advisers met to discuss 'force augmentation'. With the forces needed to defend Saudi Arabia now more or less in place, a formal decision was required on whether to continue the build up to create an 'offensive option' and to set a date for its eventual use. In practice, it was a foregone conclusion. No one at the meeting argued that sanctions would be effective within an acceptable time frame and there was no dissent from the decision to send the 200,000 extra troops required, who would be in position by mid-January 1991. It was also agreed that the administration would seek a UN resolution authorising the use of force and setting a deadline for Iraqi withdrawal.[60] Bush's public announcement of the force augmentation decision nevertheless sparked uproar in the United States, since it made clear that the administration had given up hope, if it ever had any, that sanctions were going to work. Bush sought to assure congressional leaders and the public that 'we have not crossed any Rubicon' and that he was still hopeful that sanctions would work,[61] but he was simply soft-peddling until he had the desired UN resolution authorising the use of force in place. With that secured, he would be in a much stronger position to make the case for war.

Winning support for that resolution involved Baker and Bush in an exhausting round of visits, including one for the latter to Geneva to meet President Assad of Syria, the first such meeting in thirteen years. The key to success, however, lay with the five permanent (P5) and ten non-permanent members of the UN Security Council, and particularly those who appeared reluctant to support military action, including China, Colombia, Cuba, Malaysia, Yemen and Zaire.[62] The full range of American carrots and sticks was duly brought to bear. China, the greatest threat to a successful resolution given its P5 status and veto power, was offered a return from the diplomatic and economic isolation it had been subjected to following the Tiananmen Square massacre, in the form of an invitation to the Chinese Foreign Minister to visit Washington. The non-permanent members were offered a choice of economic rewards or punishments depending on their decision (Colombia, which supported the resolution, got improved access to US markets for its cut flowers; Yemen, which did not, saw US aid cut).[63] UNSCR 678 was passed on 29 November by twelve votes to two (Cuba and Yemen), with one abstention (China). It authorised the use of 'all necessary means' to enforce existing resolutions and established a deadline of 15 January 1991 for Iraq to comply with them.[64]

Having thus secured international support for war, the Bush administration turned to the domestic front with renewed vigour. In response to the force augmentation decision of late October, Congress had initiated hearings into the administration's policy and, the week before the passage of Resolution 678, a series of former senior policy-makers had testified in favour of waiting for sanctions to work.[65] The administration now used its time before the committees to try to refute their arguments. Cheney was first on the Hill, and began by claiming that 'we do not have an indefinite period of time to wait for sanctions to produce the desired result'. While the coalition waited Iraq 'continues to obliterate Kuwait and any trace of her people' and to develop 'weapons of mass destruction'. He was followed by CIA Director William Webster who declared 'our [the CIA's] judgement' to be 'that there is no assurance or guarantee that economic hardships will compel Saddam Hussein to change his policies'. Finally, Baker told the Senate Foreign Relations Committee that 'we have to face the fact that four months into this conflict none of our efforts have yet produced any sign of change in Saddam Hussein'. Ultimately, he argued, 'no one can tell you that sanctions alone will ever be able to impose a high enough cost on Saddam Hussein to get him to withdraw'.[66]

Even now, however, Bush felt the need to demonstrate that he had pursued all possible options short of war and, on 30 November announced that, in order to 'go the extra mile for peace', he was inviting Iraq's Foreign Minister to meet him in Washington and that he would send Baker to Baghdad to meet Saddam Hussein.[67] Once again, this was a purely political gesture directed at the domestic audience – Bush had no expectation whatever that the offer would have any concrete outcome.[68] Moreover, whether Bush understood this or not, far from being a way of avoiding war, the offer only made that outcome more certain. Saddam was apparently 'ecstatic' when he heard of the offer, interpreting it as a sign that the Americans were desperate to avoid war. With anti-war protests in the United States also growing in size and frequency, his hopes that he might yet get away with his gamble were restored.[69]

With no sign of an Iraqi withdrawal, and the January deadline set in UNSCR 678 approaching, Bush faced one last domestic obstacle to war – the constitutional requirement for a congressional declaration of war. With Cheney in the lead, the administration insisted, like so many of its predecessors, that it required no further authorisation.[70] Political realities, however, argued otherwise. Given how divided Congress and the public were over the wisdom of military action, and with 60 per cent of the latter believing that Congress should have to declare war before American troops went into combat,[71] Bush ultimately decided that he had no choice other than to seek a formal congressional declaration of support.[72]

Once again, however, Bush was assisted in the pursuit of his objectives by Saddam Hussein. On 9 January 1991, presumably in the hope of slowing the momentum towards war, Tariq Aziz met with Baker in Geneva in accordance with Bush's proposal of the previous November. Baker passed to Aziz a letter from Bush to Saddam Hussein demanding unconditional withdrawal from Kuwait and warning that if he failed to do so he would 'lose more than Kuwait'. The letter also emphasised that, were Iraq to use chemical or biological weapons 'the American people will demand the strongest possible response'. Having read the letter, Aziz refused to take it to Baghdad and simply said that 'we accept war'.[73] With no sign of Iraqi withdrawal, on 12 January 1991, congressional resolutions supporting the use of force were passed by 250 votes to 183 in the House and by 52 to 47 in the Senate.

Given a choice between unconditional surrender and war, Saddam had chosen the latter. According to one account, Saddam told an Algerian official that 'I have two options: To be killed by US bombs or Iraqi officers . . . If I withdraw unconditionally from Kuwait, I will certainly have to face the second scenario.' The first scenario, in contrast, remained a good deal less certain. The American bombs could be avoided and war still held out some faint possibility of success, even if it came only in the form of a glorious defeat.[74] Desperate last-minute attempts to avoid war by UN Secretary-General Perez de Cuellar and President Mitterrand accordingly came to nothing, and war began at 7.00 p.m. Washington time on 16 January 1991.

Once fighting began, the worst case scenario for Saddam was prolonged allied bombing leading to widespread destruction within

Iraq itself, undermining morale, fomenting discontent and ultimately forcing a humiliating withdrawal without even the redemption of heroic ground combat. As soon as the air strikes began, therefore, he sought to draw the allies into an early and bloody ground battle in Kuwait. Even if Iraq lost, it would at least have fought, and could claim a glorious defeat. Saddam tried various means to achieve this end, the most serious of which were the Scud missile attacks on Israel designed to provoke Israeli retaliation and either break up the coalition or force the US into an early ground war in an effort to prevent them. The blowing up of Kuwaiti oil wells, the pumping of oil into the Gulf and the Iraqi attack on Khafji in Saudi Arabia on 29 January were all also designed to force the hand of the commanders of the forces ranged against him.[75] They, however, refused the bait. The strategic air campaign, designed to cut off Iraqi forces in Kuwait from their command and control in Iraq, degrade Iraq's defensive infrastructure and destroy sites associated with WMD development, continued from 16 January until 24 February.

On 15 February, Saddam again offered to withdraw from Kuwait but freighted the offer with unacceptable conditions, most notably the ending of other occupations in the region. Bush rejected the proposal outright but Gorbachev showed some interest and Aziz then flew to Moscow for talks, after which Iraq offered to withdraw unconditionally if the coalition suspended military operations. Having now realised that his earlier calculations were wrong, and that his army was being systematically destroyed by coalition airpower, Saddam was trying to find a way to get what was left of it out of Kuwait in one piece. The Bush administration, however, did not want to miss the opportunity to strike a decisive blow, and there was sufficient in the new proposal for it to justify a rejection. In particular, the Iraqis demanded that after their withdrawal all UN resolutions passed subsequent to UNSCR 660 be dropped. Amongst other things, those subsequent resolutions insisted that Iraq formally renounce all claims on Kuwait and pay compensation to all those who had suffered as a result of its invasion. Accordingly, on 22 February, having consulted with his international counterparts, Bush gave Iraq twenty-four hours to start withdrawing unconditionally. Despite his desperation by this point, Saddam could not be seen to leave Kuwait with nothing and the deadline passed.[76]

When the ground war came it offered no succour to Saddam.

The Iraqi army was easily and overwhelmingly defeated and ground combat lasted only a hundred hours.[77] With total defeat and disaster imminent, Saddam ordered withdrawal, supposedly in compliance with UNSCR 660, and tried, somewhat feebly, to dress this up as a glorious victory – declaring that Iraq had taken on the world and that Kuwait was part of Iraq come what may – in an effort to bolster his domestic position.[78] Nevertheless, on 27 February, the Iraqi ambassador to the UN informed the Security Council of his government's readiness to comply with all UN resolutions and on 2 March the Security Council set out formal terms for a ceasefire in UNSCR 686, requiring Iraq to rescind its annexation of Kuwait, accept liability for war damages, release all captive Kuwaiti and foreign nationals and POWs and return all property seized from Kuwait.[79]

## THE DECISION TO END THE WAR AND NOT TO REMOVE SADDAM HUSSEIN

In light of subsequent events, the Bush administration's decision to halt military action in response to the Iraqi withdrawal, rather than continuing until the Iraqi military was utterly crushed and/or Saddam Hussein was overthrown, necessarily became a source of some controversy.[80] For its part, the administration advanced a number of reasons for its decision. The extent of the victory and the fact that the destruction of the Iraqi army was coming to look 'like a slaughter' was one.[81] The fact that all objectives had been met and that going into Iraq to remove Saddam would have been 'acting beyond the [UN] resolution[s]' was also emphasised.[82] More significantly, the administration saw going into Iraq to try and topple Saddam as a recipe for turning triumph into disaster. Ironically, in view of later events, it was Cheney who expressed this reasoning most cogently:

> If we'd gone to Baghdad and got rid of Saddam Hussein – assuming we could have found him – we'd have had to put a lot of forces in and run him to ground some place. He would not have been easy to capture. Then you've got to put a new government in his place and then you're faced with the question of what kind of government are you going to establish in Iraq? Is it going to be a Kurdish government or a Shiite government or a Sunni government? How many forces are you going to have to

leave there to keep it propped up, how many casualties are you going to take through the course of this operation?[83]

Greatly reinforcing the reluctance to act was the fact that 'it was our expectation that at that point in the aftermath of the war, Saddam Hussein would not be able to survive politically, that, more than anything else, the returning Iraqi forces would overwhelm him and overthrow him'.[84]

That was an outcome, moreover, that the administration had actively encouraged. On 15 February, Bush called on 'the Iraqi military and the Iraqi people to take matters into their own hands, to force Saddam Hussein, the dictator, to step aside'.[85] Two weeks later, they appeared to be doing precisely that. On 2 March 1991, Shia insurgents, with the help of retreating Iraqi soldiers, instigated an uprising against Iraqi government forces at Nasiriyeh. Within a week most of southern Iraq had fallen under the insurgents' control. Almost simultaneously, the Kurds began rising against Iraqi forces and by 19 March most of Iraqi Kurdistan was under the control of the Patriotic Union of Kurdistan and the Kurdistan Democratic Party. One consequence of the Bush administration ending the fighting when it did, however, was that a large proportion of the Republican Guard escaped unscathed, and Saddam was now able to use these loyal troops to brutally repress the uprisings. Anywhere from 30,000 to 60,000 Shia were killed along with 20,000 Kurds, with a further 1.5–2 million of the latter displaced and fleeing their homes.[86]

Despite desperate pleas for assistance, the Bush administration did not raise a finger to help, and its failure to do so revealed the administration's most fundamental strategic calculations. In the words of George Bush and Brent Scowcroft:

> while we hoped that a popular revolt or coup would topple Saddam, neither the United States nor the countries of the region wished to see the break-up of the Iraqi state. We were concerned about the long-term balance of power at the head of the Gulf.[87]

Colin Powell was rather blunter, and a little more honest, when he stated that 'our practical intention was to leave Baghdad enough power to survive as a threat to . . . Iran'.[88]

It was the great misfortune of the Kurds and the Shia that, seen from that perspective, their uprisings were undesirable. The Kurds were fighting for independence, and Kurdish independence was unacceptable to the Bush administration because the Kurds also claimed territory inside Turkey, a key US NATO ally, and Iran. American support for the uprising would thus do grave damage to a key alliance, promote instability and conflict in the region and, not least, further weaken Iraq. A successful Shiite uprising was potentially even worse, since the Iraqi Shia were regarded by the administration and the Gulf states as actual or potential proxies of Iran, a fear seemingly confirmed when Iranian agents turned up in southern Iraqi cities to try and organise the uprising.[89] The possibility of Shiite dominance of Iraq was horrifying. The Bush administration had not gone to war to eliminate one threat only to see that war lead directly to the enhancement of the power of its other main enemy in the region.[90]

When Bush had called upon the Iraqi people and military to rise up and remove Saddam, therefore, he had been somewhat disingenuous. What he really hoped for was a nice tidy military coup which left Iraq less hostile to the US and its friends in the region but united and still capable of balancing and containing Iran. As one senior official explained the administration's thinking:

> Saddam will quash the rebellions and after the dust settles, the Ba'ath military establishment and other elites will blame him for not only the death and destruction from the war, but the death and destruction from putting down the rebellion. They will emerge then and install a new leadership.[91]

## OPERATION PROVIDE COMFORT

Though the Bush administration did not step in to assist the Kurdish uprising, it was compelled by the scale of the disaster befalling the Kurds, and by international and domestic pressure, reluctantly to provide humanitarian assistance. On 5 April the Security Council passed UNSCR 688, condemning Iraq's repression of the Kurds and insisting that Iraq 'allow immediate access by international humanitarian organizations to all those in need of assistance'.[92] Though the resolution provided no authority to enforce those demands, on 8 April the British prime minister, John Major, proposed a plan to create 'safe enclaves' inside Iraq for the refugees to return to and on 16 April the

US, the UK and France stated that UNSCR 688 entitled them to send troops to northern Iraq in order to create safe havens to aid the Kurds and deliver humanitarian aid.[93] Whilst formally rejecting 688, Saddam bowed to the realities of his situation and informally agreed to withdraw Iraqi forces from the border area. With the subsequent arrival of 16,000 Western troops and the establishment of refugee camps in the 'safe areas', the Kurds began to return home. On 7 June, the coalition forces handed over all humanitarian responsibilities to the UN High Commissioner on Refugees, but established a 'no-fly zone' (NFZ) barring Iraqi aircraft from flying above the thirty-sixth parallel in order to protect the 'safe haven'. In response, in October 1991, Iraqi troops and all government workers were ordered to withdraw from the three Kurdish provinces. Saddam's decision to thus relinquish control over the Kurdish region would appear to have been a calculated gamble. By cutting a deal with the Kurds, and not resisting Operation Provide Comfort, he gambled that Western forces would withdraw from Kurdistan sooner rather than later and that Kurdistan would remain within Iraq, to be reclaimed fully at a more opportune moment.[94]

## CONTAINING SADDAM

The NFZ in northern Iraq was imposed under UNSCR 688. After the first two months of its existence, however, it had very little to do with humanitarianism and everything to do with containing Saddam Hussein.[95] Whilst the Bush administration did not want Iraq to become so weak that it could not balance the power of Iran, nor did they wish it to become a military threat again. The war had ensured that Iraq's conventional military power and its WMD programmes had been significantly degraded, but it was imperative for the administration that things stayed that way. To that end the administration pushed, along with the UK, for the adoption of UNSCR 687, which was approved on 3 April 1991. Its main provisions were:

1. A formal ceasefire would come into effect when Iraq accepted the terms of this resolution.
2. Iraq and Kuwait must accept the 1963 UN-demarcated border.
3. Iraq must agree unconditionally to destroy or remove under international supervision all WMD and all ballistic missiles with ranges over 150 kilometres.

4. Iraq was liable for damages arising from invasion of Kuwait and a fund would be created to pay them based on a percentage of Iraqi oil revenues.

Only when Iraq had conformed to these requirements to the satisfaction of the Security Council would provisions in previous UN resolutions, including sanctions, be lifted.[96] The resolution was thus designed to ensure the elimination of Iraq's WMD programmes and that it would not be able to pose a military threat to its neighbours. Defeated and isolated, Iraq accepted the resolution on 6 April.

Iraq's perceived vulnerability to sanctions (due to its almost total dependence on oil exports), and the strength of the resolutions, meant that most states thought Iraq would comply fairly quickly and that within a year or so the sanctions would be lifted. Iraq would then be subject simply to embargoes on arms and technologies that could contribute to the development of WMD.[97] The sanctions put in place to ensure Iraqi compliance were not expected nor intended to be in place for a year, let alone ten. Nevertheless, just over a month after the adoption of UNSCR 687, Bush stated that 'we don't want to lift the sanctions as long as Saddam Hussein remains in power'.[98] In making this assertion, he was imposing an interpretation on 687 that its language could not bear and which was not shared by any other member of the Security Council, except the UK. Nothing in the resolution could justify making Saddam's removal from power a condition for the lifting of sanctions.

Bush's statement exposed the fact that his administration had no strategy in place to deal with the aftermath of the Iraqi defeat. Everything had rested on the hope that Saddam would be overthrown and replaced by a more pliable leader. As it became clear that the Iraqi officer corps was not going to, or could not, do what the Bush administration wanted, the latter was forced to cobble together a policy to deal with Saddam as best it could. The threat that sanctions would remain until Saddam fell was an extemporisation made in the hope of encouraging the Iraqi military to bring about Saddam's downfall sooner rather than later. When that failed, sanctions then became, more or less by default, the long-term centrepiece of US policy toward Iraq – a means both of denying the regime the ability to rebuild its military capability and of keeping up the pressure for Saddam's overthrow.

The NFZs were similarly manipulated for purposes other than that for which they were ostensibly designed. The northern NFZ was complimented by a southern one created in August 1992 by the US, UK and France in response to Saddam's continued repression of the Shia.[99] This action was justified on humanitarian grounds but, since it did not stop Iraqi ground forces operating in southern Iraq, it had no meaningful humanitarian benefit. In reality the southern NFZ was a tool of containment and coercion. It allowed the US to keep in place seventy aircraft, a forward headquarters and large amounts of pre-positioned equipment with which to threaten Saddam.[100]

The failure of the Iraqi military to overthrow Saddam also forced the administration into a rethink of its attitude towards the Iraqi opposition. Having initially shown no interest in making contact with Iraqi opposition groups and preferring the coup option,[101] it was now felt necessary to alter course. In November 1991, Assistant Secretary of State Edward Djerejian therefore announced the administration's support for the development of better contacts with the opposition, with a view to supporting the emergence of a representative Iraqi government.[102] The administration therefore asked Congress for an increase in funding to $40 million to support covert operations against the Iraqi regime.[103]

## A WAR FOR HEGEMONY

The Persian Gulf War of 1991 was a war to preserve American hegemony. Iraqi control of Kuwait and domination of the Persian Gulf would have destroyed the basis of the US–Saudi compact upon which the US role in the international oil system depended. That, in turn, would have undermined the ability of the United States to guarantee the oil supply to the other core states – an important aspect of its global hegemonic role. The Bush administration therefore went to war to prevent Iraqi regional hegemony and to preserve its own dominance of the Gulf and the international oil system.

The crisis also provided a demonstration of American hegemonic power, as the Bush administration translated the dependence of others upon it into political and economic support for its decision to expel Iraq from Kuwait.[104] Saudi Arabia, directly dependent on the US for its security, both funded the US war effort and increased oil production to replace that lost to the World Capitalist System from

Kuwait and Iraq. The various dependencies of the other Arab states on the US, whether, economic, diplomatic or military, similarly enabled the latter to forge a vital anti-Iraqi front amongst them (with only Jordan and Yemen staying aloof, and suffering for it). The Soviet need for American goodwill kept them in line despite occasional misgivings, whilst the Western industrialised nations readily gave their support. The ability of the United States to provide security and/or to secure the oil supply from the Persian Gulf thus lay at the core of the successful execution of its policy.

Despite being able to translate dependence into cooperation, however, the Bush administration was careful both to consult with its core allies as well as to seek the legitimising authority of the UN for its actions. In so doing it sought to exercise consensual hegemonic leadership – a process made easier by the end of the Cold War and the clear and unequivocal nature of Iraq's violation of international norms and the threat it posed to both its neighbours and the international oil system. In so doing the administration showed a clear understanding of the utility of international institutions, both in creating global order and stability and in sustaining American leadership of that order.

The war and its outcome also appeared to reinforce American hegemony. The two potential regional hegemons, Iraq and Iran, had been greatly weakened by successive wars and the Gulf oil states' continued dependence on the US had been clearly demonstrated. The exposure of their vulnerability led them into a much more overt reliance on American military power, now granting the United States the bases and treaties they had consistently denied it before the 1990s.[105] Moreover, in the aftermath of the 1991 war no one could be in any doubt that the oil weapon was a dead letter. With Iraqi oil excluded from the market by sanctions, OPEC was now dominated by the pro-Western core of Saudi Arabia, Kuwait and the UAE, who perceived their economic interests as more or less indistinguishable from those of the West.[106] Finally, the collapse of Soviet power drove the non-oil-producing Arab states in a pro-American direction. No longer able to balance between the superpowers or to rely on Soviet aid, their only hope of an acceptable Arab–Israeli peace now lay with American diplomacy. Foreign policy moderation was thus forced upon them by the realities of power.[107]

Nevertheless, the outcome of the Persian Gulf War remained problematic. One thing the first Bush war against Iraq had in common with the second was a failure to plan for the aftermath. Saddam remained in power and, having assumed that that would not be the case, the Bush administration did not have a coherent policy in place to deal with him. As a result, the policy that they did put in place was ad hoc, poorly designed and high maintenance. The sanctions were crude and harmed the Iraqi population rather than Saddam because they had not been designed to be long term. The inspections regime created by the UN to ensure the destruction of Iraqi WMD could have been better designed to secure unity at the UN and to prevent Saddam exploiting ambiguities. As a result, the Clinton administration would inherit an 'unstable containment regime that would require great skill and attention, and the repeated application of military force, to keep in place'.[108]

## NOTES

1. *The Independent*, 20 July 1988; Baghdad Radio, 18 July 1990, *Foreign Broadcast Information Service, Near East and South Asia (FBIS-NES) -90*, 18 July 1990, p. 23; Marr, 'Iraq in the 1990s', p. 13.
2. Yergin, *The Prize*, pp. 748–9; Chapman and Khanna, 'The Persian Gulf', p. 509.
3. Karsh and Rautsi, *Saddam Hussein*, p. 205.
4. *The Financial Times*, 8 September 1989; *Iraqgate*, 'Foreign economic trends and their implications for the United States: Iraq', Report FET489-98, September 1989; Lieber, 'Iraq and the world oil market', p. 95.
5. Baram, 'The Iraqi invasion of Kuwait', p. 7.
6. *Iraqgate*, 'Foreign economic trends and their implications for the United States: Iraq', Report FET489-98, September 1989.
7. Tripp, 'The foreign policy of Iraq', pp. 181, 184–5.
8. Ibid. p. 185.
9. See the comments of Tariq Aziz, *Milliyet*, 30 May 1991, *FBIS-NES-91*, 4 June 1991, pp. 13–14.
10. Wafiq al-Samara'i, *hatam al-bawaba al-sharqiyya* [The Destruction of the Eastern Gate] (Kuwait: dar al-qabas, 1997), pp. 222–3, cited in Gause, 'The international politics of the Gulf', p. 269.
11. *Iraqgate*, 'Iraqi protest: VOA editorial', 25 February 1990.
12. In March 1990 a US Customs service operation led to the seizure of a shipment of electronic capacitors with a possible use as triggers in nuclear weapons destined for Iraq. The same month Farzad Bazoft, a journalist of Iranian birth working for *The Observer*, was hanged in

Baghdad as a spy. He had been caught in late 1989 investigating an explosion at an Iraqi CW plant. These two events, and especially the execution of Bazoft, generated an outpouring of negative media coverage in the West.

13. Baram, 'The Iraqi invasion of Kuwait'; Bengio, *Saddam Speaks*, pp. 12–17; Hinnebusch, *International Politics of the Middle East*, pp. 210–12.

14. Tripp, 'The foreign policy of Iraq', p. 176; RCC Statement, Republic of Iraq Radio, 8 August 1990, *BBC/Summary of World Broadcasts/Middle East*, 10 August 1990, pp. A1–3.

15. Tripp, 'The foreign policy of Iraq', pp. 181–2; Baram, 'The Iraqi invasion of Kuwait', pp. 27–8.

16. 'Saddam Hussein's speech at the ACC Summit', 24 February 1990, *FBIS-NES-90-039*, 27 February 1990.

17. 'Saddam Hussein's speech at a ceremony honoring the Minister of Defence, the Minister of Industry and Military Industrialization, and members of the Armed Forces General Command', 1 April 1990, Baghdad Domestic Service, *FBIS-NES-90-064*, 3 April 1990. Saddam's fear of an Israeli attack was genuine. On 5 April he asked the Saudi Ambassador to the USA, Prince Bandar bin-Sultan, to seek assurances that Israel would not attack Iraq and promised in turn not to attack Israel; Woodward, *The Commanders*, pp. 202–3.

18. 'Speech by Iraqi President Saddam Hussein at the opening of the extraordinary Arab Summit in Baghdad, 28 May 1990', Baghdad Domestic Service, *FBIS NES-90-103*, 29 May 1990.

19. Jentleson, *With Friends Like These*, p. 150.

20. Baghdad Domestic Service, 18 July 1990, *FBIS-NES-90*, 19 July 1990. Saddam's complaint was not without justification. Kuwait *was* using over-production and downward pressure on the oil price in an effort to force Iraq to settle long-standing border disputes between the two countries, in particular to acknowledge Kuwaiti sovereignty over Warba and Bubiyan; Malone, *International Struggle over Iraq*, p. 54.

21. *Iraqgate*, 'Status of Iraq CCC program', 28 February 1990; 'NAC meeting on Iraq CCC program', 5 March 1990.

22. *Iraqgate*, 'Assistant Secretary Kelly's conversation with Saddam Husayn', 13 February 1990.

23. *Iraqgate*, 'Your visit to Iraq', 19 January 1990.

24. Jentleson, *With Friends Like These*, pp. 144–7.

25. *Iraqgate*, 'NAC meeting on Iraq CCC program', 5 March 1990; 'Licensing for Iraq', March 1990.

26. *Iraqgate*, 'Tensions in US–Iraqi relations: Demarche', 12 April 1990.

27. *Iraqgate*, 'NSC Deputies Committee meeting on Iraq, 16 April 1990, White House Situation Room 4.00 pm', 16 April 1990; 'Possible new

trade controls on Iraq and other chemical and biological warfare proliferators', 16 April 1990; 'Procedures for implementing expanded foreign policy controls for Iraq', 17 April 1990.

28. *Iraqgate*, 'NSC Deputies Committee meeting on Iraq', 16 April 1990.
29. *Iraqgate*, 'NSC Deputies Committee meeting on Iraq, 29 May 1990: White House Situation Room, 4.30 pm', 29 May 1990.
30. *Iraqgate*, '"US relations with Iraq", statement of Assistant Secretary John Kelly before the Senate Foreign Relations Committee, June 15 1990', 15 June 1990.
31. Baghdad Radio, 17 July 1990, *FBIS-NES-90*, 17 July 1990.
32. *Iraqgate*, 'Kuwait: Iraq keeps up the pressure', 22 July 1990.
33. 'Excerpts from Iraqi transcript of meeting between Saddam Hussein and US Ambassador April Glaspie, 25 July 1990', *New York Times*, 23 September 1990. This is the Iraqi transcript of the meeting, which Glaspie claimed left out her 'crystal clear' warnings that the United States insisted on peaceful settlement of disputes. See also the *Washington Post*, 21 October 1992, A17; US Congress, House, *United-States Iraqi relations*, 12 March 1991.
34. David Hoffman, 'US envoy conciliatory to Saddam', *Washington Post*, 12 July 1991, pp. A1, A26; Baker, *The Politics of Diplomacy*, p. 272.
35. US Congress, House, Committee on Foreign Affairs, 'Testimony of Assistant Secretary of State John H. Kelly', *Persian Gulf Crisis*, p. 126.
36. Bush and Scowcroft, *A World Transformed*, p. 309.
37. Ibid. p. 312; R. Jeffrey Smith, 'State Department cable traffic on Iraq–Kuwait tensions, July 1990', *Washington Post*, 13 July 1991, pp. A1, A26.
38. Kuwait News Agency (KUNA), 20 July 1990, *FBIS-NES-90*, 23 July 1990, p. 15.
39. Woodward, *The Commanders*, pp. 216–20; *New York Times*, 24 January 1991, p. A15; Bush and Scowcroft, *A World Transformed*, pp. 312–13.
40. Bush and Scowcroft, *A World Transformed*, p. 323.
41. BP, *BP Statistical Review of World Energy: 1989*, p. 2.
42. US Congress, Senate, Committee on Armed Services, *Crisis in the Persian Gulf Region*.
43. Brenner, 'Why the United States is at war', p. 129; Bina, 'The rhetoric of oil'.
44. Hinnebusch, *International Politics of the Middle East*, pp. 214–15; Aarts, 'The new oil order'.
45. Hinnebusch, *International Politics of the Middle East*, pp. 215–17.
46. Bromley, 'Crisis in the Gulf', p. 13.
47. US Public Broadcasting System (PBS), *The Gulf War*, interviews with Richard Haass and Brent Scowcroft; Baker, *The Politics of Diplomacy*, p. 277.

48. Hinnebusch, *International Politics of the Middle East*, p. 213.
49. UNSCR 660, www.daccessdds.un.org/Resolution/Gen/NRO/575/10/IMG/NR057510.pdf?Openelement; UNSCR 661, www.daccessdds.un.org/Resolution/Gen/NRO/575/11/IMG/NR057511.pdf?Openelement.
50. Cigar, 'Iraq's strategic mindset'.
51. 'Text of President Saddam Hussein's "Initiative on previous and subsequent developments in the region"', Baghdad Domestic Service, 12 August 1990, *FBIS-NES-90-156*, 13 August 1990.
52. *Public Papers*, 'Joint news conference of President Bush and Soviet President Mikhail Gorbachev in Helsinki, Finland', 9 September 1990.
53. Bush and Scowcroft, *A World Transformed*, p. 353.
54. 'Cheney and Powell testify to Armed Services Committee', *Congressional Quarterly Weekly Report*, 8 December 1990, pp. 4113–14.
55. Mueller, *Policy and Opinion*, Table 40, p. 208.
56. *Public Papers*, 'Address before a joint session of Congress on the Persian Gulf Crisis and the federal budget deficit', 11 September 1990; 'The President's news conference', 21 September 1990; 'Exchange with reporters in San Francisco', 29 October 1990.
57. Al Durbur, 20 September 1990, *FBIS-NES-90-113*, pp. 1–2; 'President Mitterrand's Four Point Plan', *Journal of Palestinian Studies*, 78, 1991, pp. 168–70; Herrmann, *Coercive Diplomacy*, p. 251; 'France's Six Point Plan', 14 January 1990, *Journal of Palestinian Studies*, 79, 1991, p. 136.
58. Saddam Hussein, 'Initiative on developments in the region', Baghdad Domestic Service, 12 August 1990, *FBIS-NES-90-156*, pp. 48–9.
59. Karsh and Rautsi, *Saddam Hussein*, p. 239.
60. Baker, *The Politics of Diplomacy*, p. 301; Bush and Scowcroft, *A World Transformed*, pp. 393–4; Powell, *A Soldier's Way*, pp. 488–9.
61. Bush and Scowcroft, *A World Transformed*, p. 400.
62. Hiro, *Desert Shield*, p. 257.
63. Bush and Scowcroft, *A World Transformed*, pp. 413–14; Hiro, *Desert Shield*, pp. 258–9.
64. UNSCR 678, www.daccessdds.un.org/Resolution/Gen/NRO/575/28/IMG/NR057528.pdf?Openelement.
65. Sifry and Cerf, *The Gulf War Reader*, pp. 234–7, 251–4.
66. US Congress, Senate, *Crisis in the Persian Gulf*, pp. 8–14, 23–8; US Congress, Senate, *US Policy in the Persian Gulf*, 17 October 1990, pp. 105–10.
67. *Public Papers*, 'The President's news conference', 30 November 1990.
68. Bush and Scowcroft, *A World Transformed*, pp. 419–20.
69. Karsh and Rautsi, *Saddam Hussein*, pp. 237–8.
70. US Congress, Senate, *US Policy in the Persian Gulf*, 17 October 1990, pp. 108–9.

71. *Congressional Quarterly Almanac, 1990*, p. 746.
72. Baker, *Politics of Diplomacy*, p. 334; US PBS, *The Gulf War*, Scowcroft interview. Bush did not ask for congressional 'authorisation' but 'support' and thus formally continued to insist that he already had the authority to act.
73. US PBS, *The Gulf War*, Baker interview; Bush and Scowcroft, *A World Transformed*, pp. 441–2.
74. Hiro, *Desert Shield*, p. 315; Karsh and Rautsi, *Saddam Hussein*, p. 241.
75. Karsh and Rautsi, *Saddam* Hussein, pp. 246–8.
76. Freedman and Karsh, *The Gulf Conflict*, pp. 378–85.
77. Ibid. pp. 386–400; Heller, 'Iraq's army'; Summers, *On Strategy II*; Pimlott and Badsey, *The Gulf War Assessed*; Gordon and Trainor, *The Generals' War*.
78. *Baghdad Domestic Service*, 26 February 1991; *Baghdad Radio*, 28 February 1991.
79. UNSCR 686, www.daccess.dds.un.org/doc/RESOLUTION/GEN/NRO/596/22/IMG/NRO59622.pdf?OpenElement.
80. Indeed, it was at the time: *New York Times*, 7 March 1991, p. A25; 22 March 1991, p. A33; 28 March 1991, p. A25; 29 March 1991, p. A23; *US News and World Report*, 15 April 1991, pp. 26–31.
81. Powell, *A Soldier's Way*, p. 520; US PBS, *The Gulf War*, Scowcroft interview.
82. US PBS, *The Gulf War*, Baker interview; Powell, *A Soldier's Way*, p. 521.
83. *BBC Radio Four*, 'The desert war: a kind of victory', 16 February 1992.
84. Richard Haass, quoted in US PBS, *Frontline: Spying on Saddam*.
85. *Public Papers*, 'Remarks by the President to Raytheon Missile Systems plant employees, Raytheon Missile Systems plant, Andover, Massachusetts', 15 February 1991.
86. Baram, 'The effect of Iraqi sanctions', p. 199, n; Graham-Brown, *Sanctioning Saddam*, p. 23.
87. Bush and Scowcroft, *A World Transformed*, p. 489.
88. Powell, *A Soldier's Way*, p. 531.
89. US PBS, *The Gulf War*, Richard Haass interview; Hiro, *Desert Shield*, p. 401.
90. Baker, *Politics of Diplomacy*, p. 439.
91. Anne Devroy, 'Wait and see: Bush views aiding rebels as potential morass', *Washington Post*, 29 March 1991.
92. UNSCR 688, www.daccessdds.un.org/Resolution/Gen/NRO/596/24/IMG/NR059624.pdf?Openelement.
93. Wheeler, *Saving Strangers*, pp. 147–9.
94. Malone, *International Struggle over Iraq*, p. 90.
95. Graham-Brown, *Sanctioning Saddam*, p. 121.

96. UNSCR 687, www.daccessdds.un.org/Resolution/Gen/NRO/596/23/ IMG/NR059623.pdf?Openelement.

97. Graham-Brown, *Sanctioning Saddam*, p. 57.

98. *Public Papers*, 'The president's news conference with Chancellor Helmut Kohl of Germany', 20 May 1991. See also the comments of Baker to the same effect, 'Secretary of State says sanctions must stay as long as Saddam holds power', *The Times*, 23 May 1991.

99. John Lancaster, 'US moves to toughen Iraq stance', *Washington Post*, 29 August 1992, p. A1.

100. Perry, 'Gulf security'.

101. According to Assistant Secretary of State David L. Mack: Graham-Brown, *Sanctioning Saddam*, p. 64.

102. US Congress, House, *Developments in the Middle East*, p. 15.

103. R. Jeffrey Smith, 'Turk warns against force to oust Saddam', *Washington Post*, 14 February 1992; R. Jeffrey Smith and David B. Ottaway, 'Anti-Saddam operation cost CIA $100 million', *Washington Post*, 15 September 1996, p. A1.

104. Hinnebusch, *International Politics of the Middle East*, p. 212.

105. Ibid. pp. 86–7.

106. Aarts, 'New oil order', p. 3; Odell, 'International oil'; Vasiliev, *History of Saudi Arabia*, pp. 398–404.

107. Hinnebusch, *International Politics of the Middle East*, pp. 86–7.

108. Pollack, *The Threatening Storm*, pp. 53–4.

*Chapter 4*

# DUAL CONTAINMENT, 1992–2000

## THE DEFEAT OF EASTERN REPUBLICANISM

Despite victory in the 1991 Gulf War and presidential approval ratings in the nineties following it, George H. W. Bush lost the 1992 presidential election to Democrat Bill Clinton, largely as a consequence of the combination of a short, sharp recession and a growing federal deficit, both of which fuelled a pervasive fear of American economic decline.[1] The deficit forced Bush to reverse his 1988 pledge not to raise taxes, angering large sections of the middle class, small businesses and conservative Republicans who regarded the act as a betrayal.[2] The recession then further alienated voters, and with Ross Perot entering the race and taking a fifth of the vote, mostly from Bush, Clinton was able to win the election with just 43 per cent of the vote.[3]

Bush's defeat, like Reagan's 1980 victory, marked a significant point of transition in the conservative ascendancy in American politics, representing not only a personal defeat for Bush, but also for the liberal/moderate wing of the Republican Party for which he was the standard-bearer. From this point onwards, conservative dominance of the party would advance rapidly, as indicated most clearly by the 'Republican revolution' of 1994. In the congressional elections of that year, the Republicans took eight Senate seats from the Democrats (and a ninth when Richard Shelby changed allegiances) and more than sixty in the House, giving them complete control of Congress for the first time since 1948. Another significant feature of the Republican victory was the extent to which the Democrats were wiped out across the south, which now came completely under Republican dominance. The new intake of southern and western Republicans was markedly more conservative than its predecessors, whether Democrats or Republicans.[4]

This conservatism was quickly demonstrated when, in January 1995, the congressional Republicans announced the National Security Revitalization Act, a document which made clear that the world view of the Republican right, for so long marginalised in US foreign policy-making, was now resurgent. The proposed act was both nationalist and unilateralist. Foreign aid was to be cut and defence spending increased. American soldiers would be barred from serving under UN command, a cap would be placed on US funding for UN peace-keeping, and the cost to the United States of such operations would be deducted from the annual US dues owed to the UN. A National Missile Defence (NMD) system, which the Clinton administration feared would violate the Anti-Ballistic Missile Treaty and thus undermine efforts to strengthen multilateral arms control regimes, was to be developed and deployed 'at the earliest possible moment'.[5] Overall, the message was clear. The Republicans were prepared to cooperate with others if they were prepared to do what the United States demanded. If not, America would pursue its own interests regardless.[6]

## THE END OF THE COLD WAR AND AMERICAN HEGEMONY: LIBERAL INTERNATIONALISM OR CONSERVATIVE UNILATERALISM?

In the short term, nevertheless, Bush's defeat brought to the presidential office the first Democrat since Jimmy Carter, and a man committed to the concept of consensual hegemonic leadership. Increasingly, however, the Clinton administration would find itself assailed by a Republican Party which now rejected some of the core assumptions which had underpinned American foreign policy for the best part of forty years.

A key factor energising the conservative critique of Clinton's foreign policy was the end of the Cold War and its implications for the practice of American hegemony. With the collapse of Soviet power, the world shifted from military bipolarity to unipolarity – by the mid-1990s the US defence budget was equal to those of the next five biggest military powers combined.[7] The effect of this transformation was to create new incentives to engage in unilateralism and the use of military force. For a start, the collapse of the USSR greatly reduced the degree of risk involved in the utilisation of American military power and created a permissive international environment in which to do so, as had been amply demonstrated by the Persian Gulf War of 1991.[8] In addition, unipolarity weakened the rationale for American multilateralism. During the Cold War the United States had needed allies in order to successfully pursue the containment of Soviet power.[9] In the absence of a Soviet threat, however, allies, instead of being a necessity, became optional, and once they were optional, the negative aspects of alliances weighed more heavily in the American calculus. Alliances require compromise and negotiation, and they slow things down and complicate policy implementation. Acting unilaterally thus becomes a more attractive option.[10]

Whilst military unipolarity created structural incentives toward the unilateral use of military force, however, such a recourse was incommensurate with the liberal internationalist world view of the Clinton administration. Clinton came to office 'strongly inclined to pursue a cooperative security policy', whereby the peace would be kept through international institutions wherever possible, and with the objective of strengthening those institutions and the norms they enforced. This did not imply an unwillingness to use force, but it did mean a commitment to act multilaterally, and with the imprimatur of the UN, wherever possible, as well as a belief in multilateral instruments such as arms control as a means to contain conflict.[11] The Clinton administration thus came to office determined to continue the practice of liberal, consensual hegemony which had dominated US foreign policy since 1945. Indeed, in the view of Bruce Cumings, Clinton represented the 'apotheosis' of consensual hegemony in his continual consultation of allies, courting of international opinion and emphasis on multilateralism.[12]

In practice, the Clinton administration's commitment to consensual hegemony was occasionally compromised, and its initial commitment to the UN and multilateralism would weaken to some degree. The failed intervention in Somalia in 1993 reduced the administration's enthusiasm for working through the UN, with Presidential Decision Directive 25 of May 1994 setting a very high bar for US involvement in subsequent UN peacekeeping operations.[13] In addition, the UN sometimes proved to be too weak and compromised an institution to bear the load the Clinton administration had initially wanted it to. The inherent limitations of a body which is dependent upon agreement amongst sovereign states and subject to the veto were painfully evident in policy toward the former Yugoslavia, for example.[14] In circumstances such as those, when the UN proved unable and/or unwilling to act, the temptations of unilateralism, and the advantages of military unipolarity, could become irresistible. In Bosnia in 1995, and again in Kosovo in 1999, the Clinton administration would succumb to the temptation and choose to operate through NATO rather than the UN. Nevertheless, the Clinton administration's unilateralism was sporadic, rather than habitual, and pragmatic rather than doctrinal. Clinton never openly scorned the UN the way his successor would, and his administration was often happy to support UN action where it saw it as serving American as well as global interests. Moreover, Clinton's unilateral actions were often taken in the name of enforcing UN resolutions (as in Iraq) or humanitarian exceptions (Bosnia, Kosovo). At heart, Clinton remained a multi-lateralist.[15]

Clinton's policy toward Iraq would prove to be a good example of the tensions and contradictions in his administration's practice of hegemony, being conducted within the framework of the UN and the enforcement of UN resolutions, yet with an increasing tendency to unilateralism in the face of continued Iraqi defiance and the seeming failure of the inspections/sanctions regime to achieve its objectives. Nevertheless, the Clinton administration would continue to seek to hold the international coalition sustaining sanctions together, and to seek the legitimacy of the UN's multilateral framework for its actions.

Clinton's Republican critics, in contrast, increasingly rejected multilateralism, the UN, and sanctions as ineffectual irrelevancies, demanding instead the vigorous pursuit of 'regime change' in Iraq. The 1994 elections served to confirm the dominance within the Republican Party of this unilateralist, conservative world view, but the first hint of this development emerged in the last days of the administration of George H. W. Bush, with the leaking of the 1992 Defense Planning Guidance (DPG) document. Whereas the condition of unipolarity would tempt the Clinton administration into occasional unilateralist indiscretions, the Republican right welcomed the opportunity to forge a new era of hegemony based on absolute US military predominance and the unfettered exercise of American power. Unipolarity would allow the United States to forego the constraints of ineffectual international organisations, which created rules the lawless failed to follow whilst preventing the free exercise of America's benevolent power. The DPG envisioned a future where 'the world order is ultimately backed by the US' with multilateral organisations like the UN marginalised and alliances like NATO downgraded. If the United States needed assistance, it could organise 'ad hoc assemblies' for specific crises.[16]

Such a rejection of multilateralism and international institutions would seem also to constitute a rejection of consensual hegemonic leadership, but the advocates of unilateralism sought to square it with hegemony by insisting that America was unique because its national interest 'derived its meaning and coherence from being rooted in universal principles'. That being the case, what was good for America was good for the world, which would therefore welcome the unilateral yet benevolent assertion of American power.[17]

In the absence of a global threat on the scale of the USSR, the DPG declared that the primary objective should be 'preventing the domination of key regions by a hostile power'. And no region was more important than the Persian Gulf, where 'our overall objective is to remain the predominant outside power in the region and to preserve US and Western access to the region's oil'. It therefore 'remains fundamentally important to prevent a hegemon or alignment of powers from dominating the region'.[18] The primary threat to the United States ability to remain the 'predominant power' in the Gulf was the potential combination of 'rogue states'[19] which rejected America's benevolent hegemony, and the proliferation of WMD. Those states were 'rushing to develop ballistic missiles and nuclear weapons as a deterrent to American intervention in regions they seek to dominate'[20] and 'Iraq . . . is the prototype of this new strategic threat'.[21]

There was little in that assessment that the Clinton administration would have disagreed with. Unlike the Clinton administration, however, the Republican right did not believe that a combination of arms control, sanctions, inspections and containment was adequate to deal with the threat posed by states like Iraq. The UN was a weak reed which could not be relied on to support the measures necessary to disarm Iraq, and given the ease with which certain aspects of WMD programmes could be concealed and/or were indistinguishable from legitimate civilian industrial activities, it would never be possible to guarantee the elimination of such programmes through inspections.[22] Nor was containment through deterrence an adequate solution because, unlike the USSR, the leaders of the rogue regimes now seeking WMD were irrational. Saddam's Iraq was the 'globe's most reckless power' and as such might not be susceptible to the rational logic of deterrence.[23]

Conservatives therefore advocated a two-fold response. First and foremost, they insisted on the need for a system of NMD capable of preventing small scale ballistic missile attacks on the United States. Without such a capability, they warned,

> projecting conventional military forces or simply asserting political influence abroad . . . will be far more complex and constrained when the American homeland or the territory of our allies is subject to attack by otherwise weak rogue regimes capable of cobbling together a miniscule ballistic missile force.[24]

Without NMD, in other words, a WMD-armed Iraq would be in a position to bid for regional hegemony and to deter an American response to conventional aggression such as that against Kuwait.[25] 'Building an effective, robust, layered, global system of missile defense' was therefore 'a prerequisite to maintaining American predominance'.[26]

Whilst NMD ought to be sufficient to deter rogue states from aggression, however, the possibility that such states might, nevertheless, use WMD in an irrational and suicidal fashion could not be entirely discounted. And once they possessed WMD, the elimination of such regimes would become too dangerous to contemplate. All things considered, therefore, 'the most effective form of non-proliferation' is 'an effort to bring about the demise of these regimes themselves'.[27] In place of arms control and containment, therefore, the Republican right advocated 'regime change', and nowhere more urgently than Iraq.

## DUAL CONTAINMENT

Whilst liberals and conservatives thus disagreed about the means with which to achieve them, American objectives in the Gulf were unchanging:

> The basic strategic principle in the Persian Gulf region is to establish a favourable balance of power, one that will protect critical American interests in the security of our friends and in the free flow of oil at stable prices.[28]

And Iran and Iraq remained the principal threats to that objective. Rather than regime change, however, the Clinton administration chose to adopt a policy of 'dual containment', a strategy facilitated by the altered regional and global environment. The collapse of the Soviet Union meant neither Iran nor Iraq could look to a potential super-power backer or seek to play off the superpowers against each other. The military capability of both had been significantly reduced by the two Gulf Wars, and the GCC states were now prepared to offer the United States the bases from which its military forces could contain them. The Clinton administration therefore concluded that it had the capacity effectively to contain both states simultaneously.[29]

In the case of Iraq, dual containment meant:

1. The continuation of multilateral sanctions in order to keep Iraq militarily weak, prevent it gaining access to technology and materials to rebuild military strength, and to compel its cooperation with UN inspectors.
2. UN inspections whose task was to eliminate Iraqi WMD capability.
3. Diplomatic isolation.
4. NFZs and other constraints on Iraqi military deployments.
5. A large forward US military presence in the Gulf.[30]

Whilst the Clinton administration had given it a new name, this was essentially a continuation of the policies cobbled together by the Bush administration.

At the heart of the policy was the combination of inspections and sanctions, with the latter as the means to compel Iraqi compliance with the former. For the Clinton administration, however, sanctions also served two other purposes. Firstly, as with their predecessors, they hoped that sanctions would encourage a coup against Saddam from within his inner circle. Failing that, and increasingly their central function, sanctions were a form of containment, designed to weaken the regime and keep it neutered until Saddam did eventually fall. Neither of these two alternative roles for sanctions, however, was legitimate under the terms of the UN resolutions that mandated them, nor were they shared by any other major state except the UK, a fact that would cause increasing tension and conflict within the Security Council as the decade progressed, greatly complicating American policy toward Iraq.[31]

When he formally announced the administration's Middle East

policy, Martin Indyk assured his listeners that it did not 'seek or expect a reconciliation with Saddam Hussein's regime' since it was 'a criminal regime, beyond the pale of international society and, in our judgement, irredeemable'. The administration was therefore supporting the opposition Iraqi National Congress (INC) 'as a democratic alternative to the Saddam Hussein regime'.[32] In principle, therefore, the administration was committed to regime change in Iraq. In practice, however, that commitment was barely more than rhetorical. Some in the administration, led by Indyk but also including Vice-President Gore and Ambassador to the UN Madeleine Albright, believed that regime change might be the only way to ensure that Iraq was no longer a threat to American hegemony in the Gulf. Other key policy-makers, however, led by Secretary of State Warren Christopher and National Security Adviser Anthony Lake, deemed Iraq to be a secondary issue which could be effectively dealt with by continuing the policy of containment whilst the administration focused on the bigger issues of the global economy and democratic enlargement in Russia and Eastern Europe.[33] Most importantly, Clinton shared the view of Lake and Christopher. At no point in his presidency did he treat Iraq as much more than an irritating distraction. To the extent that he was preoccupied with the Middle East, his attention was firmly on the peace process rather than the Gulf.[34]

The Clinton administration's ambivalence toward regime change in Iraq was reinforced by other considerations. Just as the Bush administration had before them, they feared the possible consequences of Saddam's fall – the break up of Iraq, regional destabilisation and/or increased Iranian influence. They also feared that support for the Iraqi opposition might lead to the United States being drawn into an unwanted military conflict in Iraq; a fear exacerbated by the fiasco in Somalia in 1993 and by their perception that the post-Cold War American public had little stomach for US military intervention.[35] Added to those considerations was the possibility that too overt a US commitment to regime change, and manipulation of the sanctions and inspections regime to that end, would lead to the collapse of international and regional support for that regime, leaving Saddam free to pursue his regional ambitions once again. The best (regime change) therefore threatened to be the enemy of the good (containment) and the Clinton administration consequently prioritised the latter over the former.

## SADDAM'S LOGIC

The reasoning which guided Saddam Hussein's actions throughout the 1990s must necessarily remain more obscure than that of American policy-makers, though he was motivated primarily, as ever, by the perceived needs of his own survival. To that end, Saddam's ultimate objective had to be the restoration of Iraqi sovereignty and with it his own freedom of manoeuvre. The ending of the regime of sanctions and inspections was thus a fundamental goal. The swiftest means to that end, however, carried its own risks.

Complete cooperation with the UN inspectors would have constituted a further humiliation, coming hard on the heels of crushing defeat in the Persian Gulf War, and a further blow to the legitimacy of Saddam's rule. Moreover, Saddam believed that acceptance of the destruction of Iraq's WMD programmes threatened his survival in other ways. As senior Iraqi officials informed US interrogators after the 2003 war, Saddam thought that possession of WMD had saved his regime in both the war against Iran and in 1991, when he believed they deterred an American advance on Baghdad.[36] It is this belief which seems to explain the central paradox of Saddam's behaviour after 1991, namely that the regime did in fact destroy its stocks of WMD, but failed to provide inspectors with full cooperation or proof of this fact.[37] Although the weapons stocks had been destroyed, Saddam apparently did not want to advertise this fact to Tehran, Washington or his domestic enemies, but rather to engage in what Lieutenant-General Raad Majid al-Hamdani descrbed as 'deterrence by doubt'.[38]

A further reason for Saddam to resist the inspections, and to seek to provoke crises over them, was the existence of divisions within the Security Council between the US and the UK – who were committed to his removal and the maintenance of sanctions until that day – and the other members of the P5 – who sought only the elimination of Iraqi WMD as a condition for the lifting of sanctions. By exacerbating those tensions Saddam sought to undermine international support for the sanctions regime. Finally, repeated American statements that they would oppose the lifting of sanctions until he was removed gave Saddam little incentive to cooperate with the inspections process.

Saddam's refusal to accept the 'oil for food' (OFF) scheme would appear to reflect similar calculations. On 15 August 1991 the Security

Council passed UNSCR 706, permitting Iraq to sell oil up to a value of $1.6 billion over a six month period. Thirty per cent of the revenue would be placed in a UN compensation fund for the victims of Iraqi aggression and the remainder in a UN escrow account to be spent on the humanitarian needs of ordinary Iraqis.[39] The Iraqi government, however, refused the deal, presumably on the basis that accepting it would facilitate American efforts to maintain sanctions indefinitely by easing their humanitarian consequences. By refusing the OFF scheme Saddam would exacerbate those consequences but hope that the suffering would be blamed on the United States and the UN and increase divisions within the international community.

Saddam's policy was effective in many ways, as will be discussed below. He failed, however, to achieve his ultimate objective of ending the sanctions regime. That failure reflected a further miscalculation on his part about the extent of American power. The unipolarity produced by the end of the Cold War had left the United States so dominant that the old tactic of playing off one great power against another was largely redundant. Moreover, his strategy contained an inherent contradiction, since the very fact of Iraq's refusal to provide full cooperation to the weapons inspectors proved to the majority of observers that Saddam was hiding, and/or bent on reconstituting, WMD, making it easier for the Clinton administration to keep sanctions in place.

## WEAPONS INSPECTIONS

The task of ensuring the destruction of Iraq's WMD programmes was divided between two organisations. Iraqi nuclear programmes would be overseen by the International Atomic Energy Agency (IAEA), whilst a new organisation, the UN Special Commission (UNSCOM), would eliminate Iraq's CW, BW and missile programmes. On 18 April 1991, as required by UNSCR 687, Iraq had submitted a weapons declaration to the UN, admitting to the possession of long-range missiles and some CW and CW precursors, but not to nuclear or BW pro-grammes.[40] However, Saddam's efforts to deceive the inspectors came unstuck almost immediately. In June 1991, IAEA inspectors caught Iraqi troops moving lorries loaded with calutrons, and in early July they found several kilos of enriched uranium. In the face of this incontrovertible evidence, Iraq admitted to enriching uranium but continued to deny it had a weapons programme.[41] On 22 September, however, IAEA inspectors found documents confirming the existence of that programme at the Nuclear Design Centre in Baghdad.[42] The inspectors' discoveries revealed that Iraq was far closer to developing a nuclear weapon than virtually anyone had believed and that IAEA inspectors had been systematically deceived throughout the previous decade. The latter fact in particular would play a significant role in the debate about Iraqi WMD programmes in 2002–3. In the meantime, however, it led the Security Council to pass UNSCR 715, authorising a more aggressive inspections regime and requiring Iraq to cooperate 'unconditionally' with the inspectors. Iraq rejected the resolution.[43]

Despite continued public defiance, however, Saddam was clearly shaken by the ease with which the inspectors had discovered his nuclear weapons programme, and this now led him to take the decision to unilaterally destroy Iraqi WMD stocks and missiles and to try to retain, and conceal, only the intellectual, rather than the material, capacity to reconstitute WMD.[44] Then, in March 1992, with UNSCOM stepping up the pressure and launching surprise inspections to try and find undeclared material, Iraq made public its destruction of its WMD stocks and invited UNSCOM to verify the claim. UNSCOM did so by inspecting the debris of the destruction, but concluded that what they were shown was insufficient to constitute all of Iraq's WMD stocks. From this point onwards, the focus of inspections would be less on hunting out hidden WMD stocks and more on verifying the Iraqi claim that those stocks had been destroyed.[45]

In ordering the destruction of Iraq's existing WMD stocks, Saddam had effectively complied with UNSCR 687, but in so doing he also sealed his own fate. The unilateral and secret destruction of Iraqi WMD, and the consequent inability to prove to the satisfaction of the inspectors that they had in fact been destroyed, would prolong the inspections process indefinitely. Disbelief of Iraqi claims was reinforced by repeated demonstrations of Iraqi lies about its WMD programmes and by its continued obstruction of the inspections process. Between 1991 and 1993, the Security Council found Iraq to be in 'material breach' of UN resolution 687 on seven occasions.[46]

## EARLY TENSIONS IN THE SECURITY COUNCIL

On 15 October 1993, the head of UNSCOM, Rolf Ekeus, reported to the Security Council that substantial progress had been made in getting Iraq to provide information about its long-range missile programmes, CW and BW, and that most requirements with regard to nuclear weapons had been met.[47] A month later, on 26 November, Baghdad finally agreed to accept the terms of UNSCR 715 and long-term monitoring of its weapons sites. These developments led France, Russia and China to recommend that Iraq be commended for progress towards meeting the conditions of UNSCR 687. In response, Albright stated that the American position was that Iraq had to comply with all Security Council resolutions, including UNSCR 833 on the border with Kuwait and UNSCR 688 requiring the cessation of terrorism at home and abroad, termination of economic warfare against the Kurds, an end to the repression of the Shia in the southern marshes and information on the fate of 623 missing Kuwaitis, before sanctions could be lifted.[48]

UNSCR 687 required the Security Council to review sanctions in view of Iraqi compliance with 'all relevant resolutions'. The Clinton administration was now deeming that to include resolutions passed after 687, an interpretation not shared by any of the other members of the P5 except the UK. This disagreement demonstrated clearly the tension between the policy of the non-Anglo-Saxon members of the P5, and American and British policy. The objective of the former was to see a successful completion of the inspections process, the disarming of Iraq and the lifting of sanctions. The Clinton administration, however, was determined that sanctions would remain in place to contain Iraq until such time as Saddam was replaced by a more acceptable regime.[49]

Whilst this disagreement was naturally framed in terms of an interpretation of the meaning of the relevant resolutions, the French, Russians and Chinese had their own self-serving motives for wanting the sanctions lifted, just as the Americans had for keeping them in place. As its economic growth accelerated, China's oil demands were increasing and the China National Petroleum Corporation had been in talks with the Iraqi oil ministry. France, for its part, had long had a close economic and military relationship with Iraq and was owed $4.5 billion by Baghdad. French oil companies Elf Aquitaine and Total had contracts to develop Iraqi oil fields that would come into operation when sanctions were lifted.[50] Russia had similarly close ties and had inherited a debt of $8 billion, owed to the former USSR, that it badly needed repaying. As Russian Foreign Minister Yevgeny Primakov complained to Madeleine Albright: 'Without sanctions, the Iraqis would sell oil and pay us; with sanctions, they sell oil and use the sanctions as an excuse not to pay us'.[51]

## MAINTAINING SANCTIONS

In August 1994, in response to American resistance to any loosening of the sanctions regime, Saddam decided to generate a crisis, warning that Iraq would reconsider its cooperation with UNSCOM if the latter continued to serve as a pawn of American policy. He also dispatched two divisions of the Republican Guard towards the border with Kuwait. With typical ham-fistedness, however, his actions only strengthened the American position and made it easier to maintain sanctions. The Clinton administration moved extra troops to the region and was able to secure support for UNSCR 949 demanding withdrawal of the Iraqi forces and full cooperation with UNSCOM.[52] In the face of this united front, Iraqi forces withdrew. Saddam's gambit nevertheless reignited debate within the Clinton administration, with some hawks arguing that the US should demand the withdrawal of Iraqi ground forces from southern Iraq altogether, creating a safe haven for the Shiite opposition to organise. Their opponents argued that this would create a power vacuum into which Iranian influence would move. In the end the decision was to maintain the status quo, and Albright was dispatched to the capitals of half a dozen key Security Council members and Arab states to demand continued support for containment.[53]

Generally, Albright found the governments she spoke to supportive, but one concern that was repeatedly expressed, particularly in the Arab states, was about the effect of sanctions on ordinary Iraqis. Accordingly, in order to lessen pressure for sanctions to be lifted, the Clinton administration decided to revive the OFF concept and to reframe it in terms likely to make it more acceptable to Baghdad. This became UNSCR 986, which was passed on 14 April 1995. Replacing UNSCR 706, it increased the permitted six-monthly oil revenue to $2 billion and made the concession of allowing Baghdad to take responsibility for distributing the humanitarian items purchased with OFF funds outside of Kurdish controlled areas. However, it still required Iraq to deposit the oil revenue in a UN account and diverted 30 per cent of the revenue to a compensation fund.[54] American objectives were made clear when Albright said that 'if it [Baghdad] refuses to implement this resolution, it will be clear for all to see . . . that the blame for the suffering of the people of Iraq rests not with the Security Council but with the government in Baghdad'.[55] Iraq nevertheless continued to reject OFF.

## INSPECTIONS AND REVELATIONS

Between mid-1993 and 1996, UNSCOM and the IAEA were able to carry out inspections in a relatively untroubled fashion and, by spring 1995, the UNSCOM monitoring and verification system was in place and operational, covering 250 sites with video cameras and chemical and temperature sensors, as well as incorporating over-flight by helicopters and American U2 spy planes. Iraq was required every six months to submit a report of any new dual-use equipment imported and UNSCOM inspectors on the ground conducted regular inspections. The inspectors were also more or less happy with regard to Iraq's nuclear, chemical and missile programmes, their one remaining concern being the Iraqi BW programme. That concern was heightened when former head of Iraqi Military Intelligence General Wafiq Jassim al-Samarrai defected in December 1994 and informed UNSCOM that Iraq had a more advanced BW programme than it had so far admitted to. Rolf Ekeus nevertheless informed the Security Council in June 1995 that once Iraq's BW declaration was verified, UNSCOM would be ready to declare its job done.[56] Sensing an opportunity, on 1 July, the Iraqis admitted for the first time that Iraq had had a BW programme and had produced anthrax and botulinum in 1989–90. Ekeus said that if UNSCOM could confirm destruction of these BW he would inform the Security Council that his job was complete.[57]

In August 1995, Saddam's son-in-law, Major-General Hussein Kamel, along with his brother and their wives (both of whom were Saddam's daughters), fled into Jordan in fear of his life, after falling out with Saddam's eldest son, Uday. In an effort to curry favour, he now revealed to UNSCOM the fact that Iraq had actually got as far as weaponising its BW programme, a fact it had failed to disclose in July.[58]

Confronted with its dissembling, Baghdad initially directed inspectors to a mass of documents it claimed, unconvincingly, that Hussein Kamel had hidden without its knowledge. It then announced a policy of complete cooperation with the inspectors, as a result of which it now admitted to having weaponised BW and having produced larger quantities of anthrax and botulinum than previously admitted. It was also revealed that Iraq had launched a crash effort to develop a nuclear weapon in 1990.[59] In his October 1995 report to the Security Council, Ekeus said Iraq had misled UNSCOM on aspects of its long-range missile programme, had sought to conceal its BW programme and had also concealed chemical missile warhead tests and attempts to develop a nuclear weapon. He accordingly demanded three new complete and full declarations of Iraq's banned programmes.[60]

The revelations of Hussein Kamel were a 'godsend' according to one State Department official.[61] Having looked as though he might be about to escape the regime of sanctions and inspections, Saddam was now back at square one.

## OIL FOR FOOD

On 20 January 1996, the Iraqi government announced that it was prepared to renegotiate terms for implementing UNSCR 986. Having previously rejected OFF on the basis that accepting it would mean that sanctions would remain in place indefinitely, Saddam's reversal of course reflected the fact that it was now clear that there was little likelihood of sanctions being lifted whether Iraq accepted OFF or not. Moreover, the continued lack of oil revenue was undermining Saddam's ability to deliver material benefits to key groups of regime supporters and thus beginning to threaten his survival. Approximately 60 per cent of Iraqis depended on the state for their income, and the inflation created by printing dinars in the absence of oil revenue had destroyed their standard of living, leading formerly loyal Sunnis to plot against the regime. In May 1995, Saddam's intelligence services discovered a conspiracy involving General Muhammad Mahdlum al-Dulaymi of the previously loyal al-Dulaymi tribe, and there were even cracks in Saddam's inner circle, as demonstrated by the defection of Hussein Kamel.[62]

Saddam therefore decided that the humiliation of accepting UNSCR 986 was the lesser of the evils now facing him.[63] In May 1996

Iraq signed a memorandum of understanding with the UN Secretary-General. Under the agreement, $2 billion worth of oil per month would be sold. Fifty per cent would go to the compensation fund, Kurdish relief and UN costs. Of the remaining 50 per cent, the vast majority would be spent on foodstuffs and medicines.[64]

## REGIME CHANGE

Despite its deeply ambivalent attitude toward regime change, the Clinton administration did extend some limited support to the Iraqi opposition – a plethora of different, competing factions loosely grouped under the umbrella of the INC. They included both Kurdish parties, the Iraqi Communist Party and the Iranian backed Supreme Council for the Islamic Revolution in Iraq (SCIRI) amongst others. One of the key figures behind the creation of the INC, and the individual in whom parts of the US national security bureaucracy invested much hope, was Ahmed Chalabi, who was attractive to many Americans because he was Westernised and lacked the narrow sectarian or ethnic interests of most of the main parties coalesced under the INC umbrella.[65] Chalabi's aim was to use Kurdistan as a base from which to launch an uprising against Saddam's regime and thus eventually to bring democracy to Iraq. Another group nominally operating under the banner of the INC was the Iraqi National Accord (INA). However, unlike the largely Kurdish and Shia parties, the INA was a Sunni-dominated organisation of ex-officers and Baathists led by Iyad Allawi. With their background and contacts inside the Iraqi military, their preferred course of action was a coup, followed by the establishment of a new authoritarian Sunni regime.[66]

Publicly, the Clinton administration expressed its support for the INC and the goal of democracy in Iraq.[67] In reality, few in the administration thought the INC had any chance of success, and feared that the possible consequences of regime change would be as bad, or worse, than the current situation. To the extent that they were prepared to contemplate regime change, they were inclined, as the previous administration had been, to believe that only a coup from within Saddam's inner circle was likely to succeed. Thus, when the CIA sent operatives into Kurdistan in 1994, ostensibly to support the efforts of the INC, they also secretly began working with the INA in its efforts to organise a coup.[68]

The INC received a boost to its plans with the defection of al-Samarrai in December 1994. In addition to revealing details of the Iraqi WMD programme, he was able to brief the INC on conditions within the Iraqi regime and the status of internal opposition to it. In collaboration with al-Samarrai, Chalabi now drew up a plan for INC forces to instigate a popular uprising in the north of Iraq in coordination with a coup staged by al-Samarrai's allies in Baghdad. Chalabi was encouraged to pursue the plan by the enthusiastic support and promises of American material assistance from CIA agent Robert Baer. Other members of the INC coalition, however, were sceptical. Kurdistan Democratic Party (KDP) leader Massoud Barzani sought confirmation from Washington that the support promised by Baer would be available. When he received flat denials that any such pledge had been made he withdrew his support for the plan.[69]

In fact, no one at a senior level in the Clinton administration had any notion of the plan's existence until informed by the KDP, and when they were informed they were horrified. They regarded Chalabi's plan as a half-baked enterprise with no chance of success that risked dragging the United States into military intervention to save the INC forces. Moreover, they soon realised that the Iraqi intelligence services were aware of the plan.[70] Anthony Lake's resulting cable to the INC leadership read: 'A. The action you have planned for this weekend has been totally compromised. B. We believe there is a high risk of failure. Any decision to proceed will be on your own.'[71] Despite this, the INC forces, with support from the Patriotic Union of Kurdistan (PUK) *peshmerga*, went ahead on 4 March 1995. The KDP, however, stopped INC forces from attacking Mosul and used the opportunity to try and recapture territory from the PUK, with which it was once more in open conflict. In the face of this, and of an incursion by Turkish forces into Kurdistan in pursuit of PKK guerrillas, the PUK withdrew, forcing the INC forces to do likewise.[72]

Whatever limited faith the Clinton administration had in Chalabi largely evaporated after this experience, though he retained his advocates in the CIA and on the Republican right. When administration supporters of regime change began pushing for more aggressive action to remove Saddam in early 1996, they therefore found themselves in a distinct minority. When they argued at a Principals meeting that Saddam's internal security situation was precarious, and that the US should move now because Saddam's position would only strengthen as time passed, their opponents were quick to remind them of the March 1995 fiasco. The latter, led by Christopher, argued that Saddam was being contained at little cost and that the administration needed to focus on more important issues such as the conflict in former Yugoslavia and the Middle-East peace process.[73]

If the Clinton administration had lost whatever enthusiasm it might have had for the INC's schemes, however, it remained open to the option of a tidy, non-destabilising coup, and gave the formal go-ahead to an INA plan in January 1996. This, however, proved no more successful than the INC effort of the previous year. After the Iraqi intelligence services intercepted CIA messages and communications equipment destined for the plotters, they bided their time in order to let the plan develop and to capture as many of those involved as possible. With the coup planned for the end of June, Iraqi intelligence began arresting the plotters in the middle of that month and by the end of it over 120 had been seized.[74]

## TENSIONS BETWEEN THE US AND UNSCOM

In early June, as it prepared to role up the INA plot, Iraq also refused UNSCOM access to a number of sites in Baghdad. Nor were the two developments unconnected. The Iraqi refusal of cooperation was at least in part because they were aware that American members of the UNSCOM teams were using the inspections process to communicate with opponents of the regime.[75] The Clinton administration now demanded a Security Council resolution finding Iraq in 'material breach' of existing resolutions, paving the way for a punitive military response. The non-Anglo-Saxon members of the P5, however, sought to find a diplomatic solution, and this led to the passage of UNSCR 1060, demanding that Iraq give UNSCOM unconditional access to all sites.[76] The Security Council then despatched Ekeus to Baghdad to secure Iraqi compliance. He was received on 19 June by Tariq Aziz, who complained about American abuses of UNSCOM and told him Iraq would no longer cooperate with inspections unless there was a 'reasonably early' end to sanctions.[77]

Rather than return to the UN and declare Iraq to be in material breach, Ekeus sought a compromise, and after two days of negotiations concluded a deal. Iraq would accept UNSCR 1060 and in return Ekeus agreed to provide a final conclusion on inspections in his next report and to observe certain 'modalities' limiting access to sites where 'the President of Iraq was present'.[78] Whilst this solution was acceptable to most members of the Security Council, Washington was furious. Ekeus had undercut its effort to find Iraq in 'material breach'.[79] This particular episode, moreover, was symptomatic of a growing disenchantment with UNSCOM within the administration, which felt that the inspectors were being too accommodating to Iraq. Some members of the administration even felt that it should no longer bother to back inspections and simply let the sanctions contain Iraq. Such a course, however, risked the collapse of the inspections process and the subsequent abandonment by most states of the sanctions regime as well. The administration therefore decided to maintain its support for UNSCOM.[80]

## THE IRAQI OPPOSITION IMPLODES

In August 1996, the simmering intra-Kurdish conflict erupted into full-scale warfare. When the KDP failed to provide the PUK with its agreed half share of the revenue from the illegal oil trade between Iraq and Turkey, PUK leader Jalal Talabani decided to trade his support against the Kurdistan Democratic Party of Iran for Tehran's backing of a PUK move against the KDP. With Iranian support confirmed, the PUK began seeking to dislodge the KDP from positions near the Iranian border in mid-August. In response, Barzani warned Washington that he might have to seek Saddam's help if the US could do nothing to halt the PUK attacks. The Clinton administration's frantic efforts to broker a ceasefire were to no avail, however, and on 31 August, Iraqi forces crossed the 36th parallel and occupied much of Kurdistan, driving out the PUK. Iraqi intelligence and security agents followed and began rounding up and killing all anti-KDP and anti-Saddam elements, including many INC people. The CIA was forced to wind up its operations in Kurdistan and withdraw its agents, evacuating over 6,000 Iraqis and Kurds who had been working with it.[81]

The Clinton administration retaliated through Operation Desert Strike. Forty-four cruise missiles were fired at Iraqi military targets in the southern NFZ, which was now extended from the 32nd to the 33rd parallel. This rather ineffectual gesture did little to disguise either the embarrassment of the administration or the fiasco that was the Iraqi opposition. As CIA Director John Deutch admitted to the Senate

Intelligence Committee on 19 September 1996, there was now 'little prospect' of removing Saddam from power in the near future.[82]

## A POLICY OF INDEFINITE CONTAINMENT

Clinton's re-election in November 1996 brought no change in American policy. In a speech at Georgetown University on 26 March 1997, newly installed Secretary of State Madeleine Albright reaffirmed the status quo. She reiterated that 'we do not agree with the nations who argue that if Iraq complies with its obligations concerning weapons of mass destruction, sanctions should be lifted'. Iraq had to fulfil all UN resolutions that applied to it, and so far it had complied with none. Moreover, 'the future threat has not been erased' because 'Iraq has yet to provide convincing evidence that it has destroyed all of these weapons' and 'under the current government, an Iraq released from sanctions would pick up where it left off half a dozen years ago'. Nevertheless, 'as long as the apparatus of sanctions, enforcement, inspections and monitoring is in place, Iraq will remain trapped within a strategic box, unable to successfully threaten its neighbors'.[83] The message, in sum, was that the policy of containment was working, and that even if Iraq fully complied with all UN resolutions, the administration would not lift sanctions unless Saddam was removed from power. The Clinton policy thus amounted to indefinite containment of Iraq whilst waiting and hoping for a successful coup and/or Saddam's death to produce a more tolerable regime.

## INSPECTIONS AND TENSIONS AT THE UN

In his last report as head of UNSCOM, Rolf Ekeus complained of an 'Iraqi policy of systematic concealment, denial and masking of the most important aspects of its proscribed weapons and related capabilities'. In particular, he was concerned about the Iraqi BW programme, noting that seventeen tons of growth media and 400 kilos of anthrax were unaccounted for, along with precursors for VX nerve agent.[84] Mohammed El Baradei of the IAEA was more optimistic. He reported in October 1997 that the IAEA had developed a 'technically coherent picture' of the Iraqi nuclear programme and that it saw 'no significant discrepancies between that picture and Iraq's latest declaration'.[85]

Even as El Baradei was issuing that report, however, the new head of UNSCOM, Richard Butler, was issuing one that would initiate a new crisis. On 25 September, UNSCOM inspectors had seized documents on the Iraqi BW programme which revealed the existence of a project to develop gas gangrene. Acting on this information, the inspectors attempted to do a 'no notice' inspection on the head-quarters of the Special Security Directorate but were refused access on the grounds that it was a 'presidential site' as defined under the modalities Ekeus had agreed with the Iraqis the previous year.[86] In his October 1997 report to the Security Council, Butler argued that this was an abuse of the concept of 'presidential sites' and emphasised the continued lack of progress on BW issues.[87]

The Clinton administration, with British support, proposed that Iraq be threatened with military action if it continued to refuse co-operation. They found little support in the Security Council, however, and were forced instead to accept the passage of UNSCR 1134, which threatened to impose a travel ban on Iraqi officials unless Iraq provided complete cooperation with the inspectors. France, Russia and China abstained from supporting even this limited measure.[88] Faced with clear evidence of division within the Security Council, and an apparent weakening of the American position, Saddam decided to try and push the coalition ranged against him to breaking point. On 29 October, Tariq Aziz announced that Iraq would no longer accept American inspectors. When UNSCOM ignored this statement of intent, Iraq expelled all US inspectors on 13 November. UNSCOM and the IAEA then withdrew all inspectors.

Saddam's actions posed a dilemma for the Clinton administration. The lack of support garnered by UNSCR 1134 meant that it would be pointless to try and seek support in the Security Council for military action. A unilateral military strike against Iraq, on the other hand, might deal a fatal blow to international support for sanctions. Doing nothing, however, would have meant allowing the inspections regime to collapse, and with it the rationale for maintaining sanctions. Desperately looking for a compromise that would keep sanctions in place, Clinton agreed to a Russian-brokered deal whereby Iraq agreed to a return of American inspectors in return for a Russian pledge to work to speed up the inspection process, diversify UNSCOM and seek a timetable for the lifting of sanctions.[89] The Russians called an emer-gency session of the Security Council on 21 November 1997 and, in coordination with France and China, sought to make good its part of the deal by securing agreement to close the files on Iraq's nuclear, missile and CW programmes. The plan failed, however, when the extensive evidence of continued Iraqi non-compliance presented to the meeting by UNSCOM persuaded most Security Council members of the need to keep the files open.[90]

This temporary victory could not disguise the parlous state of American policy. The ongoing erosion of support for the regime of sanctions and inspections meant that the administration was now desperate to avoid confrontations that would put that regime on the line. When UNSCOM inspectors went back to Baghdad in November 1997, Butler ordered them to hold off on an inspection after Albright asked him to in order to avoid a crisis that could not be controlled.[91] Saddam, for his part, remained determined to try and create just such a situation. Iraq therefore continued to deny inspectors access to eight 'presidential sites' and, in January 1998, announced that it would expel all inspectors if sanctions were not lifted within six months.

Faced with continued Iraqi defiance, the Clinton administration sought to rally support for military action, but with little effect. Russia promised to veto any resolution calling for air strikes, and when Albright and Secretary of Defense William Cohen toured the Middle East to drum up support, only Kuwait was prepared to cooperate.[92] France and Russia proposed instead that UN Secretary-General Kofi Annan go to Baghdad to try and negotiate a solution and, under the circumstances, the Clinton administration had little choice but to agree.[93] Annan flew to Baghdad and reached an agreement with Saddam on 23 February. Inspectors would be given access to presidential sites but would 'respect the legitimate concerns of Iraq relating to national security, sovereignty and dignity', and to that end would be accompanied by a group of senior diplomats.[94] On 2 March, the Security Council codified the agreement in UNSCR 1154.[95]

## REPUBLICAN ATTACKS

Annan's deal with Saddam was the last straw for many conservative critics of Clinton's Iraq policy. Indeed, even before Annan's compromise, the *Weekly Standard* had devoted a whole issue, headlined 'Saddam Must Go', to the subject of Iraq. The editorial declared that 'Saddam may well be about to acquire the weapons that will put him back in the driver's seat in the Middle East', and that with sanctions not working and the international coalition behind them collapsing, 'our policy should now aim to remove him from power by any means necessary'.[96]

This was followed in January 1998 by an open letter to Clinton under the auspices of the Project for the New American Century (PNAC), a pressure group established to make the case for a new conservative foreign policy. The letter asserted that the policy of containment 'has been steadily eroding over the past several months' and that 'our ability to ensure that Saddam Hussein is not producing weapons of mass destruction, therefore, has substantially diminished'. Moreover, it averred, even if inspectors were allowed to return, 'experience has shown that it is difficult if not impossible to monitor Iraq's chemical and biological weapons production'. And if Saddam were to re-acquire WMD, 'as he is almost certain to do if we continue along the present course, the safety of American troops in the region, of our friends and allies like Israel and the moderate Arab states, and a significant portion of the world's supply of oil will all be put at hazard'. Given that the policy of containment

> is dangerously inadequate. The only acceptable strategy is one that eliminates the possibility that Iraq will be able to use or threaten to use weapons of mass destruction. In the near term, this means a willingness to take military action as diplomacy is clearly failing. In the long term, it means removing Saddam Hussein and his regime from power. That now needs to become the aim of American foreign policy.

The authors concluded by asserting that the United States had the authority under existing UN resolutions to take all necessary steps 'to protect our vital interests in the Gulf' and that, 'in any case, American policy cannot continue to be crippled by a misguided insistence on unanimity in the UN Security Council'.[97]

The fears of both the Bush and Clinton administrations about the risks involved in removing Saddam were dismissed by the Republican right. Yes regime change might lead to the break-up of Iraq, but the threat Saddam posed meant it was worth the risk. Concerns about increased Iranian influence ignored the fact that the Iraqi Shia were not simply pawns of Iran but could be expected to pursue their own, independent, course if they became the dominant group in Iraq. The Clinton administration's lack of faith in the Iraqi opposition was also mistaken. Given sufficient support they could overthrow Saddam.[98] Ahmed Chalabi, in particular, was regarded by many conservatives as the man who had the ability to lead the Iraqi opposition to victory.

Belief in the capability of the Iraqi opposition was also politically convenient, since few in the Republican Party were, at this point, prepared to advocate direct American military action given the lack of popular support for the idea. The preferred Republican option was for the United States to increase supplies of arms and other forms of assistance to the opposition whilst using its airpower to drive out Iraqi forces and establish a 'liberated zone' in the south of Iraq to match that in Kurdistan. The Iraqi opposition would then be able to organise unmolested to overthrow the Iraqi regime.[99] In April 1998, the Republican Congress voted to provide $10 million for the establishment of a 'Radio Free Iraq' and to support the Iraqi opposition. Senate majority leader Trent Lott expressed the Republican consensus thus: 'The doctrine here has to be rollback, not containment'.[100]

## THE EFFECT OF SANCTIONS

Opposition to the Clinton administration's Iraq policy was growing elsewhere in the world as well, though for rather different reasons. By 1997, 30 per cent of Iraqi adults and children were malnourished and deaths of children under five were running at 7,000 per month, representing a trebling of the mortality rate since 1991.[101] Most of the increased mortality rate was due to disease rather than starvation and in that regard sanctions played a major role. The lack of medical supplies and equipment, the absence of clean water and effective sewage treatment (working at about 50 per cent capacity by 1996), and ongoing electricity failures (down to about 40 per cent of capacity by 1998), were all attributable to sanctions rules which barred the importation of equipment, medicines and chemicals.[102]

In the face of the evident and prolonged suffering of ordinary Iraqis, and of the failure of sanctions to force Saddam from power, international criticism of the sanctions regime grew steadily. In September 1998, Dennis Halliday, head of the UN Office of the Humanitarian Coordinator in Iraq, resigned his post. Faced with a leadership in Iraq which does not want to comply with the UN, he asked rhetorically, 'does that empower the Security Council to kill a refugee, or to sustain malnutrition? I don't think so. Killing 6,000 kids a month is like a declaration of war.'[103] The response of the United States, as always, was to insist that it was the fault of Saddam that the Iraqi people were suffering, an argument seemingly supported by a UNICEF survey which found that in Kurdistan, where the OFF programme was run by the UN rather than the Iraqi authorities, child mortality had actually fallen.[104]

Whatever the moral rights and wrongs of sanctions, however, they were certainly a failure in terms of ending Saddam's regime. Indeed, if anything, the effect was quite the opposite. The sanctions made Iraqis dependent on the regime for rations (which helped the regime to monitor the population because all recipients were on a computerised list) and 'this renders the regime stronger because the risk of having rations withdrawn is too high a price for dissent'.[105] Moreover, despite OFF and American and British efforts to blame Saddam for the suffering of ordinary Iraqis, Saddam was successfully able to depict himself as the defender of Iraqi sovereignty against the efforts of the West to crush Iraq. Both inside and outside Iraq, many Arabs were predisposed to believe him and, as a result,

> the suffering caused by the UN sanctions is creating broad Iraqi resentment of the US, Kuwait, and Saudi Arabia [and the] resulting revanchism may well survive Saddam Hussein, and could play an important role in shaping Iraqi politics and actions for several decades.[106]

Sanctions had further effects that would redound to America's long-term disadvantage as well. They crushed the professional middle classes, who were both the most likely source of opposition and the essential basis for any future democratic regime in Iraq. The salaries of professionals and civil servants were rendered worthless by inflation and doctors, teachers and civil servants now earned less than taxi drivers and street stall-holders. Over a million Iraqi professionals emigrated during the 1990s, whilst those left behind were impoverished and/or took up some other occupation (such as taxi-driving) to make a living. And the sanctions regime also contributed to a hollowing out of the Iraqi state. In order to survive, Saddam concentrated what resources he had on informal patronage networks and key security services whilst most of the formal institutions of the state were starved of revenue. As civil servants' wages collapsed, many left their jobs and, amongst those that remained, bribery and corruption became commonplace.[107] Saddam's pursuit of survival also reinforced the negative social and economic effects of sanctions by exacerbating existing sectarian and ethnic divisions. What money the state had was now distributed to a much smaller and closer network of (overwhelmingly Sunni) groups and individuals on whom its survival depended, whilst the Shia masses were increasingly kept in line by repression rather than government largesse.[108]

By the end of the 1990s, as a result of nearly a decade of sanctions, coming on top of two wars and persistent misrule by Saddam Hussein, 'the development of Iraq over the previous decades was, in effect, being set in reverse'.[109] The educated middle class had collapsed and/or gone into exile, the once powerful state had been reduced to a shadow of its former self, and Saddam's efforts to cope with sanctions through divide and rule had exacerbated existing sectarian, ethnic and tribal divides. This would be the legacy the American occupiers found themselves facing after they invaded Iraq in 2003.

## THE END OF INSPECTIONS

In April 1998, the IAEA stated that its recent inspections had 'not revealed indications of the existence in Iraq of prohibited equipment or materials or the conduct of prohibited activities', and that Iraq had 'satisfactorily completed' the 'full, final and complete' account of its nuclear programmes.[110] UNSCOM, however, was less happy. A Congressional Research Service (CRS) report summarised its position thus:

> UNSCOM has reported no firm evidence that Iraq still retains weapons or material, but the Iraqi government has not provided adequate evidence to support its claim that all its CBW arsenal has been destroyed, nor has it accounted for CBW materials known to have been in its possession.

The report also noted that American and British intelligence agencies believed Iraq has 'hidden stores of CBW agents, production equipment, ballistic missiles and missile warheads', though UNSCOM reported no evidence of this.[111]

Iraq, meanwhile, continued to try and generate the crisis which would bring an end to the regime of sanctions and inspections. On 3 August 1998, Aziz told Richard Butler that 'there is no further work to be done, nor is there any additional information for Iraq to provide concerning its past programs of weapons of mass destruction . . . Go and report to the Security Council that you have finished your job'.[112] The following day Saddam ordered the suspension of cooperation with UNSCOM and the IAEA. The initial reaction of the Clinton administration to this provocation was muted, its primary objective remaining to keep the sanctions in place. The inspections process, however, was becoming a threat to that goal by provoking Iraqi resistance and forcing the United States into a choice of either doing nothing, and encouraging further Iraqi defiance, or retaliating and risking the collapse of international support for the sanctions regime. The administration was therefore coming to the conclusion that it was better to rein in UNSCOM than to risk the whole containment regime collapsing,[113] and in August 1998 the *Washington Post* reported that for several months the administration had been pressing UNSCOM to avoid 'challenge inspections' that might have given Saddam an excuse to instigate another crisis.[114] A further consideration affecting Clinton's actions was that he was now embroiled in the Monica Lewinsky affair, as a result of which 'avoiding foreign policy crisis became an even higher priority'.[115]

As in previous crises, American policy was saved by Saddam's apparent inability not to overplay his hand. In October 1998, Kofi Annan drafted terms of reference for a comprehensive review of Baghdad's compliance with UN resolutions that would also specify a timetable for lifting sanctions. Despite this, Iraq continued to refuse cooperation with the UN and instead chose to expel ten American inspectors. This refusal to cooperate even with Annan pushed states which had previously opposed any punitive action against Iraq back into line. Eight Arab states jointly declared that Iraq alone would be responsible for the consequences of its refusal to cooperate with the inspectors.[116] Opposition from Russia and France was also muted by Iraq's behaviour.

Saddam's error of judgement created the opportunity for the United States to deliver a punitive strike against the Iraqi regime. This was initially postponed (even as the planes were in the air) when Annan and the Iraqis negotiated a further compromise allowing the inspectors to return on 14 November. The United States was not, however, to be denied. Coordinating his actions carefully, and many felt inappropriately,[117] with the Clinton administration, in December 1998 Butler submitted a report to the Security Council stating that Iraq had continued to fail to provide full cooperation with the inspections process. Seizing on the report, and freed to act by Saddam's blatant refusal to cooperate with the UN, Clinton launched Operation Desert Fox on 16 December. The air-strikes began even as Butler was presenting his report to the Security Council and without any notification or attempt to secure authorisation from that body.[118]

Desert Fox lasted for four days and involved approximately 400 cruise missile strikes and 600 sorties against a range of targets. The administration justified the attacks as an effort to 'degrade Saddam Husayn's ability to make and use weapons of mass destruction and to demonstrate the consequences of flouting international obligations'.[119] They were nevertheless widely condemned as an effort to distract attention from Clinton's domestic travails and a strategic failure which did nothing to degrade Iraqi WMD capacity or to threaten Saddam's regime. In fact, apparently fearing that the attacks were designed to support a coup, Saddam panicked and ordered wide-ranging arrests and executions, with the result that his regime was destabilised for a significant period.[120]

Operation Desert Fox did not, nevertheless, bring about the end of Saddam, but it did lead to the end of inspections. On 19 December, Iraqi Vice-President Taha Yassin Ramadan declared that UNSCOM inspections were over. Four days later, China joined Russia in demanding Butler's resignation, indicating the depth of the division within the Security Council. In January 1999, revelations about the extent of UNSCOM's witting cooperation with, and unwitting exploitation by, US intelligence further undermined support for inspections.[121] Faced with Iraqi defiance and little support in the Security Council, Butler suspended intelligence over-flights of Iraq on 12 January and in so doing effectively wound up UNSCOM. There would be no more inspections until 2002. For its part, the Clinton administration had decided to let UNSCOM die in order to ensure that sanctions would remain in place.[122]

## A NEW COMMITMENT TO REGIME CHANGE?

On 20 October 1998, in the midst of the Lewinsky scandal, and under heavy pressure from congressional Republicans, Clinton had signed the Iraq Liberation Act (ILA) This stated that 'it should be the policy of the United States to seek to remove the regime of Saddam Hussein from power in Iraq and to replace it with a democratic government', and it authorised the president to spend up to $97 million to train and arm the Iraqi opposition.[123] Two months later, in his televised address announcing the launch of Operation Desert Fox, Clinton declared that

> the hard fact is that so long as Saddam remains in power, he threatens the well-being of his people, the peace of his region, the security of the world. The best way to end that threat once and for all is with a new Iraqi government.[124]

Kenneth Pollack, who was now invited to take the post of Director for Persian Gulf affairs on the NSC staff, was told by National Security Adviser Sandy Berger that the administration had concluded that the only realistic solution to the Iraq problem left was regime change and that Pollack was being appointed to help develop the policy.[125] With support for sanctions ebbing away, the administration had seemingly decided that a policy of indefinite containment was no longer viable. On 19 January 1999, the White House certified seven Iraqi opposition groups as eligible for support under the ILA and named Frank Ricciardone as 'Special Representative for the Transition in Iraq'. A military strategy was drawn up whereby the CIA and American Special Forces would train the Iraqi opposition who, protected by US air cover, would be infiltrated into southern and western Iraq and start to seize lightly defended areas and hopefully attract defectors.[126]

In practice, the plans never got off the drawing board. The lack of enthusiasm for them was almost universal. Not even the Clinton administration itself was united behind them, with the military of the view that only a full-scale invasion would be effective and that anything short of that was likely to become a fiasco.[127] The CIA, meanwhile, had become cautious after the events of 1995–6 and was more focused on avoiding further disasters than anything else.[128] Three of the proposed recipients of American assistance (the KDP, the Movement for a Constitutional Monarchy and SCIRI) immediately rejected American aid and condemned the whole effort, whilst opposition to American plans was fairly unanimous amongst America's Arab allies.[129] For the opposition groups, too overt an association with the United States risked their being seen as imperialist pawns. The Arab states, for their part, feared chaos, civil war and a possible increase in Iranian influence. Both, moreover, saw the plan as half-baked and untenable, likely only to provoke Saddam's retribution without removing him.[130] Nor were such concerns unfounded since the plan was highly unlikely to work. The Iraqi opposition's military forces, such as they were, were almost entirely those controlled by the Kurdish parties, which had never shown any inclination to follow the INC's lead. Moreover, the PUK and KDP were still feuding and neither they, nor most of the other members of the coalition, trusted Chalabi, whose continued efforts to promote himself as the INC's leader had alienated everyone else in the opposition. Even if they could somehow agree to cooperate, and were backed by American air power, the opposition's chances of defeating the Iraqi armed forces were zero.[131]

The Clinton administration thus continued to face the problem that the best was the enemy of the good. If Washington were to move towards aggressive efforts to overthrow Saddam, with no guarantee, indeed little likelihood, of success, it ran the risk that France and Russia would then use this as a pretext to reject inspections and sanctions and undermine containment. According to Pollack, however, what really killed the plan was the Kosovo crisis. The experience of near failure and almost having to commit ground troops made senior policy-makers fearful of something similar, but worse, in Iraq.[132] The administration therefore began backing away from its renewed commitment to regime change almost immediately. When INC members came to Washington in May to ask the administration to 'loosen the rules of engagement' for US warplanes in order to help protect the opposition against Iraqi forces, Ricciardone refused to offer any promises and the administration said it aimed to emphasise 'political aspects' of opposition rather than arms.[133] In June, Deputy Assistant Secretary of State Elizabeth Jones told Congress that 'it would be unwise to arm Iraqi opposition groups right now. That could lead to more Iraqis being killed unnecessarily'.[134] By the end of the Clinton administration no military equipment had been provided to the INC and most of the $97 million provided in the ILA was unspent.[135]

## CONTAINMENT CRUMBLES

Maintaining the containment of Iraq meant keeping sanctions in place, but after the demise of UNSCOM that became increasingly difficult. The French and Russians suggested that what was to be discovered had been and that the UN should now shift from inspections to a monitoring phase and consider the lifting of sanctions. In the face of adamant Anglo-Saxon opposition to any such development, the Security Council was unable to forge a compromise and instead set up three panels under the leadership of the then president of the council, Celso Amorim, to examine the issue. The Amorim reports concluded that 'the bulk of Iraq's proscribed weapons programmes has been eliminated' but that the presence of inspectors was the best way to provide assurance of that and that the legal framework for UNSCOM should therefore remain but be 'renovated'.[136] The Iraqi government rejected the report and continued disagreement amongst the P5 about how to respond meant that not until 17 December 1999 did the Security Council adopt UNSCR 1284, with China, France and Russia abstaining.

UNSCR 1284 created a new organisation, the UN Monitoring, Verification and Inspection Commission (UNMOVIC), to replace UNSCOM and address the remaining disarmament tasks. As the abstentions indicated, however, it was essentially an Anglo-Saxon resolution. Whilst the terms of the OFF programme were eased, and the prospect of sanctions being 'suspended' if Iraq was found to have 'cooperated in all aspects' held out, 1284 offered only a temporary suspension rather than a permanent end to sanctions, and the terms for Iraqi compliance were so vague that it would always be possible for the United States to argue that they had not been met.[137] Iraq rejected the resolution and France and Russia then argued that more incentives had to be offered to secure Iraqi cooperation. They suggested that UNMOVIC specify what the key remaining disarmament issues were and that the terms for the suspending of sanctions be clarified. The Clinton administration refused to consider any such reinterpretation of the resolution.[138]

UNSCR 1284 may have bought containment a little more time but, as Clinton's second term drew to an end, support for sanctions was crumbling. This was due to both humanitarian and self-interested considerations, but also resulted from the Clinton administration's half-hearted support for regime change in Iraq. Most states took the view that if Saddam was not going anywhere then Iraq had somehow to be reintegrated back into the international system. The rot began in February 2000, when Hans von Sponeck, the head of the UN Office of the Humanitarian Coordinator in Iraq, resigned, condemning the continued punishment of the Iraqi people, followed a few days later by the head of the World Food Programme operation in Iraq, Jutta Burghardt. The Arab League called on the Security Council to discuss the continuation of sanctions in the light of the resignations.[139] On 24 March, Annan released a UN report on the humanitarian situation in Iraq which acknowledged that sanctions were contributing to the suffering of Iraqis and warned that the UN was in danger of losing the propaganda war with Saddam over who was responsible for the plight of the Iraqi people.[140] In the face of these developments the United States withdrew its previous objections to $100 million worth of contracts for various goods for Iraq and doubled the funding for equipment needed to restore Iraqi oil production.[141]

Despite these concessions, many states began openly to flout the sanctions. In August, a Russian plane brought an official delegation and humanitarian aid to Baghdad, the first such flight since August 1990. It was soon followed by others, despite American protests. France and a number of other Western European countries meanwhile began to prepare to re-establish embassies in Baghdad, and French oil companies negotiated contracts with the Iraqi government in preparation for a post-sanctions world. Arab states also moved to restore relations with Iraq. On 26 September, an official delegation from Jordan landed in Baghdad, to be followed over the next month by almost all the members of the Arab League (Kuwait and Saudi Arabia being the notable exceptions). Ten years of ostracism were then ended in October when President Mubarak invited Iraq to the emergency Arab League summit in Cairo, at which King Abdullah II of Jordan stated that his country would no longer support the sanctions against Iraq.[142] As the 2000 US presidential election approached, Iraq was being reintegrated into the Arab fold. Even the Saudis reopened their border with Iraq. Egypt upgraded its Iraqi consulate to an embassy and Jordan began weekly scheduled flights to Baghdad – followed by Egypt and Syria. In January 2001, Iraq and Egypt signed a free trade agreement, followed a few weeks later by Syria.[143]

## THE FAILURE OF DUAL CONTAINMENT

As various observers have noted, the Clinton administration had two possible options for an effective Iraq policy. It could have taken military action to remove Saddam and replace him with an acceptable regime, or it could have reconciled itself to Saddam's continued rule and focused simply on ensuring effective disarmament. That would have meant pursuing a solution that would have offered Iraq the lifting of sanctions and the NFZs in return for a system of international monitoring of its WMD programmes to ensure their non-reconstitution.[144] Instead of one or other of those choices, the Clinton administration chose to take the course of indefinite containment of Iraq, a policy with no obvious end point that was doomed to fail because the rest of the international community did not support it. As a result, by the end of Clinton's term in office he faced the worst possible outcome. Support for sanctions was failing and Saddam looked likely to escape the containment regime with inspections incomplete and no ongoing monitoring of Iraqi weapons programmes.

That the administration pursued such a wrongheaded policy was a product of a number of factors. On the one hand, reconciling itself to living with Saddam was deemed to represent an unacceptable risk, largely because the administration, along with many others, continued to believe that the inspections had not worked and that Iraq still had and was pursuing the development of WMD. Moreover, they believed that that would not change until Saddam had gone. In addition, publicly accepting that Saddam was going to remain in power was politically untenable in a domestic political context in which Saddam was international enemy number one and the Republican right were looking for any excuse to attack Clinton. On the other hand, if the American domestic context demanded at least a formal commitment to regime change in Iraq, it also made a commitment of American forces to that end very difficult. There simply was no political will in the United States for the kind of military intervention that would have been required to guarantee successful regime change. Even the Republican right were not prepared to commit to more than air support. Add to that the fear of involuntarily aiding Iran, the ineffectiveness of the Iraqi opposition, and a desire to maintain multilateral backing for US policy, and regime change was not a viable option. Containment therefore remained the default option because it held out the prospect of keeping Saddam under control, was sufficiently tough to neutralise most Republican attacks and involved none of the risks involved in the pursuit of regime change.

The paradox of Clinton's Iraq policy is that, for all its incoherence and contradictions, it was a success despite itself, at least if judged according to the criterion of Iraqi disarmament. Iraq was disarmed and it had been effectively contained. The failure of the administration (and of its Republican critics) to recognise that fact, however, meant that at the time most observers regarded it as a failure. And indeed, judged in the wider context, that conclusion was justified, since the Clinton administration's objective was not simply to disarm Iraq but to maintain American regional hegemony. By the year 2000, however, American hegemony looked a lot less secure than it had at the end of the Persian Gulf War. The dual containment of Iran and Iraq appeared to have produced nothing. Neither regime was in any way reconciled to the United States or its regional presence, Iran continued to pursue its own nuclear programme (albeit, it claimed, solely for peaceful purposes) and the multilateral regime of sanctions and containment put in place to contain Iraq was collapsing, holding out the prospect that Saddam would soon be free once again to reconstitute WMD and pursue his own ambitions for regional hegemony.

Nor had the administration's efforts to resolve the Israeli–Palestinian conflict produced any substantive progress, despite the investment of a great deal of effort. And that failure (and America's perceived pro-Israeli bias), allied to the effect of economic sanctions and the United States' continued support for repressive and autocratic regimes in the region, had served to fuel growing anti-American sentiment amongst ordinary Arabs. That sentiment, in turn, had contributed to the emergence of a new threat to American hegemony in the form of a radical Sunni Islamism. The most visible manifestation of which development was the emergence of al-Qaeda and Osama bin Laden, who announced their existence to the United States with terrorist attacks on American forces in Saudi Arabia in 1996 and on American embassies in East Africa in 1998. The gravest implication of this development, however, was not the direct threat to the United States but the danger the Sunni radicals posed to the continued rule of America's friends in the Gulf, and especially the government in Riyadh.[145]

## NOTES

1. 1987 had seen the publication of Paul Kennedy's unexpected bestseller, *The Rise and Fall of the Great Powers*, which predicted the decline of American hegemony.
2. Cox and Skidmore-Hess, *US Politics and the Global Economy*, p. 207.
3. Pomper *et al.* (eds), *The Election of 1992.*
4. Klinker, *Midterm*; Ladd, 'The 1994 Congressional elections'.
5. Lawrence T. DiRita, 'H.R.7 – The National Security Revitalization Act: Congress's defense contract with America', *Heritage Foundation*, 19 January 1995, pp. 2–6.
6. Cox, *US Foreign Policy*, pp. 14–16.
7. US Arms Control and Disarmament Agency, *World Arms Expenditures*, Figure 4, p. 4.
8. Ikenberry, 'Power and liberal order', pp. 141–2.
9. Skidmore, 'Understanding the unilateralist turn', p. 212.
10. Ibid. pp. 212–13; Wohlforth, 'The stability of a unipolar world'; Waltz, 'Structural realism'.
11. Posen and Ross, 'Competing visions', pp. 44, 23–9; Commission on America and the New World, *Changing Our Ways*; US President, *A National Security Strategy of Engagement.*
12. Cumings, 'Is America an imperial power?'.
13. PDD-25, www.fas.org/irp/offdocs/pdd25.htm.
14. Malone, 'US–UN relations', p. 78.
15. Dumbrell, 'Unilateralism and "America First"', p. 282.
16. 'Excerpts from the Pentagon's plan: "Prevent the emergence of a new rival"', *New York Times*, 8 March 1992, p. 14.
17. Kristol and Kagan, 'Toward a neo-Reaganite foreign policy', p. 23.
18. 'Excerpts from the Pentagon's plan: "Prevent the emergence of a new rival"', *New York Times*, 8 March 1992, p. 14.
19. Klare, *Rogue States.*
20. Project for the New American Century (PNAC), *Rebuilding America's Defenses*, p. 4.
21. Krauthammer, 'The unipolar moment', p. 31.
22. Gaffney, 'Making the world safe'.
23. Muravchik, 'What to do about Saddam'; Perle, 'Iraq: Saddam unbound' p. 106.
24. PNAC, *Rebuilding America's Defenses*, p. 54.
25. Khalilzad, 'United States and the Persian Gulf', pp. 98–9.
26. PNAC, *Rebuilding America's Defenses*, p. 54. See also Kagan and Kristol, 'Introduction', pp. 16–17.
27. Kagan and Kristol, 'Introduction', p. 19.

28. Lake, 'Confronting backlash states', p. 48

29. Indyk, 'The Clinton administration's approach'.

30. Byman and Waxman, *Confronting Iraq*, p. 27.

31. See comments of Phoebe Marr in 'Symposium on dual containment'.

32. Indyk, 'The Clinton administration's approach'.

33. Pollack, *The Threatening Storm*, pp. 65–7.

34. It is telling that, in several hundred pages of memoirs, Clinton gives Iraq no more than a few lines. Clinton, *My Life.*

35. Cox, *US Foreign Policy after the Cold War*, p. 12.

36. Duelfer, 'Why Saddam wants weapons of mass destruction'.

37. Iraq Survey Group, 'Comprehensive report'.

38. 'US Joint Forces Command combat study: Iraqi perspectives on Operation Iraqi Freedom, major combat operations' cited in Gordon and Trainor, *Cobra II*, pp. 73–5.

39. UNSCR 706, www.daccessdds.un.org/Resolution/Gen/NRO/596/42/IMG/NRO59642.pdf?Openelement.

40. UNSCOM, 'Chronology of main events', www.un.org.depts/unscom/chronology/chronologyframe.htm.

41. Hiro, *Neighbours not Friends*, p. 48; Blix, *Disarming Iraq*, p. 18.

42. Trevan, *Saddam's Secrets*, pp. 103–9; Ritter, *Endgame*, p. 111.

43. UNSCR 715, www.daccessdds.un.org/Resolution/Gen/NRO/596/51/IMG/NRO59651.pdf?Openelement.

44. Iraq Survey Group, 'Comprehensive Report'.

45. Ritter, *Endgame*, pp. 35–6, 46.

46. Bailey, *The UN Inspections in Iraq*, pp. 107–9.

47. *Middle East International*, 22 October 1993, p. 11.

48. Hiro, *Neighbours not Friends*, pp. 74, 79; UNSCR 833, www.daccessdds.un.org/doc/UNDOC/GEN/N93/313/44/IMG/NR9331344.pdf?Openelement.

49. Graham-Brown, *Sanctioning Saddam*, p. 78.

50. *Middle East International*, 23 July 1993, p. 10; 15 April 1994, p. 13.

51. Albright, *Madam Secretary*, p. 275.

52. UNSCR 949, www.daccessdds.un.org.doc/UNDOC/GEN/N94/401/71/PDF/N9440171pdf?openelement.

53. Pollack, *The Threatening Storm*, pp. 70–2.

54. UNSCR 986, www.daccessdds.un.org/INDOC/GEN/M95/109/88/PDF/N9510988.pdf?Openelement.

55. Albright, 'A humanitarian exception'.

56. Cockburn and Cockburn, *Saddam Hussein*, p. 111; Hiro, *Neighbours not Friends*, pp. 86–8; Ritter, *Endgame*, pp. 46–7; UN Document S/1995/494, 20 June 1995, www.un.org/Depts/UNSCOM/semiannual/srep95-494.htm.

57. Hiro, *Neighbours not Friends*, pp. 88–9.
58. Blix, *Disarming Iraq*, p. 30.
59. *Middle East International*, 8 September 1995, p. 6.
60. UN Document S/1995/S864, 11 October 1995, www.un.org/Depts/UNSCOM/sres95-864.htm.
61. Mylroie, 'US policy toward Iraq'.
62. Anderson and Stansfield, *The Future of Iraq*, pp. 92–3; Baram, *Building Toward Crisis*, p. 27.
63. Baram, *Building Toward Crisis*, pp. 68–74.
64. Hiro, *Neighbours not Friends*, p. 114.
65. Ibid. p. 58.
66. Anderson and Stansfield, *The Future of Iraq*, pp. 91–2.
67. Indyk, 'The Clinton administration's approach'.
68. Hiro, *Neighbours not Friends*, pp. 84–5; Cockburn and Cockburn, *Saddam Hussein*, p. 174.
69. Cockburn and Cockburn, *Saddam Hussein*, pp. 183–8.
70. Pollack, *The Threatening Storm*, pp. 72–3, n34.
71. Baer, *See No Evil*, pp. 171–213.
72. Cockburn and Cockburn, *Saddam Hussein*, pp. 189–90; Hiro, *Neighbours not Friends*, p. 85.
73. Pollack, *The Threatening Storm*, pp. 73–4, 78–9.
74. Hiro, *Neighbours not Friends*, pp. 103–7; Cockburn and Cockburn, *Saddam Hussein*, pp. 220, 226.
75. Hiro, *Neighbours not Friends*, p. 107.
76. UNSCR 1060, www.daccessdds.un.org/UNDOC/GEN/N96/146/81/PDF/N9614681.pdf?Openelement.
77. Ritter, *Endgame*, pp. 140–1.
78. Malone, *International Conflict over Iraq*, pp. 156–7.
79. Ibid.; Pollack, *The Threatening Storm*, pp. 79–80.
80. Blix, *Disarming Iraq*, pp. 31–2; Ritter, *Endgame*, pp. 137–45.
81. Gunter, 'The KDP-PUK conflict'; Prados, 'Iraq: post-war challenges', p. 16.
82. *Washington Post*, 20 September 1996.
83. Albright, 'Preserving principle'.
84. UN Document S/1997/301, 11 April 1997, www.un.org/Depts/UNSCOM/sres97-301.htm.
85. UN IAEA, '4th consolidated report of the Director General'.
86. Ritter, *Endgame*, pp. 124–5.
87. UN Document S/1997/774, 6 October 1997, www.un.org/Depts/UNSCOM/sres97-774.htm.
88. UNSCR 1134, www.daccessdds.un.org/UNDOC/GEN/N97/283/87/PDF/N9728387.pdf?Openelement.

89. Hiro, *Neighbours not Friends*, p. 128.
90. Ritter, *Endgame*, pp. 177–8.
91. *Washington Post*, 28 August 1998.
92. Hiro, *Neighbours not Friends*, pp. 136–8.
93. Laura Silber *et al.*, 'UN Chief in Baghdad Mission', *Financial Times*, 18 February 1998, p. 1.
94. 'Letter dated 25 February 1998 from the Secretary-General', UN Document S/1998/166, www.un.org/Depts/UNSCOM/S98-166.thm.
95. UNSCR 1154, www.daccessdds.un.org/UNDOC/GEN/N98/050/79/PDF/NN9805079.pdf?Openelement.
96. 'The end of containment', *Weekly Standard*, 1 December 1997, p. 13.
97. www.newamericancentury.org/iraqclintonletter.htm. Eleven of the eighteen people who signed the letter went on to hold senior positions in the George W. Bush administration, including Donald Rumsfeld, Paul Wolfowitz, John Bolton, Richard Perle, Richard Armitage, Elliot Abrams and Zalmay Khalilzad.
98. Perle, 'Iraq: Saddam unbound', pp. 101–3.
99. US Congress, House, 'Statement of Paul Wolfowitz'.
100. Byman *et al.*, 'The rollback fantasy', p. 25.
101. UNICEF, *The State of the World's Children*; Center for Economic and Social Rights, *Unsanctioned Suffering*; Garfield, 'Health and well-being in Iraq'.
102. Garfield, *Morbidity and Mortality*; United Nations, Security Council, *Report of the Secretary General Pursuant to Paragraph 7 of Resolution 1143*.
103. *Middle East International*, 13 November 1998, pp. 6–7.
104. Baram, 'The effect of Iraqi sanctions', pp. 204–7.
105. *Middle East International*, 10 April 1998, p. 17.
106. Cordesman and Hashim, *Iraq*, p. 4.
107. Dodge, 'Iraqi transitions', p. 709.
108. Graham-Brown, *Sanctioning Saddam*, p. 179; al-Khafaji, *War as a Vehicle*, pp. 31–2; United Nations, FAO, *Evaluation of Food and Nutrition Situation in Iraq*, Section III.
109. Malone, *International Struggle over Iraq*, p. 136.
110. 'Letter dated 9 April from the Secretary-General to the President of the Security Council', UN Document S/1998/312, www.globalsecurity.org/wmd/library/news/iraq/un/s1998312.htm.
111. Bowman, 'Iraqi chemical and biological weapons'.
112. Butler, *The Greatest Threat*, p. 184.
113. Ritter, *Endgame*, pp. 15–29, 191–2.
114. *Washington Post*, 14 August 1998.
115. Pollack, *The Threatening Storm*, p. 87.
116. Barbara Crosette, 'US welcomes Arab statement on Iraq', *New York*

*Times*, 13 November 1998, p. A14.

117. Ritter, *Endgame*, pp. 195–6; *Washington Post*, 16 December 1996.

118. Malone, *International Struggle over Iraq*, p. 160; 'Letter dated 15 December 1998 from the Secretary-General addressed to the President of the Security Council', UN Document S/1998/1172, www.un.org/ Deots/UNSCOM/s98-1172.htm.

119. Secretary of Defense William Cohen, 'Department of Defense news briefing', 16 December 1998.

120. Pollack, *The Threatening Storm*, p. 93; Ricks, *Fiasco*, pp. 19–20.

121. Blix, *Disarming Iraq*, pp. 36–7; Hiro, *Neighbours not Friends*, p. 164; Wright, 'The hijacking of UNSCOM'.

122. Malone, *International Struggle over Iraq*, pp. 161, 165.

123. The Iraqi Liberation Act, www.iraqwatch.org/government/US/ legislation/ILA.htm.

124. Clinton, 'The costs of action must be weighed', p. 209.

125. Pollack, *The Threatening Storm*, p. 95.

126. *The Times*, 24 January 1999.

127. 'Pentagon baulks at "idiotic" law urging Bay of Pigs-type invasion of Iraq', *The Guardian*, 21 October 1998.

128. Pollack, *The Threatening Storm*, pp. 95–7.

129. *Middle East International*, 12 February 1999, p. 10

130. Byman, 'After the storm', pp. 512–13.

131. Byman *et al.*, 'The rollback fantasy'.

132. Pollack, *The Threatening Storm*, pp. 98–9.

133. *Reuters*, 26 May 1999.

134. *Associated Press*, 23 June 1999.

135. See the testimony of Assistant Secretary of State David Welch, US Congress, *US Policy Toward Iraq*, 23 March 2000, pp. 11–12.

136. UN, Security Council, 'Letter dated 27 March 1999'.

137. UNSCR 1284, www.daccessdds.un.org/UNDOC/GEN/N99/396/09/ PDF/N9939609.pdf?Openelement.

138. Blix, *Disarming Iraq*, p. 55. It seems probable that at this point the administration neither believed in the possibility of, nor wanted, a successful conclusion to the inspections process.

139. Hiro, *Neighbours not Friends*, p. 181.

140. United Nations, 'Press Release SC6834', 24 March 2000.

141. Hiro, *Neighbours not Friends*, p. 183.

142. Ibid. pp. 188–9; *Washington Post*, 21 October 2000.

143. Hiro, *Neighbours not Friends*, p. 203.

144. Ritter, *Engame*, pp. 199–215; Byman *et al.*, 'The rollback fantasy', p. 38.

145. Hinnebusch, *International Politics of the Middle East*, pp. 233–6.

*Chapter 5*

# A SECOND WAR FOR HEGEMONY, 2001–2003

## THE TRIUMPH OF CONSERVATISM

Since 1979, successive American administrations had sought to stabilise the hegemonic position in the Gulf and the international oil system undermined by the fall of the Shah of Iran. By the time of the election of George W. Bush in 2000, nevertheless, the maintenance of American hegemony in the Gulf remained as problematic as ever, indeed arguably more so, with emergent Sunni Islamic militancy and terrorism now added to the challenge posed by Iraq and Iran. An increasingly large American military presence in the Gulf and repeated applications of force, both large and small in scale, had served to preserve American hegemony but were, in themselves, evidence of, and contributory to, its tenuous nature.

In the face of this unfavourable regional dynamic, and with the containment of Iraq seemingly about to collapse, the second Bush administration would choose to embark on a radical attempt to re-forge the basis of American hegemony in the Gulf and the wider Middle-East region. Whilst its actions in so doing were driven by the objective of preserving American global hegemony and by the regional developments which appeared to threaten it, two new factors under-pinned its rejection of the more cautious policies of its predecessors. In the first place, the George W. Bush administration was the first since 1945 to fully represent the interests and ideology of the Republican right and, as such, was naturally predisposed to both unilateralism and the use of military force in a way that none of its predecessors had been. The second key development was 11 September 2001. The events of that day were a critical catalyst which both pushed the administration to pursue the logic of its world view to the utmost and created a permissive domestic environment which allowed it to do so.

This combination of a long-term structural shift in American politics and the events of a single day was the key to the Iraq War of 2003.

'George W. Bush's election in 2000 marked the triumph of the conservative ascendancy'.[1] All the trends that had been marking the Republican Party's (and America's) shift to the right culminated in his election. 2000 confirmed the dominance of a white, southern, conservative, Christian coalition capable of securing victory for a presidential candidate cast in its own mould. The Republican vote was now concentrated in the south and west to a far greater extent than in 1980 or 1988, and 80 per cent of those voters considered themselves to be 'conservatives'.[2] This homogenous base enabled Bush to be the first president since 1945 to pursue a clearly conservative agenda. His corporate backers were rewarded with capital gains, corporate, individual and dividend tax rate changes as well as tort law reform and inaction on climate change. Conservative Christians, who had got little more than warm words from Reagan and not even that from the first Bush, now had a president whose overt religiosity mirrored their own as well as faith-based welfare policies, a ban on federal government funding for stem-cell research, and support for the teaching of intelligent design in schools.[3]

## CAMPAIGN 2000 AND APPOINTMENTS

Bush's victory would prove to have even more radical implications for American foreign policy than it did for domestic policy, though this was not clear to many observers at the time. To some, Bush's statements during the 2000 election campaign seemed to constitute a rejection of the Republican right's foreign policy prescriptions.[4] His criticism of Clinton for his 'promiscuous commitments' of America's armed forces, an oft-stated opposition to the use of those forces for 'nation-building', and references to the need to be 'humble', seemed to imply a foreign policy of limited ambitions.[5] However, whilst Bush's campaign statements contained elements of ambiguity (no doubt deliberately so), a careful reading clearly demonstrates an adherence to the world view of the Republican right.

Bush criticised Clinton not for using America's armed forces per se, but for using them ineffectively and for the wrong purpose. His remark in a presidential debate that 'I don't think our troops ought to be used for what's called nation building' was followed by the assertions that they should be used 'for fighting war', and that 'I think our troops ought to be used to help overthrow a dictator . . . when it's in our best interests'.[6] In an article in *Foreign Affairs*, Bush's top foreign policy adviser, Condoleezza Rice, offered a ringing defence of unilateralism, dismissing the 'symbolic agreements' and 'illusory norms' pursued by the Clinton administration and rejecting the idea that the imprimatur of the UN was required to legitimate the exercise of American power. In her view the US had a 'special role in the world', because 'American values are universal'. It should therefore feel free to act unilaterally for the greater good whenever necessary.[7]

The threat posed to American predominance by 'rogue states' armed with WMD, and the absolute necessity of building an effective National Missile Defence (NMD) system, was the central theme of Bush's national security platform. More specifically, on a number of occasions, reference was made to the need to remove Saddam from power. Rice noted that 'nothing will change until Saddam is gone, so the United States must mobilize whatever resources it can . . . to remove him'.[8] In the vice-presidential debate, Dick Cheney said that 'if, in fact, Saddam Hussein were taking steps to try to rebuild nuclear capability or weapons of mass destruction, we'd have to give very serious consideration to military action to stop that activity'.[9] Bush himself, in an interview on PBS, said 'I will tell you this: If we catch him developing weapons of mass destruction in any way, shape or form, I'll deal with him in a way he won't like'.[10]

If any doubt remained as to the administration's orientation, it should have been dispelled by Bush's appointments to the national security bureaucracy. As vice-president he chose the arch-conservative Cheney. As a congressman from Wyoming in the 1980s, Cheney had voted for the MX missile and aid to the Contras and against sanctions on South Africa. As Defense Secretary during the first Bush administration he had been the right-wing outlier amongst moderates, and found himself isolated in his distrust of Gorbachev and opposition to defence spending cuts.[11] His world view was pithily summed up by Robert Hartmann, who worked with him in the Ford administration: 'whenever his private ideology was exposed, he appeared somewhat to the right of Ford, Rumsfeld, or for that matter, Ghengis Khan'.[12]

Having secured his own position as vice-president, Cheney was instrumental in securing the appointment as Secretary of Defense of his old mentor and ideological soul-mate, Donald Rumsfeld.[13] Aside from his closeness to Cheney, Rumsfeld was appointed because he was a leading advocate of NMD and the so-called 'revolution in military affairs'. In addition, Cheney and Bush picked him for his renowned skill as a bureaucratic infighter who would be able to stand up to Secretary of State Colin Powell.[14] The combination of Rumsfeld and Cheney's ideological and personal closeness, the former's bureaucratic political skill and the latter's proximity to the president,[15] would make these two hard-line conservatives the dominant force in the administration's first term.[16]

Cheney and Rumsfeld filled the Office of the Vice-President and the Department of Defense with ideological fellow-travellers. Cheney appointed Lewis 'Scooter' Libby as his Chief of Staff, while at Defense Paul Wolfowitz once more took up the post of Deputy-Secretary and Douglas Feith became Under-Secretary. Richard Perle was apparently offered the latter job but instead took charge of the Defense Policy Board, an advisory body which also included fellow conservatives Kenneth Adelman and R. James Woolsey. In all, some seventeen 'members' of the Project for the New American Century, whose 1998 letter to Bill Clinton calling for regime change in Iraq had been signed by Rumsfeld, Wolfowitz, Perle, Woolsey, and Bolton amongst others, would take up posts in the George W. Bush administration.[17]

The only part of the national security bureaucracy that would be controlled by moderates in the mould of the first Bush administration was the State Department, where Colin Powell was supported by his close friend Richard Armitage as Deputy-Secretary. Powell, however, was appointed more because of his popularity with the American public than because Bush saw eye to eye with him. He had not been part of Bush's foreign policy team during the campaign, and he would rapidly become an isolated figure within the administration, kept carefully in check by the conservatives. Perhaps the most overt demonstration to Powell of his limited authority was the appointment of John Bolton, the hardliners' hardliner, to the number three post at the Department of State.[18] Powell's marginalisation was a very clear indication of how far to the right the centre of gravity of the Republican Party had shifted during the 1990s.

Bush's appointment of ideologically antipathetic teams to lead DOD and State was also bound to generate conflict. That, in turn, made the role of the National Security Adviser all the more important, since the primary function of that role is to ensure an effective and cohesive decision-making process. In the event, Bush's chosen appointee for the post, Condoleezza Rice, proved to be largely ineffectual, and the administration would be characterised by vicious bureaucratic infighting and a disorganised and incoherent policy process.[19] Indeed, in the view of Richard Armitage, 'there was never any policy process . . . There was never one from the start'.[20] Whilst Rice proved unable to manage bureaucratic heavyweights like Rumsfeld and Powell, however, the ultimate responsibility for the failure of the policy process lies not with her but with Bush, who failed to insist on an orderly decision-making process, with proper discussion of options and regular principals meetings.

That he failed to do so was reflective of the president's character and intellect, being a man of fixed opinions, with a black and white view of the world. Whilst intelligent, Bush is intellectually uncurious and fails to reflect on his basic assumptions. In his own words, 'I'm not a textbook player, I'm a gut player'.[21] When he decides on a course of action he sticks to it and rarely reconsiders. As he told Bob Woodward, after the Iraq War, 'I have not doubted what we're doing. I have not doubted . . . There is no doubt in my mind we're doing the right thing. Not one doubt'.[22] This combination of a reliance on instinct and absolute self-belief meant Bush was not interested in the kind of systematic policy process wherein all possibilities and angles of an issue were examined and all policy options considered. In the words of former National Coordinator for Counter-Terrorism Richard Clarke, he had 'a results oriented mind, but he looked for the simple solution, the bumper sticker description of the problem. Once he had that, he could put energy behind the drive to achieve his goal'.[23] One result would be that there was no thorough debate about the merits of the case for war against Iraq and the evidence that underpinned that case. Once Bush decided Saddam had to go that was more or less the end of the discussion.

## THE FIRST EIGHT MONTHS OF 2001

In the interlude between his election and inauguration, Bush met with Bill Clinton to discuss foreign policy. Clinton said that he had the impression that Bush's two national security priorities were NMD and Iraq; Bush replied that that was correct,[24] and that focus was confirmed when the administration held its first full NSC meeting on 30 January

2001. Rice began the discussion by stating that the issue was 'how Iraq is destabilizing the region' but might also be the key to reshaping the Middle East. She was followed by a briefing from Director of Central Intelligence George Tenet on Iraq's allegedly ongoing WMD programmes. At the end of the meeting Bush ordered the State Department to look at the sanctions regime while the DOD 'should examine our military options'. Two days later the NSC principals met again, with Powell leading the discussion and arguing for the reconfiguration of the sanctions regime. Rumsfeld, however, interjected that

> what we really want to think about is going after Saddam . . . Imagine what the region would look like without Saddam and with a regime that's aligned with US interests . . . It would change everything in the region and beyond it. It would demonstrate what US policy is all about.[25]

Clearly, whilst

> the new team did not have a preconceived plan on how to deal with Saddam's regime or a timetable for action . . . there was an assumption on the part of the president, his vice-president, and most of his national security team that something had to be done.[26]

In May, Bush outlined the rationale for regime change in Iraq in a speech at the National Defense University. He told his audience that WMD were proliferating, along with missile technology, and that those who sought them were 'some of the world's least responsible states'. These states 'seek weapons of mass destruction to intimidate their neighbors and to keep the United States and other responsible nations from helping allies and friends in strategic parts of the world'. He concluded by posing the question of whether the United States would have intervened to save Kuwait in 1990 if Saddam had had nuclear weapons.[27] The following month Rumsfeld reiterated the message: if rogue states developed WMD it would give them 'the power to hold our people hostage to nuclear blackmail – in effect to stop us from projecting force to stop aggression'. Such states, he argued, are 'not constrained by diplomatic efforts to halt their programs; they are not constrained by international "norms" and arms control regimes; and we cannot rely on them being deterred by the threat that we would use nuclear retaliation.'[28]

In inter-agency meetings during the first nine months of 2001, conservatives argued that containment of Iraq was doomed and that regime change had to be the administration's objective. Wolfowitz was busy exploring options for supporting the opposition and even inquired whether the United States could bomb dams so as to restore the marshes in the south and create a haven for opposition fighters. He also wanted the Joint Staff to establish what was needed to train and arm a sizeable Iraqi opposition force. Powell, meanwhile, made the case for 'smart sanctions' which would prevent Iraqi acquisition of WMD technologies without imposing unnecessary suffering on the Iraqi people.[29] The result was a stalemate. With the exception of Powell, the Bush administration principals wanted to remove Saddam and did not believe containment and inspections could work. Nevertheless, given the probable failure of any option short of direct American military intervention, and absent some compelling rationale for war that would win the support of the American public, the Bush administration had no more viable options for regime change than had its predecessor.

## THE IMPACT OF 11 SEPTEMBER 2001

According to George W. Bush,

> prior to September 11, we were discussing smart sanctions . . . After September 11, the doctrine of containment just doesn't hold any water . . . My vision shifted dramatically after September 11, because I now realize the stakes, I realize the world has changed.[30]

September 11 was a traumatic event, and it did change things significantly, but the assertion that it 'changed everything'[31] is clearly misleading. Rather than fundamentally altering the Bush world view, the attacks reinforced the rationale for regime change in Iraq and created a permissive domestic political environment that facilitated the pursuit of that objective. As one senior administration official put it, the importance of that day was 'not so much that it revealed the existence of a threat of which officials had previously been unaware, as that it drastically reduced the American public's usual resistance to American military involvement overseas'.[32] Regime change in Iraq was already on the agenda before 11 September, but the events of that day made it possible.

Nor were administration hawks slow to recognise this. Within hours of the attacks, Rumsfeld ordered his aide, Stephen Cambone, to get 'best info fast. Judge whether good enough hit S.H. [Saddam Hussein] @ same time – Not only UBL [Osama bin Laden] . . . Go massive – sweep it all up'.[33] The speed with which Rumsfeld concluded that this was an opportunity to eliminate Saddam clearly demonstrates that 11 September served mainly as a facilitator of existing desires rather than as a generator of new ones. At the following day's NSC meeting, Cheney argued that the administration's response should focus not only on terrorists but also on the states which supported them and Rumsfeld singled out Iraq as an example. Powell responded that they should focus on al-Qaeda. Three days later the principals met again at Camp David, where Wolfowitz claimed that there was a 10–50 per cent chance that Iraq was involved in the 11 September attacks and should therefore be a prime target for American retaliation. Powell again expressed his opposition, arguing that attacking Iraq would destroy international support for American policy. Bush concluded the debate by stating that he wanted to put Iraq to one side and focus on dealing with al-Qaeda and the Taliban regime in Afghanistan first.[34] He also made clear, however, that 'we will get this guy [Saddam] but at a time and place of our choosing'.[35]

By mid-November 2001, the Taliban had been routed and Bush's thoughts duly turned to Iraq. After an NSC meeting on 21 November, Bush ordered Rumsfeld to begin updating the existing plans for invading Iraq.[36] Two months later, in his 2002 State of the Union address, Bush again made the case for regime change in public. Branding Iraq part of an 'axis of evil' (along with Iran and North Korea), he reiterated the threat posed by rogue states with WMD, and now emphasised the added danger that those states might supply those weapons to terrorists. Terrorists, rogue states and WMD were thus conflated into a single threat, with the objective of US policy being 'to prevent regimes that sponsor terror from threatening America or our friends and allies with weapons of mass destruction'. Bush warned that 'we will not wait on events, while dangers gather'.[37]

By spring 2002 Franks and CENTCOM were working full time on

war plans for Iraq. Troops were being moved to the Gulf, and bases and infrastructure were being upgraded in Kuwait and elsewhere.[38] In March 2002, Cheney toured the Middle East in order to inform key states that the US was going to eliminate Saddam and to seek their cooperation in facilitating military action.[39] The same month Bush told a group of senators discussing Iraq policy with Rice, 'fuck Saddam, we're taking him out',[40] and when Richard Haass, the head of the State Department's Policy Planning Staff, tried to raise his concerns about the march to war with Rice in July 2002, she cut him off abruptly: '"Save your breath" she told him . . . "The president has made up his mind"'.[41] In Bush's 2002 West Point graduation address, and the *National Security Strategy of the United States* (NSS) document of which that speech was essentially a précis, the administration sought to reinforce the rationale for regime change by reiterating the nature of the threat and by seeking to discredit the alternatives. Bush warned that 'deterrence . . . means nothing against shadowy terrorist networks with no nation or citizens to defend', and that 'containment is not possible when unbalanced dictators with weapons of mass destruction can deliver those weapons or missiles or secretly provide them to terrorist allies'.[42] The latter possibility, moreover, meant that NMD, whilst still an essential priority, was no longer sufficient to provide security against attack. If defence was not possible, it followed that 'we cannot let our enemies strike first' and must 'if necessary, act pre-emptively'.[43]

## THE RATIONALE FOR WAR

Above all, therefore, the administration emphasised the combination of rogue states, WMD and terrorists as the rationale for regime change in Iraq.[44] In the aftermath of the Iraq War, however, Paul Wolfowitz gave an interview to *Vanity Fair* in which he asserted that the administration emphasised the WMD threat posed by Iraq 'for reasons that have a lot to do with the bureaucracy'.[45] Remarks such as that, when added to the absence of WMD in Iraq and the administration's manipulation and distortion of the intelligence (see below), have led some observers to question the claim that the Iraq War was about WMD at all.[46] The administration itself, of course, insisted that it was about WMD but with the primary focus now on the danger posed by WMD-armed terrorists. Regime change in Iraq was depicted as part of the so-called 'global war on terror', rather than as an attempt to reassert American hegemony.

The idea that the Iraq War was not about WMD flies in the face of both evidence and logic. The Republican right had been obsessed by the threat posed by WMD-armed rogue states for a decade before 11 September. Moreover, they had long seen Iraq as the prototypical example of that threat and advocated regime change as the solution. American policy throughout the 1990s had been driven by the objective of preventing Iraqi possession of WMD and there was a widespread consensus that Iraq had still not fully disarmed.[47] The Bush administration's actions and statements before 11 September 2001 demonstrated that they shared those concerns. As Wolfowitz himself noted, in the same interview quoted above, it was 'the one issue that everyone could agree on'.[48] Finally, 'had administration officials not sincerely believed that at least some weapons [of mass destruction] were there, it would have been imprudent at the least . . . to have based their entire propaganda strategy on their presence'.[49]

The argument that, after 11 September, regime change in Iraq was about terrorism rather than hegemony, is more plausible on its surface. Certainly, there can be no question that the Bush administration did develop a newfound preoccupation with Islamic terrorism and with the prospect of those terrorists gaining access to WMD. Nor should we doubt that that danger made regime change in Iraq all the more compelling to many members of the administration. Nevertheless, this did not imply an alteration in the fundamental rationale for Saddam's removal. As Dick Cheney stated in a speech to the Veterans of Foreign Wars (VFW) convention in August 2002, a WMD-armed Iraq

> could then be expected to seek domination of the entire Middle East, take control of a great portion of the world's energy supplies, directly threaten America's friends throughout the region and subject the United States or any other nation to nuclear blackmail.[50]

Cheney's statement demonstrated that his fundamental preoccupation with American hegemony in the Gulf had not altered. Donald Rumsfeld's testimony to the Senate Foreign Relations Committee in September 2002 explains why. He noted that even some critics of the administration had conceded that Saddam

'seeks weapons of mass destruction . . . to deter us from inter-
vening to block his aggressive designs'. . . imagine for a moment
that Iraq demonstrated the capacity to attack US or European
populations with nuclear, chemical or biological weapons. Then
imagine you are the president of the United States, trying to put
together an international coalition to stop their aggression, after
Iraq had demonstrated that capability. It would be a daunting
task. His regime believes that simply by possessing the capacity
to deliver WMD to Western capitals, he will be able to prevent
. . . the free world from projecting force to stop his aggression.

The significance of 11 September, he went on, was that rogue states
like Iraq

> have discovered a new means of delivering these weapons –
> terrorist networks. To the extent that they might transfer WMD to
> terrorist groups, they could conceal their responsibility for attacks.
> And if they believe they can conceal their responsibility for an
> attack, then they would likely not be deterred.[51]

The attacks of 11 September did not, therefore, create a new, *sui
generis*, rationale for regime change in Iraq in the form of a fear of
WMD-armed terrorists. Although that fear was real enough, such
terrorists were perceived primarily as another potential delivery
system that rogue states might use to try and deter an American
response to a bid for regional hegemony. Indeed, that was the only
possible reason that Saddam might arm terrorists. The fundamental
rationale for regime change in Iraq was thus unaltered. Rather than
being subsumed or displaced by the 'war on terror', it was the war on
terror which was subsumed by, and used as a rationale for, the
preservation of American hegemony in the Gulf.

Nevertheless, as Wolfowitz's remark implied, some members of
the administration had additional, complimentary, rationales for war
which went beyond the mere elimination of a WMD-armed rogue
state. In the view of some of its advocates, regime change in Iraq
'would revolutionize the situation in the Middle East in ways both
tangible and intangible, and all to the benefit of American interests'.[52]
The key to that revolution, it was widely agreed, was using regime
change in Iraq as a lever to engineer the spread of market-democracy

in the wider region. This was an argument that had been widely touted by so-called neoconservatives for some time and which derived its logic from the 'democratic peace' theory.[53] According to this reasoning, the United States could best preserve its hegemonic position in the Middle East by remaking the latter in its own, democratic, image because 'the lesson of history is that democracies don't initiate aggression'.[54]

This idea had been largely absent from the Bush administration's thinking before 11 September. Over the course of the next fifteen months, however, it began to feature in Bush's speeches more and more often, with the most extensive statement in February 2003:

> the world has a clear interest in the spread of democratic values, because stable and free nations do not breed the ideologies of murder. They encourage the peaceful pursuit of a better life . . . A new regime in Iraq would serve as a dramatic and inspiring example of freedom for other nations in the region.[55]

The promotion of market-democracy in Iraq and the rest of the Middle East was thus seen by some within the Bush administration as a kind of universal panacea to the problems of American hegemony in the region. According to this logic, it was the continuation of closed, autocratic regimes with inefficient statist economies which was the source of all America's problems. Such regimes were prone to violence, whilst their repression and lack of economic opportunity bred resentment that easily transformed into Islamic radicalism and terrorism. Washington's support for such regimes ensured that those resentments were then directed towards America as well as its regional clients. The spread of market-democracy, in contrast, would eliminate inter-state violence and the source of the frustrations that underpinned anti-Americanism and terrorism. It would facilitate the ending of the provocative presence of American forces in the region and a resolution of the Israeli–Palestinian conflict, whilst isolating Iran and increasing the pressure on it to follow the path of democratic reform.[56]

This new-found enthusiasm for democracy in the Middle East thus represented a recognition on the part of some members of the administration (Cheney and Rumsfeld never showed any interest in democracy promotion, instead preferring to rest American hegemony solely on overwhelming military predominance and a demonstrated willingness to use it) that the fundamental weakness of American hegemony in the Gulf, and in the Middle East more generally, was the continued absence of the shared norms, rules and values that made hegemonic leadership consensual. In the absence of such shared norms, the United States was forced to rely solely on coercion which, whilst effective in many ways, had failed to provide any fundamental resolution to the various regional threats to American hegemony.

The inability of the United States to develop a consensual hegemony in the Middle East is explicable largely in terms of the relative autonomy of many Middle-Eastern states, which have been able to use their oil wealth to maintain autonomy both from their own societies and from the WCS.[57] That autonomy meant that, unlike most of the rest of the periphery, those states had been able to repress demands for democracy and liberalisation at home whilst also resisting external pressure to integrate their economies more fully into the WCS and to restructure them in line with its imperatives. As a result, whilst liberal, democratic and market norms had spread throughout much of the periphery over the previous two decades, the Middle East remained largely immune from that development.[58] And in the absence of market-democratic norms, there was no basis upon which Washington could hope to create consensual hegemony.

For some in the Bush administration, therefore, regime change in Iraq became the means by which American hegemony in the Middle East could be re-forged on a consensual basis. Saddam's regime would be replaced by a market-democracy which would serve as an exemplar and catalyst for change in the rest of the region, which would also come under direct pressure from Washington to move in a similar direction. The resulting spread of market-democracy would enable the United States to maintain its regional dominance with the active consent of the region's states and population. The need to maintain hegemony through coercion would be largely eliminated, placing it on a more stable footing.[59] The United States, in short, would engage in a decisive act of coercion in the short term in order to preclude the need to do so again in the longer term.

## SELLING THE WAR

Having decided on regime change, in early autumn 2002 the Bush administration began a sustained campaign to persuade the American public, Congress and the wider world of its necessity. It did so at least partly in response to the emergence of the first significant criticisms of its policy. In August 2002, the *Wall Street Journal* published an article by former National Security Adviser (and close friend of the president's father) Brent Scowcroft in which he argued that the threat posed by Saddam was being exaggerated. Threatening the United States with WMD would be suicidal and, he averred, Saddam was certainly not that, being rather a 'power-hungry survivor'. Scowcroft also warned that attacking Iraq would 'seriously jeopardize, if not destroy, the global counterterrorist campaign we have undertaken' by alienating the Arab world, reducing international cooperation and fuelling terrorism.[60] Scowcroft's arguments were supported by both James Baker and Lawrence Eagleburger, who called on Bush to work through the UN, avoid unilateralism and seek the return of the weapons inspectors, considering war only if such a return was refused.[61]

These criticisms provoked the Bush administration into an aggressive effort to play up the threat posed by Iraq, at the heart of which were the claims that Iraq already had WMD, would shortly have nuclear weapons, and was connected to al-Qaeda and the attacks of 11 September 2001. None of these claims, it would turn out, was true,[62] which inevitably raises the question of why the Bush administration went to war on a false prospectus. Two possible explanations offer themselves, namely that the intelligence was simply wrong, or alternatively, that the Bush administration deliberately misrepresented the evidence.

The first of these explanations is certainly true. The US intelligence community (IC) overestimated the threat posed by Iraq and were far from alone in that error.[63] As the Carnegie Endowment for International Peace noted, 'most national and international officials and experts believed that Iraq likely had research programs and some stores of hidden chemical or biological weapons and maintained interest in a program to develop nuclear weapons'.[64] To some extent, therefore, the Bush administration was simply misled by the mistaken intelligence consensus, particularly when it came to claims about Iraqi possession of CW and BW. The Carnegie Endowment also concluded, however, that 'administration officials systematically misrepresented the threat from Iraq's WMD and ballistic missile programs',[65] and that the greatest misrepresentations, moreover, occurred in precisely those areas – nuclear weapons and ties to al-Qaeda – which were most central to the public case for war.

In his speech to the VFW, Cheney stated that 'many of us are convinced that Saddam will acquire nuclear weapons fairly soon', while the following month he said that 'we do know, with absolute certainty, that [Saddam] is using his procurement system to acquire the equipment he needs in order to enrich uranium to build a nuclear weapon'.[66] Bush, in a major speech in October 2002, similarly asserted that 'the evidence indicates Iraq is reconstituting its nuclear weapons program'.[67] On 16 March 2003, Cheney went further, stating that 'we believe he has, in fact, reconstituted nuclear weapons'.[68] To support these claims, two pieces of 'compelling evidence' were repeatedly emphasised by the administration. The first was an order for aluminium tubes which the administration insisted could be 'only . . . for nuclear weapons programs, centrifuge programs'. The second was a report that Iraq had sought to purchase 'yellowcake' uranium ore from Niger.[69]

The certainty of these claims and of the evidence cited to support them, however, went well beyond the available evidence and failed to reflect the disagreements and uncertainties of the IC. A National Intelligence Estimate (NIE) of 1 October 2002[70] stated that Iraq would 'probably have nuclear weapons during this decade', but also contained a dissent from the State Department's Bureau of Intelligence and Research (INR) stating that there was no evidence to make a 'compelling case' that Iraq was pursuing 'an integrated and comprehensive approach to acquire nuclear weapons'.[71] With regard to the yellowcake claim, the NIE stated that a 'foreign government service' had claimed that Iraq was seeking up to 500 tons of yellowcake from Niger but that 'we do not know the status of this arrangement' and 'we cannot confirm whether Iraq succeeded in acquiring uranium and/or yellowcake'. State's INR described the claim as 'highly dubious',[72] and the IC was sufficiently uncertain about the truth of the story for Tenet to insist it be taken out of Bush's speech in Cincinnati.[73] Despite that, it reappeared in the 2003 State of the Union address and elsewhere in administration statements. With regard to the aluminium tubes, both the Department of Energy and INR argued that they were not for centrifuges but were far more likely to be for rockets, a view shared by the IAEA.[74]

The greatest misrepresentation of the intelligence, however, was in regard to Iraqi links to al-Qaeda. In his Cincinnati speech Bush claimed that 'we know that Iraq and al Qaeda have high-level contacts that go back a decade . . . We've learned that Iraq has trained al Qaeda members in bomb-making and poison and deadly gases'.[75] The crucial assertion, however, was that Iraq was somehow linked to the 11 September attacks, and the key piece of evidence used to support that claim was an alleged meeting between hijacker Mohammed Atta and an Iraqi intelligence official in Prague, a meeting Cheney described as 'pretty well confirmed'.[76] In practice, the vast majority of the analysis produced by the IC expressed doubts about these claims.[77] With regard to the Iraqi connection to 11 September, the CIA concluded that 'we have no credible information that Baghdad was complicit in the attacks' and as to the claim of a meeting between Iraqi intelligence agents and Mohammed Atta: 'the most reliable reporting to date casts doubt on this possibility'.[78]

In addition to thus misrepresenting the intelligence provided, the administration also manipulated the intelligence process in an effort to produce evidence supporting the case for war. Rather than allowing the IC to make their own judgements, the administration demanded that it focus on a limited number of issues that it saw as supporting regime change.[79] Moreover, in summer 2002 Cheney, in unprecedented behaviour, personally visited CIA headquarters on a number of occasions in an attempt to pressure analysts to find evidence supporting the administration's arguments.[80] The pressure was such that, in January 2003, Deputy-Director for Intelligence Jami Miscik threatened to resign if she was compelled to rewrite a report on the connection between Iraq and al-Qaeda after already responding to multiple demands to do so from the Office of the Vice-President.[81] When the IC still failed to come up with the evidence it wanted, the administration responded by creating its own intelligence 'shop' in the form of the Policy Counterterrorism Advisory Group (CAG) in the DOD.[82]

The administration's misrepresentation of the evidence can be explained in a number of ways, the least plausible of which is that they simply knew that their claims were untrue but made them anyway. In fact, it was precisely the absolute, almost theological, certainty that Saddam did have active WMD programmes that was the primary cause of the administration's actions. Study of the available evidence demonstrates that there was no point at which that assumption was

seriously questioned or discussed amongst the administration principals. Neither Bush nor Rice bothered to read the whole of the
October 2002 NIE, so certain were they of their case.[83] After all, as
Cheney argued, 'why in the world would he [Saddam] subject himself for all those years to UN sanctions and forego an estimated
$100 billion in oil revenue? It makes no sense!' unless he had
something to hide.[84] In addition to that assumption of Iraqi guilt, the
administration's actions were shaped by long-standing belief that the
IC had 'repeatedly underestimated the weapons capabilities of threatening states'.[85] Twice, in recent decades, conservatives had established
parallel intelligence efforts when they were unhappy with the IC
consensus. In the 1970s, they formed 'Team B' to evaluate the Soviet
threat and, in the 1990s, established a commission on the threat posed
by WMD and ballistic missile proliferation.[86] The creation of the CAG
was simply a third such effort to produce intelligence that proved
what they already believed to be the case.

This combination of absolute certainty about the existence of Iraqi
WMD and distrust of the IC led to what Greg Theilmann of the INR
bureau described as a 'faith-based' approach to intelligence: 'we know
the answers, give us the intelligence to support those answers'.[87] Any
scepticism about the existence of Iraqi WMD on the part of the IC was
dismissed as evidence of their perpetual failings and credulity about
the threats facing the United States. The deliberate misrepresentation
of the intelligence, meanwhile, was rationalised on the basis that,
since the administration knew that Saddam had WMD and posed a
major threat to American interests, exaggerating the evidence in order
to sell the war was entirely justified.

The administration's efforts were effective. Polling in the first nine
months of 2003 demonstrated that large numbers of Americans
believed that Iraq was directly involved in the events of 11
September.[88] Faced with the combination of the effectiveness of
the administration's propaganda and imminent mid-term elections,
sceptics about the necessity of regime change could not find a strategy
to oppose the march to war that would not be politically damaging.
Congress therefore took the path of least resistance and on 10 and
11 October 2002 the House and Senate gave Bush the authority to use
the American military 'as he determines necessary and appropriate' to
deal with the threat from Iraq.[89]

## GOING THE UN ROUTE?

Even as his administration sought to lay the basis for military action, Bush was being pushed toward calling for a return of UN inspectors by political considerations, chief amongst which was his desire to retain the support of the UK in any future war. The UK government feared that American unilateralism would make it impossible for them to persuade the British public to support war against Iraq, but that 'it would make a big difference politically and legally if Saddam refused to allow in the UN inspectors . . . If the political context were right, people would support regime change'.[90] The British therefore concluded that it was necessary to secure the return of the UN inspectors as a prelude to war. They assumed that Saddam would probably admit the inspectors but then obstruct them, creating grounds for a UN resolution authorising the use of force.[91] They were supported by Colin Powell who, having lost his struggle against war, now sought to at least secure international support and multilateral legitimacy for military action. He told Bush that it was imperative to secure a new UN resolution demanding the return of weapons inspectors.[92]

Once again, Powell found himself pitted against administration hardliners who were adamantly opposed to any course that might limit their freedom of action and terrified that Saddam might actually cooperate (or give the appearance of cooperation) with the inspectors, and in so doing undermine the rationale for war. With Bush due to address the UN General Assembly on 12 September, the argument within the administration swung back and forth. Ultimately, however, Powell's argument won the day, largely because Bush was aware that the few foreign leaders who were prepared to back his policy of regime change all wanted to legitimate it in this fashion.[93] When he addressed the General Assembly, therefore, Bush delivered an ultimatum: 'If the Iraqi regime wishes peace' it must unconditionally agree to eliminate all WMD, end all support for terrorism, stop persecuting its people, release or account for all POWs and missing persons from the 1990–1 war and end all illicit trade outside the 'oil for food' programme. His administration would

> work with the UN security council for the necessary resolutions. But the purposes of the United States should not be doubted. The Security Council resolutions will be enforced . . . or action

will be unavoidable. And a regime which has lost its legitimacy will also lose its power.[94]

In the face of such an unambiguous threat, Iraq announced four days later that it would accept the return of inspectors without conditions. Inspections could not recommence, however, until the terms of the new resolution under which they would be acting had been agreed. The resulting negotiations once again brought the US and the UK into conflict with the non-Anglo-Saxon members of the P5, with the former seeking a tripwire for regime change and the latter to ensure that the inspections process was actually allowed to run its course. Two issues were central to the argument: firstly, what would constitute a failure of the inspections process and, secondly, what would happen if the inspections were deemed to have failed. The Bush administration wanted a resolution that would authorise individual member states to determine non-compliance and to then take action, but France and Russia insisted that the United States had to go back to the Security Council for a further resolution to authorise military action. The resulting resolution, UNSCR 1441, passed on 8 November, was a compromise, stating that in the event of Iraq being found to be in 'material breach', the Security Council would reconvene to 'consider the situation' and 'impose serious consequences'.[95] Left unresolved were who would decide when a material breach had occurred and what those 'serious consequences' would be.[96]

On 13 November, Iraq accepted the resolution and on 7 December, in accordance with the timeline laid down therein, submitted a new 'complete and final' weapons declaration. Having studied it, the UNMOVIC inspectors concluded that it contained little that was new and proved nothing one way or the other.[97] The Bush administration, in contrast, claimed to have identified a series of omissions in the declaration which in themselves constituted material breaches.[98] Bush's attitude toward the new inspections process was summed up a few days later when he told Spanish Prime Minister José Maria Aznar: 'At some point we will conclude enough is enough and take him [Saddam] out. He's a liar and he's no intention of disarming'.[99]

## PLANNING FOR THE POST-WAR SITUATION

Whilst all aspects of Bush's Iraq policy were afflicted by bureaucratic conflict and the lack of a coherent policy process, nowhere were the consequences of this more significant than in relation to planning for the post-war situation in Iraq. The fundamental causes of the inadequacy of American post-war planning were a systematic lack of attention, deriving from an abiding hostility to 'nation-building' and over-optimistic assumptions about the conditions that would follow an American invasion.

'On assuming office few administrations were less prepared' than that of George W. Bush to engage in nation-building.[100] Most of the administration principals were fundamentally opposed to the involve-ment of the United States in such a process. The job of the United States and its armed forces was to maintain international order and to crush challenges to American hegemony, not to tidy up afterwards.[101] In the 2000 campaign Bush had stated that 'I don't think our troops ought to be used for what's called nation-building' and had called for the withdrawal of US forces from Kosovo and Bosnia.[102] September 11 and regime change in Afghanistan had not altered this perspective, with Bush telling his advisers that 'once the job [removing the Taliban regime] is done . . . we ought to put in place a UN protection force and leave' because 'we don't do police work'.[103]

Complementing this belief, and mutually reinforcing it, was an ideologically driven assumption that there would be no need for nation-building in Iraq. In the view of most senior administration officials, converting Iraq to a market-democracy was going to be easy. It was assumed that there would be no significant post-war armed resistance, and that Iraqis would welcome the American invasion and the political transition to a new democratic Iraq with open arms.[104] Indeed, it was a central tenet of Bush and many of his advisers that the Middle East contained 'hundreds of millions of Muslims . . . who aspire to enjoy the blessings of freedom and democracy and free enterprise'.[105] Moreover, they believed that Iraq was a relatively advanced society with a sizeable professional middle class and a strong, capable state. They would therefore pursue a 'decapitation strategy' in which Saddam and his close supporters would be removed from power 'but the institutions would hold, everything from ministries to police forces . . . You would be able to bring in a new leadership but we were going to keep the body in place'.[106] A new interim government, composed of the leaders of the Iraqi opposition in exile and led by Ahmed Chalabi, would draft a constitution and arrange elections for a new government which would assume sovereign power, all in a matter of months.[107] Reconstruction costs would be paid for out of Iraqi oil revenue.[108] With almost no actual knowledge of the Iraqi state and society, the Bush administration thus projected upon it its own ideological fantasy of 'how the world should be and would be upon the application of American power'.[109]

This combination of an innate antipathy to the idea of nation-building and a blithe assumption that it was unnecessary meant that there was little or no attention paid to the issue on the part of the president or of most of his senior advisers. That, in turn, ensured that what post-war planning did occur was sporadic and uncoordinated. The State Department initiated its own effort, the Freedom of Iraq Project (FOIP), but it was the DOD which would ultimately be given authority over post-war planning by Bush, and 'no one was less interested in the future of Iraq than Donald Rumsfeld'.[110] Asked during the war in Afghanistan about the nature of the new regime in that country, Rumsfeld had responded that 'I don't think [the invasion] leaves us with any responsibility to try to figure out what kind of government that country ought to have'.[111] Just in case anyone had misunderstood, on 14 February 2003, Rumsfeld gave a speech entitled 'Beyond nation-building'. Citing Bosnia and Kosovo as examples wherein a lengthy American occupation had created a 'culture of dependence', he approvingly contrasted Afghanistan as a model of the way it should be done. There should be no major US involvement; instead the locals should be left to manage things themselves: 'Iraq belongs to the Iraqis and we do not aspire to own it or run it'.[112] In addition, Rumsfeld's innate distrust of Powell and the State Department, and his conviction that the latter did not really support regime change in Iraq, ensured that he did all that he could to systematically exclude the agency of the federal government with the most experience and expertise in post-war reconstruction from the post-war planning process.[113]

On 20 January 2003, less than two months before the invasion of Iraq, Bush signed National Security Presidential Directive 24, establishing the Office of Reconstruction and Humanitarian Assistance (ORHA) within the DOD. All planning done so far by State and any other agencies was to be handed over to ORHA, which would be headed by retired General Jay Garner.[114] What Garner found, however, was that there was very little planning to be handed over. He claimed to have received no plans from the DOD, nor even to know that anyone in DOD had been responsible for post-war planning until ten days after he arrived in Baghdad. DOD also failed to inform him of the existence of the FOIP, prevented him from liaising with CENTCOM, and denied several of his personnel requests, mainly for State Department staffers. ORHA's staff was assembled in a rush from whoever could be found, most of them without relevant Middle East experience and some of them assigned tasks outside their areas of expertise.[115]

In February, Garner ran a 'rock drill' to go over existing plans and see how things stood. The notes of one participant summarised the situation with considerable acuity. ORHA had been set up 'far too late', there were not enough troops in the military plan to secure major urban areas 'let alone for providing an interim police function'. As a result 'we risk letting the country descend into civil unrest, chaos whose magnitude may defeat our national strategy of a stable new Iraq'.[116] When Garner then briefed Bush and the administration principals on 28 February, not one of them asked a single question, even after he had said that his team did not have the resources to do four of the key tasks it had been assigned.[117]

## THE MARCH TO WAR

In January 2003, Saddam directed his officials to cooperate with UNMOVIC and the IAEA in the hope of depriving the Bush administration of a *causus belli*. Despite that decision, according to General Hamdani, Saddam remained determined to avoid appearing weak and still, therefore, sought to maintain an element of ambiguity. His behaviour was influenced by the fact that he still failed to perceive a direct threat to his own position. According to Tariq Aziz and other senior Iraqis, Saddam did not believe American forces would come all the way to Baghdad. At worst he thought there would be an extensive air assault and a limited ground invasion to establish an enclave for the opposition in southern Iraq.[118]

On 27 January, after the new inspections process had been in place for a month, UNMOVIC chief Hans Blix reported to the Security Council that 'Iraq appears not to have come to a genuine acceptance . . . of the disarmament which was demanded of it and which it needs to carry out'. He said that Iraq appeared to have decided to cooperate on process but not yet on substance and that there remained a lack of evidence which had to be resolved.[119] A week later he was followed to

the UN by Colin Powell, who presented the Council with an impress-
ively detailed and lengthy summation of all the administration's
claims about Iraq's WMD programmes and collaboration with
al-Qaeda, virtually none of which would turn out to be true, though
they were persuasive to many observers at the time.[120] A week after
that, Blix and El-Baradei reported to the Council again. Blix stated that
UNMOVIC had found no WMD, though some weapons remained
unaccounted for. El-Baradei, for his part, said there were 'no unresolved disarmament issues' with regard to nuclear weapons.[121]

Heedless of the inspectors, the Bush administration now demanded
a new UN resolution, again largely at the behest of the British government, which had already lost a vote on the use of force in parliament.
Most other members of the Security Council, however, felt that whilst
a new resolution was required before military action could be taken, it
was not necessary to pass one at this point because the inspections
process had not been given sufficient time to produce results. They
also believed, correctly, that the United States simply wanted to create
a tripwire for war and, to that end, would seek to impose conditions
Iraq could not possibly meet.[122] On 24 February, the United States, the
UK and Spain nevertheless tabled a draft resolution stating that the
Security Council 'decides that Iraq has failed to take the final opportunity afforded it in resolution 1441 (2002)'.[123] On 5 March the French,
German and Russian foreign ministers responded with a joint statement in which they said that they supported the 'full and effective
disarmament of Iraq' but that 'we consider that this objective can
be achieved by the peaceful means of the inspections . . . In these
circumstances we will not let a proposed resolution pass that would
authorize the use of force'.[124] Two days later a Security Council meeting
produced no progress, with a French proposal to allow a further 120
days for inspections rejected by the US.

On 16 March, Blair, Bush and Aznar met in the Azores. It was now
clear to them that they could not rally enough votes in the Security
Council even for a creditable defeat. Accordingly, they decided to
withdraw the resolution tabled on 24 February. The following day
Bush declared that 'Saddam Hussein and his sons must leave Iraq
within 48 hours. Their refusal to do so will result in military conflict,
commenced at a time of our choosing.'[125] When Saddam failed
to comply, the invasion of Iraq began on 21 March and on 9 April
American forces entered Baghdad.

## NOTES

1. Critchlow, *The Conservative Ascendancy*, p. 286.
2. Miller and Klobucar, 'The role of issues'.
3. Greenstein, *The George W. Bush Presidency*; Morgan and Davies, *Right On*.
4. William Kristol, 'For the defense', *Washington Post*, 31 August 2000, p. A31.
5. 'Heavyweight "Vulcans" help Bush forge a foreign policy', *Washington Post*, November 19, p. A2; 'The second Gore Bush presidential debate', 11 October 2000, www.debates.org/pages/trans2000b.html; Dunn, 'Myths, motivations and misunderestimations', pp. 282–3; Halper and Clarke, *America Alone*, p. 135.
6. 'The second Gore–Bush presidential debate', 11 October 2000, www.debates.org/pages/trans2000b.html.
7. Rice, 'Promoting the national interest', pp. 47–9.
8. Ibid. p. 60.
9. 'Leiberman-Cheney vice-presidential debate', 5 October 2000, www.debates.org/pages/trans2000d.html.
10. Baker, 'Condi and the boys', p. 10.
11. Fitzgerald, 'George Bush and the world'.
12. Nichols, *The Rise and Rise of Dick Cheney*, p. 59.
13. Mann, *Rise of the Vulcans*, pp. 58–68.
14. Ibid. p. 58.
15. Barbara Slavin and Susan Page, 'Cheney is power hitter in White House lineup', *USA Today*, 28 August 2002.
16. Daalder and Lindsay, *America Unbound*, p. 15.
17. Halper and Clarke, *America Alone*, pp. 105–6.
18. Daalder and Lindsay, *America Unbound*, pp. 57–8; Mann, *Rise of the Vulcans*, p. 275.
19. Burke, 'The contemporary presidency'; Baker, 'Condi and the boys'.
20. Suskind, *The One Percent Doctrine*, p. 225.
21. Woodward, *Bush at War*, p. 342.
22. Woodward, *The War Within*, p. 430.
23. Clarke, *Against all Enemies*, p. 243.
24. Gordon and Trainor, *Cobra II*, p. 15.
25. Suskind, *The Price of Loyalty*, pp. 72–5, 85.
26. Gordon and Trainor, *Cobra II*, p. 15.
27. George W. Bush, 'Remarks by the President to students and faculty at National Defense University', Fort Lesley J. McNair, Washington, DC, 1 May 2001, www.whitehouse.gov/news/releases/2001/05/20010501-10.html.

28. 'Prepared testimony to the Senate Armed Services Committee by Secretary of Defense Donald H. Rumsfeld', 21 June 2001, www.defenselink.mil/speeches/2001/s20010607-secdef.html.

29. Gordon and Trainor, *Cobra II*, p. 16; Pollack, *The Threatening Storm*, p. 105; Lynch, 'Smart sanctions'; Woodward, *Plan of Attack*, pp. 20–2.

30. 'Press conference: Prime Minister Tony Blair and President George Bush', 31 January 2003, www.number10.gov.uk.page1767.

31. Dick Cheney on NBC's *Meet the Press*, 14 September 2003; see also Halper and Clarke, *America Alone*, pp. 137–8; Kaplan and Kristol, *The War over Iraq*, p. 72.

32. Lemann, 'The next world order'.

33. Packer, *Assassin's Gate*, p. 40.

34. Woodward, *Bush at War*, pp. 82–5.

35. Gordon and Trainor, *Cobra II*, p. 19.

36. Woodward, *Plan of Attack*, pp. 1–3, 40–4, 53–65.

37. George W. Bush, 'The President's State of the Union address', Washington, DC, 29 January 2002, www.whitehouse.gov/news/releases/2002/01/20020129-11.html.

38. Woodward, *Plan of Attack*, pp. 136–7.

39. Gordon and Trainor, *Cobra II*, pp. 45–9.

40. Murphy and Purdum, 'Farewell to all that'.

41. Lemann, 'How it came to war'.

42. George W. Bush, 'Remarks by the President at 2002 graduation exercise of the United States military academy', West Point NY, 1 June 2002, www.whitehouse.gov/news/releases/2002/06/20020601-3.html.

43. *The National Security Strategy of the United States of America*, The White House, September 2002, www.usinfo.state.gov/topical/pol/teror/secstrat.html.

44. George W. Bush, 'Address on Iraq: remarks in Cincinnati, Ohio', 7 October 2002, www.whitehouse.gov/news/releases/2002/10/20021007-8.html.

45. 'Deputy Secretary Wolfowitz interview with Sam Tannehaus, Vanity Fair (interview conducted May 2003)', www.defenselink.mil/transcripts/2003/tr20030509-depsecdef0223.html.

46. Khalidi, *Resurrecting Empire*, pp. ix–x; Pillar, 'Intelligence, policy and the war in Iraq'.

47. Cirincione *et al.*, *WMD in Iraq*, p. 15.

48. 'Deputy Secretary Wolfowitz interview with Sam Tannehaus, Vanity Fair (interview conducted May 2003)', www.defenselink.mil/transcripts/2003/tr20030509-depsecdef0223.html.

49. Danner, *The Secret Way to War*, p. 76.

50. Richard B. Cheney, 'Vice-President speaks at VFW 103rd National

Convention', 26 August 2002, www.whitehouse.gov/news/releases/2002/08/20020826.html.

51. 'Prepared testimony of US Secretary of Defense Donald H. Rumsfeld before the House and Senate Armed Services Committees regarding Iraq', 18–19 September 2002, www.defenselink.mil/speeches/2002/s20020918-secdef.html.

52. Robert Kagan, 'Saddam's impending victory', *Weekly Standard*, 2 February 1998, pp. 22–5.

53. Russett, *Grasping the Democratic Peace.*

54. 'Richard Perle: the making of a neoconservative', *PBS Think Tank with Ben Wattenberg*, www.pbs.org/thinktank/transcript1017.html; see also Abrams, *Security and Sacrifice*; Kristol and Kagan, 'Toward a neo-Reaganite foreign policy'; Muravchik, *Exporting Democracy.*

55. George W. Bush, 'President Bush discusses the future of Iraq', American Enterprise Institute, 26 February 2003, www.whitehouse.gov/news/releases/2003/02/20030226-11.html.

56. Ibid.; Richard Haass, 'Reflections a year after September 11', remarks to the IISS 2002 annual conference, 13 September 2002, www.state.gov/s/p/rem13442.htm; 'Remarks by Deputy-Secretary of Defense Paul Wolfowitz', Ronald Reagan Building and International Trade Center, Washington, DC, 14 November 2001, www.defenselink.mil/speeches/2001/s2001114-depsecdef.html; 'President Bush discusses Iraq policy at Whitehall Palace in London', 9 November 2003, www.whitehouse.gov/news/releases/2003/11/20031119-1.html.

57. See the Introduction, pp. 3–4.

58. Dodge, 'The Sardinian'; Henry, 'The clash of globalisations in the Middle East'.

59. 'Dr Condoleezza Rice discusses the President's National Security Strategy', Waldorf Astoria Hotel, New York, 1 October 2002, www.whitehouse.gov/news/releases/2002/10/20021001-6.html; Richard Haass, 'Reflections a year after September 11', remarks to the International Institute of Strategic Studies annual conference, 13 September 2002, www.state.gov/s/p/rem13442.htm.

60. Brent Scowcroft, 'Don't attack Saddam', *Wall Street Journal*, 15 August 2002.

61. James A. Baker III, 'The right way to change a regime', *New York Times*, 25 August, 2002; *CNN*, 'Crossfire', 19 August 2002, www.edition.cnn.com/transcripts/020819/cf.00.html.

62. Iraq Survey Group, 'Comprehensive report'; Cirincione *et al.*, *WMD in Iraq*; US Congress, Senate, *Postwar findings about Iraqi WMD programs.*

63. US Congress, Senate, *Postwar findings about Iraqi WMD programs.*

64. Cirincione *et al.*, *WMD in Iraq*, p. 15.

65. Ibid. p. 8; see also, Pfiffner, 'Did President Bush mislead'; Pfiffner, 'Intelligence and decision-making before the war with Iraq'; Judis and Ackerman, 'Selling the Iraq War'; Prados, *Hoodwinked*, pp. 51–93.

66. 'Vice-President speaks at VFW 103rd National Convention', 26 August 2002, www.whitehouse.gov/news/releases/2002/08/20020826.html; 'Transcript of interview with Vice-President Dick Cheney on "Meet the Press"', 8 September 2002, www.mtholyoke.edu/acad/intel/bush/meet.htm.

67. George W. Bush, 'Address on Iraq, remarks in Cincinnati, Ohio', 7 October 2002, www.whitehouse.gov/news/releases/2002/10/20021007-8.html.

68. Barton Gellman and Walter Pincus, 'Depiction of threat outgrew supporting evidence', *Washington Post*, 10 August 2003, pp. A1, A9.

69. George W. Bush, 'President delivers "State of the Union"', 28 January 2003, www.whitehouse.gov/news/releases/2003/01/20030128-19.html; US Department of State, 'Illustrative examples of omissions'; Condoleezza Rice, 'Why we know Iraq is lying', *New York Times*, 23 January 2003, p. A25.

70. US, CIA, 'Iraq's continuing programs'.

71. Ibid. pp. 5, 8, 9, 14.

72. Ibid. pp. 24, 84.

73. Woodward, *Plan of Attack*, pp. 201–2.

74. US, CIA, 'Iraq's continuing programs'; Pfiffner, 'Did President Bush mislead', p. 35.

75. George W. Bush, 'Address on Iraq, remarks in Cincinnati, Ohio', 7 October 2002, www.whitehouse.gov/news/releases/2002/10/20021007-8.html.

76. Dana Millbank and Claudia Deane, 'Hussein link to 9/11 lingers in many minds', *Washington Post*, 6 September 2003, p. 1.

77. US, CIA, 'Iraq and Al-Qaeda: interpreting a murky relationship', 21 June 2002; US, CIA, 'Iraqi support for terrorism', 29 January 2003.

78. US, CIA, 'Iraqi support for terrorism', pp. 24–5; Murray Waas, 'Key Bush intelligence briefing kept from Hill panel', *National Journal*, 22 November 2005.

79. Pillar, 'Intelligence, policy and the war in Iraq'.

80. Walter Pincus and Dana Priest, 'Some Iraq analysts felt pressure from Cheney visits', *Washington Post*, 5 June 2003, p. A1.

81. Suskind, *The One Percent Doctrine*, p. 190.

82. Hersh, 'Selective intelligence'; Hersh, 'The Stovepipe'; Goldberg, 'A little learning'; James Risen, 'How pair's finding on terror led to clash on shaping intelligence', *New York Times*, 28 April 2004, p. A1.

83. Ricks, *Fiasco*, p. 61.

84. Woodward, *Plan of Attack*, p. 298.

85. 'Prepared testimony of US Secretary of Defense Donald H. Rumsfeld before the House and Senate Armed Services Committees regarding Iraq', 18–19 September 2002, www.defenselink.mil/speeches/2002/s20020918-secdef.html.

86. US, CIA, 'Intelligence community experiment in competitive analysis'; 'Commission to assess the ballistic missile threat to the United States', www.fas.org/irp/threat/bm-theat.htm; Paul Wolfowitz was a member of both 'Team B' and the Commission, which was headed by Rumsfeld.

87. Julian Borger, 'White House "lied" about Saddam threat', *The Guardian*, 10 July 2003.

88. Halper and Clarke, *America Alone*, p. 194.

89. 'Joint resolution to authorise the use of United States armed forces against Iraq', www.whitehouse.gov/news/releases/2002/20021002-2.html.

90. 'The Downing Street Memo', 23 July 2002, in Danner, *The Secret Way to War*, p. 76.

91. 'Iraq: conditions for military action', 21 July 2005, in Danner, *The Secret way to War*, p. 158.

92. Woodward, *Plan of Attack*, pp. 150–2.

93. Ibid. pp. 174–6, 180–3.

94. George W. Bush, 'President's remarks at the United Nations General Assembly', 12 September 2002, www.whitehouse.gov/news/releases/2002/09/20020912-1.html.

95. UNSCR 1441, www.daccessdds.un.org/doc/UNDOC/GEN/N02/682/PDF/NO268226.pdf?openelement.

96. Malone, *International Struggle over Iraq*, p. 194; Blix, *Disarming Iraq*, p. 89.

97. Blix, *Disarming Iraq*, p. 107.

98. US Department of State, 'Illustrative examples of ommissions'; Condoleezza Rice, 'Why we know Iraq is lying', *New York Times*, 23 February 2003, p. 25.

99. Woodward, *Plan of Attack*, p. 240.

100. Bronson, 'Reconstructing the Middle East', p. 271.

101. Krauthammer, 'Why America must not go into Bosnia'.

102. 'The second Gore-Bush presidential debate', 11 October 2000, www.debates.org/pages/trans2000b.html.

103. Woodward, *Bush at War*, pp. 237, 310.

104. Dodge, 'Iraqi transitions'; Rathmell, 'Planning post-conflict reconstruction in Iraq', p. 1022.

105. 'Bridging the dangerous gap between the West and the Muslim world', remarks prepared for delivery by Deputy Secretary of Defense Paul Wolfowitz at the World Affairs Council, Monterey, CA, 3 May 2002, www.defenselink.mil/speeches/2002/s20020503-depsecdef.html.

106. Gordon and Trainor, *Cobra II*, p. 163.
107. 'Testimony of Deputy-Secretary of Defense Paul Wolfowitz, prepared for the Senate Armed Services Committee: the future of NATO and Iraq', 10 April 2003, www.armed-services.senate.gov/statement/2003/April/ Wolfowitz.pdf. These assumptions, it should be noted, were far from universally held, and there was plenty of expert advice contradicting them which the administration chose to ignore; Ricks, *Fiasco*, pp. 71–2; Gordon and Trainor, *Cobra II*, p. 667.
108. Eric Schmitt, 'Pentagon contradicts general on Iraq occupation force's size', *New York Times*, 28 February 2003, p. A1.
109. Dodge, 'Coming face to face with bloody reality', p. 259.
110. Packer, *Assassin's Gate*, p. 42.
111. 'Secretary of Defense Donald H. Rumsfeld's news conference', 9 October 2001, www.defenselink.mil/news/oct2001/tl10092001-tl1009sd. html.
112. 'Beyond nation building', remarks as delivered by Secretary of Defense Donald H. Rumsfeld at the 11th Annual Salute to Freedom, Intrepid Sea-Air-Space Museum, New York City, 14 February 2003, www. defenselink.mil/speeches/2003/sp20030214-secdefoo24.html.
113. Packer, *Assassin's Gate*, pp. 78–9; Pollack, 'Seven deadly sins'.
114. Woodward, *Plan of Attack*, pp. 280–4.
115. Chandrasekaran, *Imperial Life*, pp. 32–4; Fallows, 'Blind into Baghdad'; Galbraith, *The End of Iraq*, p. 92; Woodward, *State of Denial*, pp. 126–9.
116. Ricks, *Fiasco*, pp. 101–2.
117. Ferguson, *No End in Sight*, pp. 83–5; Woodward, *State of Denial*, pp. 131–4.
118. US Joint Forces Command Combat Study, 'Iraqi perspectives on Operation Iraqi Freedom, major combat operations', in Gordon and Trainor, *Cobra II*, pp. 75, 138–9.
119. UNMOVIC, 'Briefing, 27 January 2003'.
120. 'Transcript of Secretary of State Colin Powell's UN Presentation, 6 February 2003', www.cnn.com/2003/us/02/05/sprj.irq.powell. transcript.10/index.html.
121. UNMOVIC, 'Briefing, 14 February 2003'; United Nations, IAEA, 'Status of nuclear inspections, 14 February 2003'.
122. Malone, *International Struggle over Iraq*, p. 180.
123. US Department of State, 'Iraq: U.S./U.K./Spain Draft Resolution'.
124. 'Iraq's disarmament can be achieved by peaceful means', in Sifry and Cerf, *The Iraq War Reader*, pp. 501–2.
125. George W. Bush, 'Address to the nation on war with Iraq', remarks in Washington, DC, 17 March 2003, www.whitehouse.gov/vews/ releases/2002/200303-17-7.html.

*Chapter 6*

# THINGS FALL APART, 2003–2008

=====

## THE COLLAPSE OF THE IRAQI STATE

In 2003 the Bush administration's plans for the future of Iraq fell apart, along with the country itself. Having assumed that they would simply decapitate the Iraqi regime and graft a new regime onto the still-functioning torso of the Iraqi state, the administration instead found itself confronted by the total collapse of that state and the fragmentation of political power along ethnic, sectarian and geographical lines. It then faced a massive task of state-building for which it was totally unprepared.

As American troops advanced across Iraq in March 2003, looting broke out in their wake. Not sporadic, opportunistic theft, but rather systematic pillage, in which government buildings and basic infrastructure were stripped of everything that could be physically moved, right down to the light bulbs. Many were then burned to the ground.[1] ORHA had drawn up a list of buildings which needed protecting, but CENTCOM failed to transmit it to the commanders in Baghdad and most of them were looted and/or burned down.[2] That coalition forces were taken aback by the extent of this pillage, as they were, was indicative of a lack of planning and ignorance of Iraqi history, since looting is 'an Iraqi tradition born of tribal raiding and poverty'. Iraqi forces had systematically looted Kuwait in 1990 and Shia rebels had looted government buildings in southern Iraq in 1991.[3] That they would do so again in 2003 was predictable.

The immediate reason that coalition troops failed to stop the looting was that they were unprepared for it and had no orders to do so. Had they been given different orders, they could certainly have protected some of the key sites identified by ORHA at the very least. Nevertheless, even with the best will, they would have had great difficulty in establishing security and order across the whole country, because they did not have enough troops to do so.[4] And the reason for that lack of troops was the administration's assumption that the transition to a market-democracy in Iraq was going to be wholly unproblematic. That unquestioned assumption meant that Rumsfeld went unchallenged (except by parts of the uniformed military itself) as he consistently pressured CENTCOM to reduce its force projections during the pre-war planning process. In consequence, the final plan for the invasion of Iraq had half the troops originally envisaged by the CENTCOM planners.[5] Extrapolations from a RAND Corporation study of previous occupations estimated that 400–500,000 troops would be necessary to establish security in Iraq, but there would be just 116,000 personnel in the actual invasion force.[6]

The looting of Iraq was both symptom and cause of a more fundamental problem facing the occupiers, namely the collapse of the Iraqi state. As Toby Dodge has argued, in assuming that Iraq was possessed of a relatively modern, functional state which would survive the invasion, 'US planning for post-war Iraq was based on a funda-mental misperception'.[7] In fact, two wars and a decade of sanctions meant that the Iraqi state had been progressively hollowed out until it was little more than a shell.[8] The 2003 invasion then caused that shell to collapse. The army and the police took off their uniforms and went home to avoid being killed, facilitating the looting. Civilian state employees chose to stay at home to protect their families from the looting and crime and then had no place of work to go back to because it had been destroyed by the looters. Within a very short space of time, therefore, 'the Iraqi state failed to exist in any meaningful form'.[9] Instead of simply installing a new government and going home, the United States found itself faced with the task of completely reconstructing the Iraqi state from the ground up.

The collapse of the state, and the inability of the coalition to re-establish security and order, was the primary source of America's problems in Iraq. The most fundamental requirement of any state – that it exercise an effective monopoly of violence within its own borders – ceased to exist in Iraq.[10] The invasion produced a political and security vacuum in which power fragmented and devolved into the hands of whichever group could muster the personnel and weaponry to assert control of a given geographical area. Organised criminal gangs, Sunni insurgents and sectarian and tribal militias became the new centres of power. In the effective anarchy into which Iraq descended after April 2003, ordinary Iraqis had to look to something other than the state to provide security, employment and other fundamental needs. The destruction of Iraqi civil society by Saddam's totalitarian state, and the hollowing out of that state by war and sanctions, meant that Iraqis had already been driven increasingly to seek resources from tribal and communal sources.[11] Now, those preexisting sectarian and ethnic identities became the basis of political mobilisation, as sectarian and tribal leaders were able to exploit the needs and fears of the populace in their own pursuit of power.[12] Or, as George W. Bush put it, Iraqis 'found themselves in a situation where they had to rely on the local cat with the big gun'.[13] The collapse of the state thus fuelled the emergence of sectarian conflict in Iraq.

## FROM THE OFFICE OF RECONSTRUCTION AND HUMANITARIAN ASSISTANCE TO THE COALITION PROVISIONAL AUTHORITY

In early May 2003 the British political representative in Iraq sent a cable to London describing the situation in Baghdad:

> Crime is widespread . . . Carjackings are endemic . . . Last week the Ministry of Planning was re-kitted out ready to resume work; that night it was looted again. The evening air is full of gunfire. There is still a climate of fear on the streets, because of the level of crime, and that is casting a shadow over all else.

Coalition forces, he concluded, had been 'widely welcomed, but are gradually losing public support'.[14] Their inability to provide security seemed to show either weakness or utter contempt for the wellbeing of ordinary Iraqis. Whichever was the case, respect for the occupiers was undermined.[15]

Sawers also had harsh words for ORHA: 'Garner's outfit, ORHA, is an unbelievable mess. No leadership, no strategy, no co-ordination, no structure, and inaccessible to ordinary Iraqis'.[16] His criticism misses the point, however, which is that ORHA was set up to fail by the false assumptions of policy-makers in Washington, having been given insufficient time and resources to prepare even for the limited mission assigned to it, let alone for the mammoth and wholly unexpected task it found itself facing. As one Defense Department official put it,

Garner was simply the 'fall guy for a bad strategy'.[17] Having assumed that everything would just fall into place, the chaos in Iraq meant that the Bush administration was now reduced to making policy on the hoof. Garner was always going to be replaced by a permanent representative, but the administration now decided to make both he and ORHA the scapegoats for the chaos that had resulted from their lack of planning. Garner was brusquely informed that he was being replaced, and that ORHA would give way to the Coalition Provisional Authority (CPA). The man chosen to head the CPA was L. Paul Bremer III, whose appointment seems to have been determined largely by his reputation as a loyal Republican, since he had no experience in the Middle East, spoke no Arabic, and had no post-war reconstruction experience.

Despite facing a wholly unexpected situation, Garner had sought to fulfil his brief for a rapid transfer of power, announcing on 5 May that he would form the basis of an interim government within ten days and planned to hold elections within ninety. Bremer arrived in Iraq on 12 May, and four days later he announced that there would be no Iraqi interim government and no early handover of power. This reversal of Garner's policies was determined by two principal considerations. In the first place, the collapse of the Iraqi state had clearly rendered the original plan null and void. In addition, however, it was clear to Bremer that the Iraqi exiles whom the Bush administration had hoped would form the basis of an interim government were unpopular with Iraqis.[18] He therefore concluded that a prolonged occupation would be necessary to create the conditions for a successful handover of power. Whilst understandable under the circumstances, this decision never-theless served further to alienate many Iraqis, a majority of who by June believed that the United States had invaded in order to establish imperial control over Iraq.[19]

## COALITION PROVISIONAL AUTHORITY ORDERS 1 AND 2

On the same day that he announced there would be no rapid transfer of power, Bremer issued CPA Order Number 1, which stated that all 'full members' of the Baath Party would be removed from their posts and barred from future government employment. A week later he issued CPA Order Number 2, disbanding all the Iraqi security forces (ISF) except the police.[20]

Once again, Bremer was abandoning the administration's pre-war plans, wherein the Iraqi military was to have been left intact and de-Baathification confined to the most senior party members.[21] Bremer later claimed that both decisions had been carefully discussed and approved by the administration principals.[22] Every other source, however, indicates that this was a unilateral decision on his part or one taken only in consultation with the Pentagon. Neither Rice nor Powell was apparently aware of Bremer's intentions,[23] and when an interviewer asked Bush how he had responded to CPA Order Number 2, he said 'I can't remember, I'm sure I said "this is the policy [keeping the army intact], what happened?"'.[24]

When informed of the orders, the CIA station chief in Iraq told Bremer that the de-Baathification order would create some 50,000 dangerous enemies who would go into outright opposition to the occupation.[25] The same objections applied, and were made, with regard to the disbanding of the Iraqi security forces. Bremer and his chief military adviser, Walter Slocombe, argued that the original policy had been overtaken by events, because the army had effectively dissolved itself. They further argued that, since it had been a conscript army of Shias officered by Sunnis, the former would not have accepted its reconstitution, making it was necessary to start from scratch.[26] Whatever the validity of those claims (and they are widely disputed),[27] what is certain is that Bremer's orders had two major consequences. In the first place, they destroyed what was left of the Iraqi state, with the de-Baathification order purging the civil service not just of senior party members but also of all senior administrators and technocrats. The second, equally significant, consequence was to alienate much of the Sunni population of Iraq. To most Sunnis the de-Baathification order was effectively a 'de-Sunniisation' order. It led to something like 100,000 people losing their jobs, the majority of them ordinary Sunnis for whom party membership had been necessary to progress in their careers. The decision to allow Ahmed Chalabi to take charge of the de-Baathification Commission only further persuaded Sunnis that this was a sectarian process. Another 700,000 people lost their jobs as a result of CPA Order Number 2, at a time when unemployment was already running at something like 70 per cent and Iraqis faced widespread poverty and hunger.[28] Some of those dismissed would find new employment with the Sunni insurgency, others with the Shiite militias.

## DEMOCRATIC FANTASIES

In thus sweeping away the remnants of the Iraqi state at a moment when his most fundamental objective should have been to restore its capacity to deliver security and public goods, Bremer made a major contribution to the ongoing disintegration of the Iraqi polity. In so doing, however, he was acting in accordance with the ambitions of those within the Bush administration who intended to turn Iraq into a model market-democracy.[29] In eliminating the last vestiges of the old order, Bremer was also removing potential obstacles to the building of the new model Iraq.[30] That task, in turn, was comprised of two main objectives. Politically, Bremer intended to oversee the drafting of a constitution enshrining secular, liberal principles. Only after such a constitution had been written and legitimated by referendum would elections be held for a new government and sovereignty transferred.[31] Equally important, however, was the creation of a free market economy open to foreign investment.[32] This was necessary to reinforce the transition to democracy, fundamentally alter the relationship between the state and the private sector, and to ensure the integration of Iraq into the World Capitalist System. Bremer's intention was thus to create 'facts on the ground' before handing power back to Iraqis.[33]

The CPA's economic plan called for the immediate reconstruction of the Iraqi economy along market lines in a fashion similar to the 'shock therapy' applied in the former USSR in the early 1990s. There would be currency reform, investment laws that opened up the economy to foreign investors, tariff cuts, tax reductions and privatisation of state enterprises.[34] Iraq was to be an 'ideal model of neoliberal reform'.[35] This ideologically driven agenda took no account of the economic realities of Iraq, whose physical infrastructure had been substantially destroyed by war and sanctions, and whose social and human capital had been severely depleted by the flight into exile of a large proportion of Iraq's best-educated and most highly skilled citizens.[36] Iraqis, moreover, were used to living under a regime where the state provided everything, from jobs to food, and were psychologically unprepared for a market economy. Most Iraqis wanted the creation of more government jobs, rather than private sector employment.[37] The anarchy and violence which characterised the new Iraq further undermined the CPA plan by inducing the further flight of those with marketable skills and deterring foreign investors. Finally, the CPA simply didn't have the resources to make the plan work, with just three people assigned to the privatisation programme.[38]

The consequences of the CPA's reforms were almost wholly negative. Whilst privatisation was soon abandoned because the CPA simply did not have the capability to pursue it, the CPA instead resorted to simply cutting all subsidies to state-run enterprises and agriculture. The main effect of this was to gut the state-owned industries and to put more Iraqis out of work, whilst Iraq's first post-war harvest was the worst for half a century. The lifting of tariffs, for its part, simply produced a flood of imported goods which helped further to hollow out the Iraqi economy.[39] Five years after the invasion, unemployment remained at a level barely below where it was in the immediate aftermath of the war, whilst the share of Iraqi GDP contributed by non-oil activities had not altered at all.[40] It is at least arguable, moreover, that CPA economic policies contributed to the growth of sectarian conflict in Iraq, most obviously in the fundamental failure to generate employment, which produced resentment, particularly amongst Sunnis, some of whom joined the insurgency simply in order to make a living. In addition, the failure of economic reform drove into exile precisely those secular, educated Iraqis who should have constituted the basis of the civil society which was crucial to the development of a non-sectarian, democratic Iraq.[41]

The existence of civil society is a basic precondition for the development of liberal democracy. An even more fundamental requirement, however, is a state that has a monopoly over the legitimate use of coercion.[42] That precondition was clearly absent in Iraq in 2003 and remained so five years later. As for civil society itself, the interest groups, independent media, universities and trade unions which serve to check and constrain the institutions of the state[43] had been systematically eliminated by Saddam: 'There was no civil society in Iraq before the US military reached Baghdad'.[44] A third precondition for democracy is the development of a democratic political culture wherein family structure, religion, moral values and traditions all have to adapt to democratic values.[45] In this regard as well, the new Iraq would be starting from scratch.

Many advocates of a democratic Iraq cited the successful post-war American occupations of Germany and Japan as examples of what could be done. But as Eva Bellin has pointed out, the differences between those two cases and that of Iraq are more marked than the similarities. Germany and Japan were advanced industrialised societies which were able to achieve economic recovery relatively rapidly after the Second World War. Iraq, in contrast, was a relatively backward country which lacked the human and social capital for such development. Given that there is a clear correlation between a country's level of economic development and the evolution of durable democracy, this did not bode well for Iraq.[46] Democratic theory further suggests that ethnic homogeneity is an important factor in democracy-building, helping to prevent the conflict of democratic politics from creating more fundamental societal divisions. Germany and Japan were both ethnically homogenous nations whilst Iraq, clearly, is not. It is also an empirical fact that the countries with most success in democratising are those that have had some prior experience of democracy. Germany and Japan fell into this category, but Iraq has no history of democracy beyond the charade that existed under the monarchy.[47] Overall, the conclusion drawn by Simon Bromley under slightly different circumstances would still seem to have held good in 2003: 'In Iraq, none of the conditions for democratic rule exist'.[48]

## THE IRAQI GOVERNING COUNCIL

Bremer's intention was to retain American control until the infrastructure of a neoliberal market-democracy was in place. Nevertheless, the UN representative in Iraq, Sergio Viera de Mello, emphasised to him the necessity of creating a body embodying Iraqi sovereignty in order to win popular backing for the process of state-building.[49] Bremer therefore reluctantly agreed to create an Iraqi Governing Council (IGC) in July 2003.

Having argued that the exile leaders were unpopular and not representative of Iraqis, Bremer now proceeded to make them the core of the IGC, whose leading members included Ahmed Chalabi, Iyad Allawi, Ibrahim al-Jaafari of Dawa, Abd al-Aziz al-Hakim of SCIRI and the Kurdish leaders Massoud Barzani and Jalal Talabani. This decision reflected a basic dilemma confronting Bremer. Whilst the exiles might not have been representative, there were as yet no significant indigenous political parties or leaders in Iraq and the exiles were the only Iraqis he or the Bush administration knew anything about. He thus had little choice but to rely on them.

Bremer added eighteen other members to the nucleus described above in a bid to make the IGC more 'representative', but the lie to that was given by a State Department poll which revealed that only seven of the twenty-five members were sufficiently well-known for more than 40 per cent of Iraqis to have an opinion about them. In addition, despite seeking to make the IGC a more faithful reflection of the Iraqi population, Bremer only included a single Sunni tribal leader, further convincing Sunnis of America's ill intent.[50] Bremer also chose to define 'representativeness' in explicitly sectarian terms, allocating seats on the IGC in accordance with the demographic representation of groups in the population.[51] He thus 'elevated sectarian and ethnic identity to the rank of primary organising political principle',[52] whilst Iraqis generally deplored this introduction of overt sectarianism into Iraqi politics.[53] Finally, the fact that Bremer unilaterally added eighteen new members to the IGC reflected another fundamental problem with that body, namely that it was transparently no more than a fig leaf for his exercise of power. The creation and composition of the IGC thus reinforced the developing trend of sectarianism in Iraqi politics whilst doing nothing to convince Iraqis of American intentions to relinquish control.[54]

## THE FAILURE OF RECONSTRUCTION

After the provision of security, the most fundamental objective for an occupying power is to try and improve the lives of ordinary people quickly. Whilst the CPA formally made the improvement of basic infrastructure one of its main priorities,[55] in practice reconstruction was either slow or non-existent. The CPA aimed to get electricity production back to pre-war levels by October 2003 and up to 6,000MW by June 2004. As of December 2008, however, production was still below 5,000MW and residents of Baghdad were receiving fewer hours of electricity per day than before the war.[56] It was a similar story with regards to water and sanitation. In June 2004 the CPA claimed 90 per cent of Iraqis would have access to clean drinking water within two years, but by September 2005 the US General Accounting Office estimated that the actual figure would be 50–60 per cent.[57] Overall, rather than improving, living standards in Iraq collapsed even further, with Iraqis facing chronic malnutrition, low life expectancy and declining standards of health and literacy in addition to the ever-present threat of violence.[58]

The causes of these failures were multiple. As with every other aspect of American policy, mistaken assumptions and a lack of planning was a factor. The Bush administration had vastly underestimated the damage done by sanctions whilst assuming that what reconstruction needed to be done could be paid for out of Iraqi oil revenues. Congress accordingly appropriated just $2.5 billion for reconstruction in April 2003 whilst later that summer World Bank teams estimated $55–75 billion was required.[59] The looting that followed the invasion massively increased the scale of the reconstruction required and the anarchy and violence that continued to characterise Iraq greatly complicated reconstruction efforts. Reconstruction of the oil industry was undermined by repeated sabotage of pipelines by insurgents and smuggling, with the Iraqi authorities estimating that illegal exports accounted for 25 per cent of output in January 2004.[60] Facilities were rebuilt only to be stripped by looters and security concerns meant that foreign contractors hired for reconstruction projects regularly withdrew from Iraq for long periods of time.[61]

The CPA also proved to be a very poor manager of the reconstruction process, though to some extent this was not the fault of Bremer and his staff. The ad hoc nature of the CPA's creation meant that it never had enough staff and for most of its existence operated with half the number it was supposed to have.[62] Many, if not most, of those personnel, moreover, were not experts in their fields and/or had no post-conflict reconstruction experience in part, at least, because of the Bush administration's insistence on putting partisan loyalty before competence as a criterion for employment.[63] The CPA therefore simply did not have the institutions or the personnel necessary to run an effective post-conflict reconstruction in place.[64]

The one international institution which did have the necessary experience and expertise to run such an operation was the UN, but the Bush administration's hostility to that organisation, and its assumption that it did not need its assistance, led it to insist that the reconstruction effort be under the firm control of the CPA. The UN was unwilling to commit to a major effort under those conditions, and most of the staff they did send were withdrawn after the bombing of the UN building in August 2003 (see below).[65] As a result, planning and management of reconstruction was weak, nowhere more obviously so than in the area of finance. Money appropriated was not spent, spent without proper oversight, and/or misappropriated. In

October 2003, Congress appropriated $18 billion in supplemental spending for Iraq but only $366 million had actually been spent by June 2004.[66] Where money was spent, there was a glaring absence of procedures to ensure that it was spent effectively. In its first report, the International Advisory and Monitoring Board stated that it had found that contracts had been awarded with no public tenders and no record of bidding, absence of evidence of goods being supplied, use of funds for prohibited activities, and that half of the $5 billion spent from the Development Fund for Iraq by the CPA could not be accounted for.[67] As a result of this lack of oversight and accountability, the reconstruction process was rife with corruption.[68]

## THE INSURGENCY

The factor which undermined CPA reconstruction efforts more than anything, however, was the inability to establish security in Iraq in the face of escalating violence. For most Iraqis, the primary source of insecurity was the simple lack of law and order and the prevalence of criminal gangs who were able to operate with impunity.[69] From the summer of 2003 onwards, however, coalition forces and the CPA increasingly found themselves under attack from an organised insurgency.

The insurgents were a mixture of groups and individuals with different motives and objectives, but the one thing they had in common was that they were Sunnis. Having been the dominant group in Iraq, and having come to identify the Iraqi state with themselves, Sunnis had suddenly seen that dominance and identity destroyed, and that was a situation most were simply not ready to reconcile themselves to. In those circumstances, some opposition to the occupation was always likely, but the insurgency was powerfully fuelled by de-Baathification and the dissolution of the armed forces, which Sunnis regarded as deliberately punitive and sectarian actions.[70] The composition of the IGC only reinforced suspicions that the CPA planned to hand Iraq over to the Shia and the Kurds. The heartland of the resistance that consequently emerged was the so-called 'Sunni triangle' bounded by Baghdad, Ramadi and Tikrit.

The Bush administration would make much of the centrality of foreign fighters and al-Qaeda to the insurgency, but it was overwhelmingly an indigenous phenomenon. In 2004, of 8,000 suspected insurgents detained, 127 had foreign passports.[71] Whilst small in number, however, the foreign fighters had an importance beyond mere numbers. They introduced a powerful religious ideology to parts of the insurgency and bolstered the influence of Salaafist extremism within the Sunni community. They also deliberately sought to fuel sectarian warfare by targeting Shias, whereas the indigenous insurgents initially focused their attacks on coalition forces. Moreover, whilst the goal of the indigenous insurgents was to drive the United States out of Iraq and to prevent Shia domination of the country, the objective of foreign religious extremists like Abu Musab al-Zarqawi, who became the leader of 'al-Qaeda in Mesopotamia' (AQM), was also to transform Iraq into a base for terrorist operations in the wider region. In the long run, the tensions between these objectives would lead many indigenous Sunnis to turn against the foreign fighters but, initially, cooperation, if at times uneasy, was the norm.[72]

A number of factors facilitated the success of the insurgency. The lack of coalition troops in large areas of the country gave them freedom to organise and allowed foreign fighters to enter the country at will. The insurgents also had access to millions of dollars in cash seized by senior Baathists before they went into hiding. To this was added ready access to the huge caches of weaponry stored in depots across Iraq which the coalition lacked the troops to secure. Most importantly of all, they had the support of a large and growing section of the population. Three opinion polls taken in 2004–5 showed between 45 and 85 per cent of respondents in Sunni areas supporting insurgent attacks on coalition forces.[73]

In August 2003, using car bombs, the insurgents attacked the Jordanian embassy, the UN headquarters (killing, amongst others, Sergio Viera de Mello), the headquarters of the Red Cross and the Italian base at Nasiriya. Within two months, the number of foreign UN personnel in Iraq fell from 650 to forty and CPA staff were forced into the Green Zone. Iraqis who worked for the CPA or coalition forces felt compelled to conceal their jobs even from their own families.[74] By mid-2004, insurgent attacks on coalition forces and the institutions of the new Iraqi state were running at 500 a week.[75] The Bush administration's response to the insurgency was nevertheless one of denial, repeatedly insisting that the insurgents were just a handful of Baathist 'dead-enders' and foreign 'jihadis' whose 'last throes' were in sight.[76] Even when the CIA told Bush in November 2003 that the United

States faced an organised insurgency in Iraq, he continued to resist the idea.[77]

That denial of the reality of what the United States was facing in Iraq undermined the response of coalition forces. Initially, the American military's response to the insurgency was hampered by a lack of pre-war planning, as General Jack Keane admitted: 'We did not see it coming. And we were not properly prepared and organized to deal with it.'[78] The coalition commanders in Iraq did not have sufficient troops to establish security. Nor were the troops they did have trained or prepared for a counter-insurgency war that no one had planned for, lacking Arabic speakers and interpreters and having virtually no sources of intelligence amongst the population and none at all inside the insurgency itself.[79] Such weaknesses might have been overcome had the Bush administration acknowledged the nature of the problem it faced and adjusted its strategy accordingly. But an effective counter-insurgency strategy would have involved a massive increase in coalition forces in order to secure the population from violence, and it would have meant accepting that the United States was facing a 'long war' that could take years or even decades to win.[80] The Bush administration, however, and the DOD in particular, remained wedded to a 'short-war' strategy in which American forces were to remain relatively small in number (until 2007 the US never had more than 150–155,000 troops in Iraq) and to be replaced by reconstituted ISF at the earliest possible opportunity.[81]

In the absence of sufficient troops to conduct an effective counter-insurgency strategy, coalition commanders chose instead to concentrate on actively pursuing the insurgents, an option which also coincided with the American military's preference for conventional warfare.[82] The ensuing operations, however, were counter-productive in a number of ways. Lacking adequate intelligence, coalition forces relied on a policy of cordoning off large areas and arresting the whole male population within those areas in the hope that the actual insurgents would be picked out during the subsequent processing of those detained. Large numbers of innocent Sunnis were consequently held for weeks or months without charge[83] and as one US officer observed, 'ninety percent . . . [of those arrested] were not the enemy. But they are now'.[84] Meanwhile, lacking the forces to retain a presence in the area swept, the coalition would withdraw and the insurgents, most of whom had simply evaded the cordon and sweep operation, would return to take control. Whilst coalition forces were pursuing these fruitless efforts in the 'Sunni triangle', they were consequently absent from large parts of the rest of the country, leaving the militias and criminal gangs to cement their control.[85]

Alongside operations against the insurgents, the other main strand of the Bush administration's strategy was 'Iraqisation'. Unwilling to commit more American troops, and lacking allies willing to make up the shortfall, the administration looked to Iraqis themselves to fill the gap. Having dismantled the ISF (bar the police) in May, by autumn 2003 the CPA was being ordered to rebuild them post haste. The original plan for creating a new Iraqi army called for nine new battalions to be trained in twelve months, but this was now changed to twenty-seven battalions in just nine months. Meanwhile, the creation of the wholly unplanned for Iraqi Civil Defence Corps (ICDC) was announced.[86] The result was a disaster. The desire to transfer responsibility as quickly as possible meant training was perfunctory. Whereas in Kosovo the new police force were trained for five months and then received four months of close supervision in the field, in Iraq most of the police force and the ICDC got a twenty-one-day training course. They were hopelessly unprepared for the tasks expected of them and, for the most part, loyal primarily to the sectarian and ethnic militias from which they had been drawn, rather than to the nascent Iraqi state.[87] Of the 120,000 ISF personnel who existed on paper by January 2005, coalition commanders estimated 5,000 could be relied on.[88]

The Bush administration's response to the failure of its strategy would, for three years, be one of denial, with evidence of continued failure met by a redoubling of effort – speeding up training and assigning more advisers – rather than a questioning of the strategy itself.[89] Only in 2006, as the insurgency evolved into civil war, would the administration finally acknowledge its failure.

## REVERSING COURSE AGAIN

Between May and November 2003, Bremer's strategy for a long occupation and the administration's short-war strategy were in contradiction with each other.[90] After November 2003, however, the political strategy was brought into line with the security strategy as the Bush administration returned to its original insistence on a swift transfer of sovereignty. A variety of factors underpinned this shift, including increasing media criticism of the IGC, the insurgency, UN pressure for a return of Iraqi sovereignty, and the increasing alienation of Iraqis from the occupation.[91] The primary causes, however, were political considerations in Washington and the balking of Bremer's plans by the political manoeuvrings of Grand Ayatollah Ali al-Sistani.

Sistani was the most influential Shia leader in Iraq. Sometimes depicted as a 'quietist' who did not demand a political role for the clergy in the manner of Khomeini, he nevertheless clearly believed in the need for clerical influence in political life and expected the new Iraqi constitution to have a central place for Islam.[92] He also wanted to ensure Shia dominance of the new Iraqi state, and had responded to Bremer's plans for drawing up a new constitution by issuing a fatwa demanding that the document be written by elected Iraqis. Initially, Bremer simply ignored the fatwa, assured by the Shiite leaders on the IGC that they could talk Sistani round. It soon became clear, however, that Sistani was the real power amongst the Shia and the IGC members, fearful of becoming even more unpopular, backed Sistani's demand for elections.[93]

Bremer was also coming under pressure to change course from Washington. With a presidential election just a year away, Rice told Bremer that the political situation in Washington could not accept another year of the status quo.[94] In response, the CPA produced a new plan, which was announced on 15 November. Under it, the IGC would draw up an interim constitution or Transitional Administrative Law (TAL), after which an Iraqi Transitional National Authority (TNA) would be selected by a process of caucuses. The TNA would then select an Iraqi Transitional Government, which would assume full sovereignty on 30 June 2004. The plan then provided for the election of delegates to a Constitutional Convention by 15 March 2005. The convention would write a new constitution to be approved by referendum and, with that approval, national elections would be held by 31 December 2005.[95] Having hoped to maintain control of the writing of the constitution, Bremer was thus forced to hand that task over to Iraqis, hoping only that the TAL could be infused with secular and liberal principles that would somehow find their way into the final document. Through the caucus system, the CPA sought once more to dilute the power of the exiles and encourage the emergence of indigenous Iraqi leaders.

Sistani, however, encouraged by the Shia parties on the IGC and perhaps fearing that the caucuses were a device to dilute Shia power, remained unmollified. In January 2004, he issued a new fatwa condemning the 15 November agreement and calling for the TNA to be chosen by elections.[96] Bremer insisted that it could not be done within the time frame, but was only able to persuade Sistani of this with the assistance of UN representative Lakhdar Brahimi, who was brought into the negotiating process at the behest of Washington. Brahimi persuaded Sistani to accept a process whereby an Iraqi Interim Government would be appointed by the UN representative, in consultation with Iraqi leaders and the CPA, by 30 June 2004. Elections for the TNA would then be held by 30 January 2005, the TNA would produce a constitution by 15 August 2005, a constitutional referendum would be held by 15 October 2005 and, if the constitution was approved, elections for a permanent government would take place by 15 December 2005.

Brahimi's plan was to lay the basis for a new Iraqi state by creating a government of apolitical technocrats and to exclude the unpopular IGC members from power. Despite his considerable doubts as to their merits, however, Bremer now insisted on the inclusion of the IGC members on the grounds that if they were excluded they would simply try and wreck the whole process. He nevertheless insisted that the CPA's 'main objective' was to ensure that the appointment of the new government led to a broadening of its base.[97] The two objectives, however, were essentially antithetical. In the end Bremer did manage to adjust the balance of power in the new government, most notably by ensuring the appointment of secular Shiite, and former Baathist, Iyad Allawi to the post of prime minister. Allawi was a leading critic of the first two CPA orders and had already begun rehabilitating former Baathists by giving them jobs in his party and the new Iraqi intelligence services which he oversaw as chair of the IGC security committee.[98] Bremer's move could thus be seen, on one level, as an attempt to address the concerns of Iraq's Sunni population. On the other hand, and more importantly from Bremer's point of view, Allawi was secular and pro-American. In insisting on his appointment he thus sought to maintain American influence in Iraq even as the country moved towards a return of sovereignty.

Bremer's efforts to retain American power could not disguise the fact that he had failed in his original objective of broadening the base of the Iraqi government, which was simply a rehash of the IGC. Bremer had been defeated by the Bush administration's rush to transfer sovereignty and Sistani's political manoeuvring. Unable to develop alternative, indigenous, political representatives, he had ultimately fallen back on the only Iraqis he knew. The consequences of this for the future of Iraq would be immense. The exile parties would use the position handed them by the United States to cement their dominance of Iraqi politics and to exclude potential rivals from power, by fair means or foul, and form the basis of all subsequent governments, both elected and unelected.

The actual power of those governments would nevertheless be extremely limited because, even as it sought to create a viable Iraqi state, the CPA was presiding over the decentralisation and fragmentation of the Iraqi polity.[99] In the absence of sufficient forces to maintain security, the coalition continued to tolerate, and even encourage, the emergence of local militias as long as they were deemed to be maintaining order. In so doing the coalition in many cases co-opted and empowered local leaders who, in turn, sought to exploit coalition support to strengthen their position and their autonomy from the national government. Even where those militias were connected to parties at the centre, as was the case with the Kurdish and some of the Shiite militias, the effect was still to encourage the pursuit of local autonomy and power bases at the expense of the central state.[100] Bremer was thus engaged in the process of creating a government in Baghdad whose authority did not stretch beyond the 'green zone' in which it was physically located.

## SADDAM AND WMD

On 13 December 2003 Saddam Hussein, who had been in hiding since the invasion in March, was captured by coalition forces. American optimism that this would lead to a weakening of the insurgency would prove to be misplaced. Just over a month later, the man appointed to search for Iraqi WMD in the aftermath of the invasion told Congress that 'we were almost all wrong, and I certainly include myself'. With 85 per cent of the inspection work done, he said he had no reason to believe that any WMD would be found in Iraq. The final report of the Iraq Survey Group, published later in the year, concluded that Iraq had destroyed its WMD, the materials to produce them, and its missiles, in 1991–2 and that none of those programmes had been reconstituted since.[101]

## SADR, FALLUJAH AND ABU GHRAIB

In spring 2004, the United States launched two offensives whose failure served only to re-emphasise the parlous condition of the occupation. The first was against the Jaish al-Mahdi (JAM), or Mahdi army, of Moqtada al-Sadr. Sadr was the scion of one of the most important clerical families in the Shia world, and both his father and his uncle had been assassinated by Saddam's regime. With Saddam's fall he sought to translate that legacy into a position as the dominant Shiite cleric in Iraq, in the process demonstrating that Iraq's divisions did not fall solely along sectarian lines. Sadr's primary appeal was to the Shia urban dispossessed, the poorest part of the Iraqi population which had suffered most under Saddam. He bolstered that support by immediately declaring his opposition to the occupation and seeking to couch his rhetoric in nationalist terms, openly attacking Sistani and the exile Shia parties for their cooperation with the CPA. The JAM soon became a powerful force in Shia-dominated east Baghdad (Sadr City) and the main Shiite cities of the south. The other main Shiite parties, Dawa and SCIRI, meanwhile, drew most of their support from the mercantile middle classes, and chose to cooperate with the occupation rather than to oppose it. Only Sistani had anything like cross-class appeal amongst the Shia.[102]

Bremer saw Sadr as a threat to his plans for a new Iraq, but coalition commanders resisted any move against him on the grounds that they did not have the resources and were backed by Rumsfeld.[103] However, on 26 March 2004, when Sadr gave a sermon praising the attacks of 11 September, Bremer ordered Sadr's paper, *Hawza*, shut down. This was swiftly followed by the arrest of one of Sadr's chief aides. Fearing that this presaged a full-scale move against him, Sadr called the JAM onto the streets. The scale and ferocity of the resulting uprising was completely unanticipated by the CPA and the US military had no plan to deal with it. The JAM seized control of Sadr City and several southern cities, including Najaf. Fighting continued for several weeks before a ceasefire was agreed, with the CPA dropping its demands for Sadr's arrest and the dissolution of the JAM.[104]

On 31 March 2004, four security guards working for the private contractor Blackwater were killed by Sunni insurgents in Fallujah. Against the advice of local commanders, Bush and Rumsfeld ordered that the city be cleared of insurgents immediately.[105] The subsequent assault led to approximately 800 deaths, 572 of them civilians, and produced a storm of protest.[106] Several Sunni members of the IGC resigned and Brahimi was threatening to do so as well. With the whole political process in danger of collapse, Bremer pleaded with Washington to allow a ceasefire and negotiations, which duly occurred on 8 April.[107] That was followed by an agreement under which American forces withdrew and were supposedly replaced by the 'Fallujah Brigade' of former Iraqi army officers. In practice Fallujah was returned to the control of the insurgents.[108]

The coalition's legitimacy suffered a further blow with the revelation in May 2004 of prisoner abuse at the Abu Ghraib detention centre.[109] Whilst a handful of individuals would subsequently be held responsible for these events, the reality, like so much else in Iraq, was that they represented a fundamental failure of policy. The detention facilities and those manning them were simply swamped by massive numbers of detainees. CPA and military officials had been aware that there was a problem but failed to do anything about it, and the 'thousands of prisoners would eventually overwhelm the under-manned, undertrained, underequipped, undersupervised and incompetent Army Reserve unit running the prison'.[110]

## TRANSFERRING SOVEREIGNTY AND HOLDING ELECTIONS

Power was formally transferred to the Interim Iraqi Government on 28 June 2004, two days earlier than planned, in order to catch the insurgents off-guard. Bremer was replaced as the chief US representative in Iraq by a new ambassador, John Negroponte. The coalition's military leadership was also transferred, with General George Casey taking command. His primary focus would be on an increased effort to train the ISF in order to accelerate the transfer of responsibility for security.[111]

In the short term, however, Casey's objective was to ensure that the January 2005 elections to the TNA were held in conditions of relative security. To that end, coalition forces once more moved against Sadr and Fallujah. In August 2004, with the active encouragement of Allawi, US forces attacked the JAM forces in Najaf. The Sadrists were spared destruction, however, when Sistani negotiated a five-point peace plan for the demilitarisation of Najaf and Kufa and the withdrawal of the JAM. Sadr subsequently stood the JAM down and backed away from confrontation with the United States.[112] The Najaf assault was followed in November 2004 by Operation Phantom Fury. This time American forces did take control of Fallujah, but only at the cost of flattening it and making the vast majority of the population refugees. Nor did they break the insurgents, many of whom slipped away before the attack began.[113] Overall, the operation further hardened Sunni opinion against the coalition and reinforced their determination to boycott the upcoming elections.[114]

The CIA warned Bush that those elections were likely to fuel sectarian divisions, but the president refused to consider postponement.[115] In his view, and that of most of his senior advisers, the elections were the key to legitimating the new Iraqi regime and thus undermining support for the insurgency. One result of this insistence on keeping to schedule was that, lacking an accurate census and having no time to hold one, the CPA had established an electoral system whereby the entire country was treated as a single constituency with one list of parties. The effect was to encourage the creation of large multi-party blocs built along sectarian lines and to disadvantage smaller parties and local candidates.[116] Understanding this, Sistani encouraged the creation of a single Shia list, the United Iraqi Alliance (UIA), incorporating SCIRI, Dawa and the Sadrists, who had now decided to join the political process.

On polling day, the UIA took 140 of the 275 TNA seats available, with the Kurdistan Alliance taking seventy-five. The secular Iraqi list led by Iyad Allawi, the Bush administration's favoured party, took just forty seats. The UIA took three-quarters of the Shia vote, the Kurds voted for the Kurdistan Alliance and the vast majority of Sunnis boycotted the election altogether.[117] Bush hailed the elections as a triumph for Iraqi democracy, but they were nothing of the sort.[118] In the absence of civil society and a democratic political culture, with sectarian divisions deepening and no progress towards establishing a consensus on the basic principles which would underpin the future Iraqi state, the elections only served to reinforce sectarian divisions, making the process of political reconciliation even more difficult.[119]

Having pinned its hopes on Allawi, the Bush administration now pressured the Kurds to ally with his list in the hope of preventing the

UIA from dominating the TNA.[120] The Kurds, however, reasoned that their interests lay in forming an alliance of convenience with the Shia. The accommodation thus reached meant that the Kurds would be allowed to maintain the quasi-independent status of the Kurdish provinces, in return for which they would allow the UIA to dominate in Arab Iraq. Talabani became president and Ibrahim al-Jaafari of Dawa prime minister. UIA parties took control of the oil, interior and finance ministries whilst the Kurds contented themselves with foreign affairs. Nine Sunnis were given minor or ceremonial positions. The new government was 'an alliance of two empowered sects against a third disempowered one'.[121]

The January 2005 elections had produced a TNA in which Sunnis played virtually no part but which was now supposed to draft a constitution for the whole country. In an effort to retrieve the situation, Washington insisted that a group of Sunnis, selected by the United States, be brought onto the drafting committee, but to little effect. The proposed constitution affirmed that Islam would be 'a main source' of legislation and that experts in Islamic law would sit on the federal Supreme Court. In addition, two or more provinces could join together to form autonomous 'regions' which would be self-governing across a wide range of spheres, including the maintenance of internal security forces.[122] It thus reflected the main interests of the Shia and Kurdish parties and was not endorsed by any of the Sunni representatives on the committee. Sunni opposition was driven by a strong ideological commitment to a centralised Iraqi state as well as by resource concerns, fearing that under the new constitution the oil-rich southern and Kurdish regions would retain oil revenue and leave the Sunnis of the centre with nothing.[123] The Sunnis were joined in their opposition to the constitution's decentralising emphasis by Moqtada al-Sadr, who saw it as designed to facilitate a SCIRI-dominated region in the south and a threat to the Shia of the centre and Baghdad who were his core constituency.[124]

In the subsequent referendum on the constitution, Sunni leaders called either for a no vote or a boycott. Each of the Kurdish governorates approved the constitution with 99 per cent support and the yes vote in the nine Shia southern governorates ranged from 95 to 98 per cent. The Sunni-dominated governorates of Salahhadin and Anbar voted 81 per cent and 97 per cent against respectively. With a two-thirds vote in three governorates required to veto it, the constitution was only approved because Sunnis made up just 60 per cent of the population of Nineveh province, which consequently saw only 54 per cent of its population oppose the constitution.[125]

The entrenching of sectarian divisions was confirmed by the December 2005 elections for a new Iraqi parliament. This time, most of the insurgent groups declared a ceasefire and Sunni leaders urged their followers to vote in order to challenge Shia domination of the political system. The main Sunni party bloc to emerge was the Iraqi Accord Front or Tawafuq, which took forty-four seats. The UIA never-theless still held 128 of the 275 seats and the Kurds fifty-three, and their coalition therefore continued to dominate. Allawi's non-sectarian National Iraqi List took just 9 per cent of the vote.[126] Formation of a new government proved problematic, however, as the UIA parties fought amongst themselves over who should become prime minister of the new government. Dawa wanted Jaafari to continue, but SCIRI wanted him replaced by their candidate Adil Abd al-Mahdi. The United States and the Kurds both preferred the SCIRI candidate. The deadlock continued until April 2006 when American pressure forced Jaafari's resignation. The limits of American influence were clearly demonstrated, however, when Jaafari was replaced by another Dawa candidate, Nuri al-Maliki.[127]

## 'HANDING IT OVER TO IRAN'

In a speech to the Council on Foreign Relations in September 2005, Saudi Foreign Minister Prince Faisal al-Saud warned that 'we are handing the whole country [Iraq] over to Iran without reason'.[128] Faisal thus expressed a growing fear amongst the Sunni states of the Persian Gulf that regime change in Iraq had led to the emergence of a 'Shia crescent'. Not only were Shia parties now in control in Iraq, but in Lebanon Hizbollah held seats in the government after deciding to enter the political process in 2005. With Iraq and now perhaps Lebanon about to line up alongside Iran and Syria, Sunni leaders feared a shift in the balance of power in the Gulf.[129]

As with everything else, 'the United States went into Iraq with little or no understanding of the Shi'a factor in Iraqi politics'.[130] Ahmed Hashim, who spent six months working on Iraq policy before the invasion of March 2003, found that US policy-makers had no knowledge of the Shia and made little effort to gain one. There was a widespread belief that the Iraqi Shia and clerics were different to those in Iran: that their past oppression would make them supportive of democracy, and that the Iraqi clerical hierarchy was 'quietist' and did not seek a significant political role.[131] Asked about the danger of Iraq becoming a theocracy in the Iranian mould, Paul Wolfowitz replied that

> fifty percent of the Arab world are women. Most of those women do not want to live in a theocratic state. The other fifty percent are men. I know a lot of them. I don't think they want to live in a theocratic state.[132]

Apart from the questionable assertion that he knew 'a lot' of the male population of the Arab world, Wolfowitz was probably telling the truth when he said that the Iraqi Shia leaders he knew did not want to live in a theocracy. However, after the 2005 elections, the Shia leaders he knew were not running Iraq. Wolfowitz and the rest of the Bush administration had pinned their hopes on Westernised, secular Iraqis like Ahmed Chalabi and Iyad Allawi, but they, and others like them, had been marginalised by the increasingly sectarian politics of post-war Iraq. Rather than Chalabi and Allawi, the Shia the United States ended up putting in power in Baghdad were the leaders of the two Iranian-backed theocratic parties, Dawa and SCIRI.

Whilst it had little choice but to support the government that had thus emerged from the electoral process it had created, the Bush administration increasingly came to accuse Iran of being responsible for much, if not most, of the violence in Iraq, alleging that it was arming Shiite militias and supplying the improvised explosive devices (IEDs) that were used in some of the most deadly attacks on coalition forces.[133] Whilst it would have made little sense for Iran to have supplied IEDs to Sunni insurgents who would then use them against an ISF largely comprised of the Shiite militias of Tehran's allies,[134] there is little question that Iran has sought to exercise a decisive influence over developments in post-war Iraq.

Iran's initial response to the invasion of Iraq had been one of fear. It took little imagination to suspect that a successful implantation of an American client regime in Baghdad would be followed by an attack on Iran. Iran's goals, once Saddam was overthrown were, accordingly, to ensure that such an attack did not take place and, to that end, to foster the emergence of a pro-Iranian regime in Baghdad. The resulting Iranian policy blended cooperation and defiance. In the first place, it was obvious to Tehran that rapid movement towards elections and a transfer of sovereignty were in its interest, since they were likely to result in Shia dominance in Baghdad. It therefore encouraged the Shiite parties to cooperate with the CPA.[135] This, along with the obvious demographic logic of doing so, helps to explain the willingness of SCIRI and Dawa to participate in the IGC and the US-backed political process in Iraq.

In addition, however, Tehran soon realised that, rather than a threat, the US occupation of Iraq was becoming an opportunity. The catastrophic nature of the occupation meant that the Bush administration was clearly going to be in no position to attack Iran. Moreover, Iranian influence in Iraq would be a powerful lever to be used to deter such an attack. As well as seeking influence with the government in Baghdad therefore, Iran has also extended support and finance to the Shiite militias in southern Iraq and generally sought to ensure that the United States remains bogged down in a failing occupation. Tehran also responded to threats by Bush to bomb Iranian nuclear facilities by warning that it would turn Iraq into a graveyard for American troops.[136]

## DESCENT INTO CIVIL WAR

The December 2005 elections led to Nuri al-Maliki becoming prime minister, but he was hardly in charge of his own government, let alone the country. The electoral system, with its incitement to the formation of large, multi-party blocs, left the prime minister as little more than a broker between the factions that comprised the UIA and between it and the other parties. The parties, for their part, treated the government as a spoils system with control of ministries as the prize. Those ministries were treated as party fiefdoms, staffed with party members and supporters, and used to deliver benefits to the ethno-sectarian group the party represented rather than to the citizens of Iraq as a whole. No 'government', understood as a unitary entity with a common purpose, existed. Instead there was rather an incoherent collection of largely autonomous and conflicting ministries and agencies each pursuing its own agenda as defined by the relevant party leader rather than the prime minister.[137]

Whilst those party agendas were diverse, one thing the majority had in common was a determination to utilise control of the government in the interests of the Shia. State radio and television became more Shiite in their religious programming, Shiite religious holidays were made national holidays, and Shiite provisions on marriage and inheritance started to enter the legal system.[138] The de-Baathification Commission, shut down under Allawi, was restored and civil servants reinstated by Allawi demoted or fired. Iraqi ties to Iran were also improved. In July 2005, Iraq signed an agreement with Iran for the latter to train and supply the ISF and the new government later apologised for starting the Iran–Iraq War and offered to pay compensation, as well as agreeing to share intelligence and oil pipeline connections.[139] None of this was calculated to reassure Sunnis.

The key factor deepening sectarian conflict, however, was Shiite control of parts of the security forces, most notably the Ministry of the Interior. Prior to the formation of the first UIA-dominated government in May 2005, organised Shia retaliation against Sunnis in response to insurgent attacks had been relatively rare, for a number of reasons including the urging of restraint by Sistani and Iran, the fact that the Shia were clearly the winners in the new Iraq, and a lack of control over the means of coercion. Once SCIRI took control of the Interior Ministry, however, they began to transform parts of the police force into Shia death squads and to take systematic revenge on former Baathists and any Sunni suspected of supporting the insurgency.[140]

What had been a combination of largely criminal violence and an insurgency against the occupying forces was thus being transformed into an emergent civil war. Then, on 22 February 2006, Sunni insurgents blew up the al-Askari shrine in Sammara and the civil war became a full-blown one. Within hours of the attack the JAM began to exact revenge in Baghdad, and over the following week 184 Sunni mosques were destroyed or attacked and over 1,000 Iraqis died. The Shia militias, with the active support of the police, now began systematic sectarian cleansing of mixed neighbourhoods. Estimates put the number of extra-judicial killings of Sunnis at 1,000 per month and over 100,000 Iraqis fled their homes in the first four months of 2006.[141] By the end of the year, ten formerly mixed Baghdad neighbourhoods were now entirely populated by the Shia, whose share of Baghdad's population had risen from 65 to 75 per cent.[142] The UN calculated that 34,452 civilians were killed in Iraq in 2006.[143]

The Maliki government did nothing to try to halt the violence, nor could it, beholden as it was to the parties who were behind the sectarian assault on the Sunnis, and lacking any effective security forces of its own. Moreover, the civil war only reinforced the dominance of the parties and the militias as each served as the protector of its own community in the absence of an effective central government and ISF. CIA Director Michael Hayden's analysis of the Iraqi political situation at the end of 2006 was that

> the government is unable to govern . . . The inability of the government to govern seems irreversible. We have placed all our energies in creating a center, and the center cannot accomplish anything. The levers of power are not connected to anything.[144]

## THE NATIONAL STRATEGY FOR VICTORY IN IRAQ

As Iraq descended into civil war, the Bush administration continued to deny what was happening. In November 2005 the administration released a *National Strategy for Victory in Iraq*.[145] The document itself was largely vague and rhetorical, designed more to create the impression that there was a strategy than to actually define one. Bush's speech announcing the *Strategy*, however, was revealing in its complete disconnection from the realities of Iraq. He claimed that despite problems, Iraq had seen real progress over the previous year. In particular, he focused on the transfer of responsibility for security to Iraqis. One hundred and twenty Iraqi police and army battalions were now operational, he asserted, with forty of them operating independently or with only limited US support. He therefore looked forward optimistically to a situation where all frontline security operations would be transferred to the ISF, limiting the American role to training and support.[146]

In reality, Casey's efforts to improve security and 'stand up' the ISF continued to meet with failure. As soon as American forces left an area they had cleared the insurgents regained control as the ISF, who were supposed to hold it, crumbled without American support.[147] Regardless, Casey proceeded to hand over responsibility for security in Baghdad to the ISF. From an average of 360 American patrols per day in June 2005 the figure fell to ninety-two per day by February 2006. By summer 2006, the ISF were responsible for security in 70 per cent of Baghdad and controlled all its checkpoints,[148] a development which hugely facilitated Shia sectarian cleansing of the city. As the violence escalated, Casey presented his plan for a drawdown of American forces to Bush, envisioning a reduction to five or six American combat brigades by December 2007.[149]

Casey's plan was suspended within a month of its being outlined, and American troop numbers increased from 125,000 to 142,000 to cope with the rising tide of sectarian violence. Casey now sought to try and regain control of the capital by swamping it with security forces and creating effective population security. The operation foundered once again, however, on the lack of reliable forces and the inability and/or unwillingness of the ISF to perform. By early autumn 2006, American commanders determined that 'Operation Together Forward' had been a failure. Violence had continued to increase and insurgents were returning to the areas that had been cleared.[150]

## THE SURGE

By mid-2006, Bush could no longer deny that US policy in Iraq was failing disastrously. The president's 20 July 2006 Iraq update said that

> the deteriorating security situation is outpacing the Iraqi government's ability to respond . . . spiralling sectarian violence by Sunni and Shia extremists, including some elements of the Iraqi Security Forces, is becoming the most immediate threat to Iraq's progress . . . Violence has acquired a momentum of its own and is self-sustaining.

By August, Rice was warning Bush that the fabric of Iraqi society was being ripped apart and that there was a real danger that this could become terminal for American goals in Iraq.[151] The belief that something had to change was increasingly shared by most of the senior members of the administration except Rumsfeld, who continued to insist on the need to transfer responsibility to Iraqis as quickly as possible.[152]

In September 2006, the NSC staff initiated a review of Iraq strategy. The DOD continued to argue Rumsfeld's case that the US needed to leave the Iraqis to their own devices. Rice was also inclined to the view that more pressure had to be put on the Maliki government to fulfil its responsibilities, possibly by threatening to withhold US support and troops,[153] an argument that was also advanced by the Iraq Study Group (ISG) set up by Congress. As well as urging the Bush administration to engage Iraq's neighbours diplomatically in an effort to stabilise the country, the ISG argued that the United States should push the Iraqis to take charge of their own destiny and not make an open-ended commitment to remain in Iraq, rather making it clear to the Iraqi government that it would be withdrawing its forces come what may.[154]

The NSC staff, however, felt that the situation in Iraq was now so bad that the ISF were likely to collapse if given responsibility too early, and that if that occurred rebuilding them might be impossible. The option they therefore came to favour was a short-term 'surge' of US forces.[155] This was also Bush's inclination, and had been even before the review started, so in January 2007 he announced the dispatch of 21,500 extra troops to Iraq. Conceding the failure of American policy to this point, he argued that the new American troops would enable coalition commanders to create a secure environment in Iraq in which 'daily life will improve, Iraqis will gain confidence in their leaders, and the government will have the breathing space it needs to make progress in other critical areas'. He nevertheless emphasised, in a sop to the State Department and the ISG, that the US would hold the Iraqi government to a series of political benchmarks which it itself had announced, including taking responsibility for security in all Iraqi provinces by the end of 2007; legislation on oil-revenue sharing; the holding of provincial elections by the end of 2007; reform of de-Baathification laws; and a process for amending the constitution.[156]

In addition to extra troops, Bush replaced Casey with General David Petraeus, who planned to move many of the extra troops he now had into Baghdad and to establish some thirty-six small bases throughout the city. The aim was to clear and hold ground in order to provide population security. This time the American troop presence amongst the Iraqi population, and alongside the ISF, would be permanent rather than temporary. The US forces would serve both to bolster the ISF and to monitor them to prevent their engagement in sectarian violence.[157] This strategy of embedding American units amongst the population was complemented by a more aggressive campaign against both the insurgents and the JAM. From June 2007, American forces launched a series of operations to clear insurgent forces from the 'Baghdad belts' of northern Babil, eastern Anbar and south Baghdad and then from north-west of Baghdad. This was followed by a concerted effort to hold these areas after they had been cleared.

For the first time since 2003, the results of an American military operation in Iraq were encouraging. Civilian casualty levels began to decline and attacks on coalition forces also began to fall. According to American commanders, by autumn 2007 AQM had been crippled in Baghdad and Anbar province and degraded by 60–70 per cent nationwide since the start of the year.[158] By the end of 2008, civilian casualty levels were below 500 a month, one-seventh of their peak in 2006 and lower than at any time since the American invasion. All the security indicators were now heading in the right directions.[159]

Whilst the change in American tactics was undoubtedly a significant factor in the improving security situation in Iraq, it was not the most important one. The key development had actually preceded the Surge, in the form of the so-called 'Sunni Awakenings'. These were the product of an intra-insurgency conflict between Iraqi Sunnis and AQM stemming from divergent political objectives and AQM's depredations on the Sunni tribes, including infringement of the illicit economic activities which were the source of much of their income. The specific catalyst was AQMs declaration of the existence of an Islamic State of Iraq in October 2006, a move which crystallised its growing divergence from indigenous Sunni insurgents, since it would only facilitate the fragmentation of Iraq and thus play into the hands of the Kurds and the Shia.[160]

In response, the Albu Risha tribe formed the Anbar Salvation Council, and its leader, Ahmed Abu Risha, proclaimed an 'Iraqi awakening'.[161] Petraeus and his commanders seized on this opportunity to divide the insurgents and isolate AQM. Coalition officers were give discretion to negotiate with local Sunni leaders, resulting in a proliferation of ceasefires and deals with tribal sheikhs and other 'community leaders', usually involving large cash payments, in which the latter agreed in return to secure their own areas and fight AQM. The resulting groups, effectively Sunni militias, became known as Concerned Local Citizens (CLCs) and received a monthly stipend from the American military.[162] As a result of internal divisions within the insurgency, the United States was thus able to co-opt a large part of it and use it in the fight against AQM. This was the main reason for the dramatic reduction in violence in 2007–8.

## POLITICAL PROGRESS?

Whilst unquestionably a significant development, the improvement in security created by the combination of the Surge and the Awakenings was no more than a means to an end. The ultimate goal was to create a context in which political reconciliation amongst Iraq's divided communities would occur, in turn laying the basis for a stable and functional Iraqi state. In this regard, developments since early 2007 have been much more ambiguous, with the main trends being a lack of reconciliation between ethno-sectarian groups, the fragmentation of pre-existing political alliances and a relative increase in the power of the central state.

In formal terms, national reconciliation was supposed to take the form of a number of 'benchmarks'. By the end of 2008, however, progress on these was patchy at best. Most of the progress related to security issues, but when it came to political progress, the picture was significantly bleaker. Revision of the constitution, an oil revenue-sharing law, a law on militia demobilisation and a resolution of the status of Kirkuk all remained stalled. De-Baathification reform and an amnesty law, both intended to reconcile Sunnis to the new regime, were passed in early 2008. However, whilst the new de-Baathification law restored the rights of some former Baathists, it also allowed for the prosecution of others and the firing of about 7,000 from the new ISF, leading Sunnis to actively oppose a law supposedly designed to help them.[163] Of the 17,000 detainees formally approved for release under the amnesty law, less than a thousand had actually been freed. A provincial elections law was finally passed in September 2008 and a 31 January 2009 date set for the elections, but agreement was only made possible by excluding Kirkuk and the three Kurdish provinces from the process.[164]

This lack of progress at the legislative level reflected the continued distrust that existed between the various ethnic and sectarian communities represented in the Iraqi parliament and the weakness of Iraq's central political institutions, which remain incapable of sustaining the kind of serious negotiations required to address the fundamental divisions and conflicts of interest involved. The Political Council for National Security, created specifically as a forum for this purpose, rapidly became moribund, whilst withdrawal from the political process and the government continued to be common.[165]

The Bush administration's response to this lack of political progress was to return to denial and evasion. In response to the lack of progress toward the various benchmarks, the administration initially sought to downplay their significance by claiming that they were not necessarily useful or reliable indicators of progress.[166] Instead, it increasingly sought to focus on what it termed 'bottom-up' reconciliation.[167] According to the administration and its supporters, rather than seeking sweeping changes at the national level, reconciliation was better achieved incrementally at a local level. With Sunnis increasingly being brought into the political process via the Awakenings, they could be slowly integrated into the state and thus given a stake in it.[168]

The evidence cited by Bush and others as evidence of bottom-up reconciliation – the emergence of the Awakenings and the formation of the CLCs – however, was anything but. The Sunnis in these organisations made a tactical decision to reconcile with the coalition in order to deal with AQM and to protect themselves against the Shia onslaught unleashed in 2006, but many were not reconciled to continued Shia domination. Abu Abed, leader of the so-called Amariya Knights, declared that 'after we finish with al-Qaida here, we will turn toward our main enemy, the Shia militas. I will liberate Jihad, then Saadiya and the whole of West Baghdad'.[169] Others, more pragmatically, seemed prepared to accept the reality of Shia power in Baghdad if they could secure political control over their own regions, guaranteed access to oil revenue and, crucially, a significant percentage of the posts in the new ISF.

The government in Baghdad, however, had thus far shown little inclination to meet those terms. In particular, it was deeply reluctant to integrate what it, with some justification, saw as a potential fifth column, into the ISF.[170] In principle it had agreed to allow Sunnis to constitute up to 20 per cent of the ISF, in line with their representation in the country as a whole. That, however, was well below what the Awakenings were demanding and in practice the government was reluctant to meet even that target. At the end of 2007, US commanders submitted 3,000 names to the government for incorporation into the ISF, the majority of them Sunnis from the Awakenings. Four hundred were accepted, and all were Shias.[171] In spring 2008, Maliki then brought the operation of the Reconciliation Committee set up to integrate the Awakenings fighters into the ISF to a halt. This was followed by the use of ISF units loyal to him to begin dismantling those elements of the Awakenings that he deemed a threat to his political position. Leaders of the so-called Sons of Iraq, including Abu Abed, who had been organising to fight the upcoming provincial elections, were arrested or forced into exile and their organisations disbanded. Maliki then demanded that the Americans turn over control of the entire reconciliation process to him.[172]

These developments reflected another significant development in Iraqi politics, namely the relative increase in the power of the central government. To a significant extent, this was a result of American efforts to create an effective ISF finally coming to fruition, thus allowing the Iraqi state to begin to recover its monopoly of coercion. The consequence, however, was less to move Iraq toward political reconciliation than to embolden Maliki, who sought to utilise the newfound strength of the state to cement his own grip on power. In so doing he demonstrated a clear understanding of the precariousness of his own political position. With perhaps twelve loyal supporters in parliament, and no militia of his own, he was entirely dependent on the support and goodwill of SCIRI (now renamed the Islamic Supreme Council of Iraq or ISCI) and the Kurdish parties. He now set out to rectify that situation.

His move against the Sons of Iraq was part of that process, but it was not the first. In March 2008, with the support and encouragement of both ISCI and the US, Maliki sought to oust the JAM from Basra, following this up with further moves against the JAM in Sadr City. In both cases the ISF met with considerable success, and the Bush administration proclaimed this as evidence of both the progress of the ISF and of the increasingly non-sectarian nature of the Iraqi government.[173] The reality, however, was that it was primarily another move in the intra-Shia feud between Dawa/ISCI and the Sadrists which had little to do with acting in the national interest and a lot to do with attempting to use the coercive power of the state to crush a political rival.

Whilst ISCI was happy with Maliki's move aginst Sadr, with whom it had been struggling bloodily for control of southern Iraq throughout 2007,[174] it was deeply unhappy with another of Maliki's actions. One of Maliki's primary relative weaknesses, vis à vis his coalition partners, was the lack of a loyal party militia. To some extent that problem was rectified by the development of the ISF, parts of which, such as the special forces, report directly to Maliki's office rather than to the

Defence Ministry. In addition, however, Maliki began to create so-called Tribal Support Councils. He sought to depict these as an extension of the Awakenings, a claim made superficially plausible by the fact that, having eliminated many of the stronger Awakenings and their leaders, he was now able to integrate some of the weaker Awakenings, who could see no viable alternative, into these new organisations. The reality, however, was that the Tribal Support Councils were a personal militia, loyal to Maliki and paid by the prime minister's office. ISCI and the Kurdish parties condemned the creation of the councils, viewing them as part of a concerted effort by Maliki to establish a dictatorship. The three-man presidency also ordered Maliki to disband them, to no effect.[175]

Further evidence of Maliki's power-grab and the resultant break-up of the former UIA-Kurdish alliance came in the form of Maliki's moves against the Kurds. In this case, Maliki would appear to be seeking to exploit Iraqi nationalist and anti-Kurdish sentiment, particularly amongst Sunnis, in an effort to broaden his base of support. Conflict had in any event been developing for some time as Kurdistan continued to act like an independent state, signing deals with foreign oil companies and contractors and issuing visas. The problematic status of Kirkuk, claimed by the Kurds as part of Kurdistan, also remained unresolved. When the provincial elections law, drawn up by the Shiite-dominated parliament, included a provision that in the Kirkuk Governerate, rather than one man one vote, Kurds, Arabs and Turkomen would each have one-third of the council seats, despite a Kurdish demographic majority, President Talabani vetoed the law. In response, Maliki has sought constitutional reforms designed to strengthen the central government at the expense of autonomous regions such as Kurdistan, and in early September 2008 he sent the Iraqi army into the peaceful Kurdish-administered town of Khanaqin and expelled the Kurds.[176]

## THE US–IRAQ STATUS OF FORCES AGREEMENT

Whilst largely avoiding public criticism, much of what Maliki was doing was distinctly unwelcome from an American point of view. The Kurds against whom Maliki was now positioning himself were the United States' closest allies in the new Iraq, whilst the American cultivation of the Awakenings Councils and their careful efforts to support reconciliation by integration had been summarily dismantled. That the Bush administration did, and could do, nothing to prevent these developments, reflected the 'commitment trap' in which it now found itself. Having chosen to back Maliki and committed itself to the survival of his regime, the administration consequently had little or no leverage over the Iraqi prime minister. Any threat to withdraw support would be regarded as hollow since Maliki knew that the administration would not risk the collapse of the country into a renewed bout of sectarian conflict or an increase in Iranian influence in Baghdad.[177] Recognition of that reality, allied to the fact that Maliki could increasingly rely on the ISF and the Tribal Support Councils to maintain security, led the prime minister to take an increasingly assertive line not only in his dealings with fellow Iraqis but also with the United States, a change evident in the negotiations over the US–Iraq Status of Forces Agreement (SOFA).

Throughout the chaos of the American occupation of Iraq, Bush never wavered from his commitment to do 'whatever it takes' to achieve his objectives, informing one interviewer that it 'is going to take forty years'.[178] Most Americans, however, did not share his commitment. Even after violence began to decline significantly in late 2007, 73 per cent of Americans said two years was the maximum they would be willing to keep large numbers of American troops in Iraq.[179] After regaining control of both houses of Congress in November 2006, the Democrats then passed a bill in April 2007 that would have required the withdrawal of all US combat troops from Iraq by August 2008, forcing Bush to veto it. Subsequent attempts by congressional Democrats to impose a timetable for troop withdrawal similarly fell foul of Republican filibusters in the Senate and short of veto-proof majorities, but the writing was on the wall.

Facing increasing pressure for withdrawal, and with the security situation in Iraq improving, Bush moved to begin negotiations on a SOFA. Such an agreement could be depicted as a step towards withdrawal of American forces whilst simultaneously establishing the legal basis for a long-term US presence in Iraq. Maliki, for his part, was keen to secure an agreement which he then deemed vital to his survival. In April 2008, a leaked draft of the SOFA demonstrated the extent to which the Bush administration planned to retain a permanent and powerful American presence in Iraq. Conditions in the document included full US control of Iraqi airspace, legal immunity for

US military and private contractors, and the right to conduct armed operations throughout Iraq without securing the consent of the Iraqi government.[180] The Bush administration also said it was not discussing a deadline for withdrawal of combat troops but rather that any decision on withdrawal would be 'conditions based'.

In June 2008, however, Maliki announced that negotiations had 'reached a dead end' because the US demands for immunity from prosecution for coalition troops were unacceptable,[181] and he now also insisted on a deadline for the withdrawal of US troops. The change in Maliki's stance reflected both his newfound confidence in his ability to survive and a recognition that, if he was to cement his position in a political environment in which a substantial majority of Iraqis wanted US troops to leave,[182] he had to take an assertively nationalist stance in the negotiations. The consequence of his shift then demonstrated the clear alteration in the balance of power between him and his American patrons, as the Bush administration was forced into a series of concessions. Under the terms of the SOFA ratified by the Iraqi parliament on 27 November 2008, coalition combat forces would withdraw from Iraqi cities by 30 June 2009 and from all of Iraq by the end of 2011. US training and coordination forces would, however, remain. In addition, the agreement now contained a ban on US troops entering Iraqi homes without ISF approval, the right of Iraq to prosecute American troops and foreign contractors, and a clause barring the United States from using Iraq as a base to attack other countries (i.e. Iran).[183]

## NOTES

1. Ferguson, *No End in Sight*, pp. 104–13.
2. Cockburn, *The Occupation*, pp. 74–6; Ferguson, *No End in Sight*, pp. 106–10.
3. Cockburn, *Muqtata al-Sadr*, p. 161.
4. Gordon and Trainor, *Cobra II*, pp. 529, 537–8.
5. Gordon and Trainor, *Cobra II*, pp. 32–3, 77–8, 84–5.
6. Dobbins *et al.*, *America's Role in Nation-Building*; Woodward, *Plan of Attack*, p. 406.
7. Dodge, 'Iraqi transitions', p. 708.
8. See Chapter 4, pp. 138–9.
9. Dodge, 'Iraqi transitions', pp. 708–10; see also Diamond, 'What went wrong'; Rathmell, 'Planning post-conflict reconstruction'.

10. Dodge, 'Iraq: the contradictions of exogenous state-building'; Pollack, 'Seven deadly sins'.
11. Yousif, 'Economic restructuring in Iraq', p. 46.
12. Dodge, 'Causes of US failure in Iraq'; Herring and Rangwala, *Iraq in Fragments*, pp. 155–8; Wimmer, 'Democracy and ethnic-religious conflict'.
13. Woodward, *The War Within*, p. 86.
14. Gordon and Trainor, *Cobra II*, pp. 676–9.
15. Ricks, *Fiasco*, p. 136; Galbraith, *The End of Iraq*, p. 113.
16. Gordon and Trainor, *Cobra II*, p. 676.
17. Packer, *Assassin's Gate*, p. 147.
18. Bremer, *My Year in Iraq*, pp. 48–9.
19. Cockburn, *The Occupation*, p. 107.
20. CPA Order Number 1, www.cpa-iraq.org/regulations/20030516_CPAORD_1_De_Ba_athification_of_Iraqi_society.pdf; CPA Order Number 2, www.cpa-iraq.org/regulations/20030823_CPAORD_2_dissolution_of_entities_with_Annex_A.pdf.
21. Gordon and Trainor, *Cobra II*, pp. 184–5.
22. L. Paul Bremer III, 'How I didn't dismantle Iraq's army', *New York Times*, 6 September 2007.
23. Ferguson, *No End in Sight*, pp. 154–6, 190–224; Gordon and Trainor, *Cobra II*, pp. 553–5; Woodward, *State of Denial*, pp 196–7.
24. Jim Rutenberg, 'In book, Busk peeks ahead to his legacy', *New York Times*, 2 September 2007.
25. Woodward, *State of Denial*, pp. 193–4.
26. Chandrasekaran, *Imperial Life*, pp. 82–3; Ferguson, *No End in Sight*, pp. 168–70.
27. Ferguson, *No End in Sight*, pp. 171–83; Ricks, *Fiasco*, p. 161.
28. Chandrasekaran, *Imperial Life*, pp. 80–1; Ferguson, *No End in Sight*, pp. 156–7; Cockburn, *The Occupation*, pp. 70–1.
29. Bremer, *My Year in Iraq*; Tripp, 'The United States and nation-building', pp. 546–8.
30. Dodge, 'Coming face to face with bloody reality', pp. 267–71.
31. L. Paul Bremer III, 'Iraq's path to sovereignty', *New York Times*, 8 September 2003.
32. Chandrasekaran, *Imperial Life*, p. 68.
33. Herring and Rangwala, *Iraq in Fragments*, p. 222.
34. Foote *et al.*, 'Economic policy'.
35. Mahdi, 'Neoliberalism, conflict and oil', p. 12.
36. Yousif, 'Economic restructuring in Iraq', pp. 47–8.
37. Foote *et al.*, 'Economic policy', p. 68.
38. Chandrasekaran, *Imperial Life*, pp. 127–33.

39. Ibid. pp. 134–9; Pelham, *A New Muslim Order*, pp. 79–80.
40. Brookings Institution, *Iraq Index*, December 2008, pp. 42, 45.
41. Yousif, 'Economic restructuring in Iraq'.
42. Bromley, *Rethinking Middle East Politics*, p. 168; Bellin, 'The Iraqi intervention', p. 599.
43. Fukuyama, 'Primacy of culture'.
44. Dodge, 'Causes of US failure', p. 94.
45. Fukuyama, 'Primacy of culture'.
46. Przeworski *et al.*, *Democracy and Development*, p. 98.
47. Bellin, 'The Iraqi intervention', pp. 598–601.
48. Bromley, *Rethinking Middle East Politics*, p. 168.
49. Packer, *Assassin's Gate*, pp. 215–16.
50. Pollack, 'Seven deadly sins'.
51. Bremer, *My Year in Iraq*, p. 93.
52. Pelham, *A New Muslim Order*, pp. 104–5.
53. Dodge, 'Iraqi transitions', p. 715, n.
54. Tripp, 'The United States and nation-building', p. 548.
55. Bremer, *My Year in Iraq*, pp. 115–16.
56. Herring and Rangwala, *Iraq in Fragments*, pp. 69–73; Brookings Institution, *Iraq Index*, December 2008, p. 41.
57. US GAO, 'US water and sanitation efforts', p. 14.
58. UNDP and Iraqi Central Organization for Statistics, *Iraq Living Conditions Survey*.
59. Bremer, *My Year in Iraq*, p. 117.
60. 'Oil ministry cracks down on smugglers', *Iraq Press*, 14 January 2004, www.iraqpress.org/english.asp?fname=ipenglish%5c2004-01-14%5CO.htm.
61. Wheelock and McGuckin, 'Iraqi power sector'.
62. In March 2004, only 56 per cent of CPA positions were actually occupied. Inspector General, *Audit Report*, p. 1.
63. Galbraith, *The End of Iraq*, p. 127.
64. Rathmell, 'Planning post-war reconstruction', p. 1031.
65. Pollack, 'Seven deadly sins'.
66. Herring and Rangwala, *Iraq in Fragments*, pp. 76–7; Tarnoff, 'Recent developments', p. 2.
67. IAMB, 'Development Fund for Iraq'.
68. Galbraith, *The End of Iraq*, pp. 130–1; Waxman and Dorgan, 'Halliburton's questioned and unsupported costs'.
69. Dodge, 'The causes of US failure', p. 90.
70. Hashim, *Insurgency and Counter-Insurgency*, pp. 17–29, 69, 99.
71. Ibid. p. 139.
72. Ibid. pp. 138–72.

73. Eisenstadt, 'The Sunni Arab insurgency'.
74. Herring and Rangwala, *Iraq in Fragments*, p. 20; Packer, *Assassin's Gate*, pp. 217–18.
75. Brookings Institution, *Iraq Index*, December 2008, p. 6
76. 'Rumsfeld blames Iraq problems on "pockets of dead-enders"', www.usatoday.com/news/world/iraq/2003-06-18-Rumsfeld_x.htm; 'Iraq insurgency in "last throes" Cheney says', www.edition.cnn.com/2005/US/05/30/Cheney.iraq/.
77. Woodward, *State of Denial*, pp. 266–7.
78. Stephen Hedges, 'Former General says US military didn't expect Iraqi insurgency', *Chicago Tribune*, 15 July 2004.
79. Ricks, *Fiasco*, pp. 193–4.
80. Galula, *Counter-Insurgency*.
81. Woodward, *War Within*, pp. 20–2, 131.
82. Pollack, 'Seven deadly sins'; Ricks, *Fiasco*, pp. 175–6, 192.
83. ICRC, *Report of the ICRC*, pp. 3, 13.
84. Douglas McGregor, 'War strategy: dramatic failures require drastic changes', *Saint-Louis Post Dispatch*, 19 December 2004.
85. Hashim, *Insurgency and Counter-Insurgency*, pp. 333–8; Pollack, *A Switch in Time*, pp. 28–41.
86. Pollack, 'Seven deadly sins'.
87. Hashim, *Insurgency and Counter-Insurgency*, pp. 330–3.
88. Ewen MacAskill, Richard Norton-Taylor and Rory McCarthy, 'US and UK look for early way out of Iraq', *The Guardian*, 22 January 2005.
89. Eric Schmitt, 'General seeking faster training of Iraqi soldiers', *New York Times*, 23 January 2005, p. 1.
90. Bremer, *My Year in Iraq*, pp. 167–72, 183, 186.
91. Dodge, 'Iraqi transitions', p. 716.
92. Noorbaksh, 'Shiism'; Rahimi, 'Ayatollah al-Sistani'.
93. Chandrasekaran, *Imperial Life*, pp. 209–12.
94. Bremer, *My Year in Iraq*, p. 188.
95. Katzman and Elsea, 'Iraq: transition to sovereignty'.
96. Pollack, 'Seven deadly sins'.
97. Bremer, *My Year in Iraq*, pp. 347–9.
98. Pelham, *A New Muslim Order*, pp. 164–7.
99. Tripp, 'United States and nation-building'.
100. Herring and Rangwala, *Iraq in Fragments*, pp. 111–27; Tripp, 'United States and nation-building'.
101. Iraq Survey Group, 'Comprehensive Report'.
102. Cockburn, *Muqtada al-Sadr*, pp. 107–8; Pelham, *A New Muslim Order*, pp. 144–7.
103. Bremer, *My Year in Iraq*, pp. 129–31, 135–6.

104. Cockburn, *Muqtada al-Sadr*, pp. 180–6.
105. West, *No True Glory*, pp. 58–62.
106. Iraq Body Count, 'No longer unknowable'.
107. Bremer, *My Year in Iraq*, pp. 333–6; Woodward, *State of Denial*, pp. 296–300.
108. Laura King, 'Insurgents and Islam now rulers of Fallouja', *Los Angeles Times*, 13 June 2004.
109. Hersh, 'Torture at Abu Ghraib'; National Public Radio, 'Article 15-6 investigation'.
110. Ricks, *Fiasco*, pp. 199–200.
111. Ibid. pp. 393–4, 413.
112. Cockburn, *Muqtada al-Sadr*, pp. 194–202.
113. Patrick Cockburn and Andrew Buncome, 'Fallujah did not break the back of the insurgency', *The Independent*, 8 December 2004.
114. Herring and Rangwala, *Iraq in Fragments*, p. 36.
115. Woodward, *The War Within*, p. 26.
116. Chandrasekaran, *Imperial Life*, pp. 275–6.
117. Independent Electoral Commission of Iraq, www.ieciraq.org/english/frameset_english.htm.
118. 'Bush proclaims election results "resounding success" vows support', www.lubbockonline.com/stories/013105/nat_01310549.shtml.
119. Ottaway, 'Iraq: without consensus', p. 5.
120. Galbraith, *The End of Iraq*, p. 188.
121. Pelham, *A New Muslim Order*, p. 185.
122. Katzman, 'Iraq: politics, elections', pp. 1–2.
123. Herring and Rangwala, *Iraq in Fragments*, pp. 39–40.
124. Hashim, *Insurgency and Counter-Insurgency*, pp. 267–8.
125. Independent Electoral Commission of Iraq, www.ieciraq.org/english/frameset_english.htm.
126. Ibid.
127. Cockburn, *Occupation*, pp. 212–15; Woodward, *State of Denial*, pp. 457–8.
128. Robert Gibbons, 'Saudi says US policy handing over Iraq to Iran', *Reuters*, 20 September 2005.
129. Pelham, *A New Muslim Order*, pp. 209–15; Alterman, 'Iraq and the Gulf States'.
130. Hashim, *Insurgency and Counter-Insurgency*, p. 230.
131. Ibid. pp. 231–2.
132. Packer, *Assassin's Gate*, p. 115.
133. US Congress, House, Committee on Foreign Affairs, 'Statement of Ambassador Ryan C. Crocker'; Petraeus, 'Report to Congress', 10–11 September 2007.

134. Ferguson, *No End in Sight*, pp. 446–7, 452–3; Cockburn, *Muqtada al-Sadr*, p. 211.
135. Taremi, 'Iranian foreign policy'.
136. Ibid.; Cockburn, *Muqtada al-Sadr*, pp. 210–11; Ferguson, *No End in Sight*, p. 455.
137. Dodge, 'Causes of US failure', pp. 97–8; Herring and Rangwala, *Iraq in Fragments*, pp. 131–2.
138. Galbraith, *The End of Iraq*, p. 173.
139. Pelham, *A New Muslim Order*, p. 189; Taremi, 'Iranian foreign policy'.
140. Cockburn, *Muqtada al-Sadr*, pp. 223–4.
141. Brookings Institution, *Iraq Index*, December 2008, p. 4; Dodge, 'Causes of US failure', p. 90; Cockburn, *Occupation*, p. 208; Galbraith, *The End of Iraq*, pp. 1–2, 178.
142. Leila Fadel, 'Security in Iraq still elusive', www.mcclatchydc.com, 7 September 2001.
143. Damian Cove and John O'Neil, 'UN puts '06 Iraq toll of civilians at 34,000', *International Herald Tribune*, 17 January 2007.
144. Woodward, *War Within*, pp. 217–18.
145. US, National Security Council, *National Strategy for Victory in Iraq*.
146. George W. Bush, 'President outlines strategy for victory in Iraq', 30 November 2005, www.whitehouse.gov/news/releases/2005/11/20051130-2.html.
147. Comments of Lieutenant-General David Petraeus at a press briefing on 5 October 2005, www.dod.gov/transcripts/2005/tr20051005-4021.html.
148. Dexter Filkins, 'Baghdad's chaos undercuts tack pursued by US', *New York Times*, 6 August 2006.
149. Gordon and Trainor, *Cobra II*, pp. 594–5; Woodward, *War Within*, p. 7.
150. Multinational Force (MNF) -1, press briefing, 19 October 2006, www.mnf-iraq.com.
151. Woodward, *War Within*, pp. 72–3, 85–6.
152. Ibid. *passim.*
153. Ibid. 232–3, 267.
154. *Iraq Study Group Report.*
155. Feaver, 'Anatomy of the Surge'; Woodward, *War Within*, pp. 233–4.
156. George W. Bush, 'President's address to the nation', 10 January 2007, www.whitehouse.gov/news/releases/2007/01/20070110-7.html; on the benchmarks, see Katzman, 'Iraq: politics, elections', pp. 3–4.
157. Petraeus, 'Report to Congress on the situation in Iraq', 10–11 September 2007; Ricks, *Fiasco*, pp. 445–9.
158. Thomas E. Ricks and Karen DeYoung, 'Al-Qaeda in Iraq reported crippled', *Washington Post*, 15 October 2007; Damien Cave, 'Militant group is out of Baghdad, US says', *New York Times*, 8 November 2007.

159. Brookings Institution, *Iraq Index*, December 2008.
160. Stephen Negus, 'Call for Sunni state in Iraq', *Financial Times*, 15 October 2006; Kahl *et al.*, 'Thinking strategically about Iraq'; Simon, 'The price of the Surge'.
161. Trudy Rubin, 'A powerful awakening shakes up Iraqi politics', *Philadelphia Inquirer*, 12 December 2007.
162. US DOD, 'Measuring security and stability in Iraq', p. 17; Sudarsan Raghaven, 'New leaders of Sunnis make gains in influence', *Washington Post*, 8 January 2008.
163. Waleed Ibrahim, 'Iraq VP says won't ratify key Baathist law', *Reuters*, 31 January 2008.
164. Katzman, 'Iraq: politics, elections'; US National Security Council, *Benchmark Assessment Report*.
165. James Denselow, 'Saying goodbye to what's left of Iraq', *The Guardian*, 16 January 2009, www.guardian.co.uk/commentisfree/cifamerica/2009/jan/16/george-bush-iraq-war-farewell; Francke, 'Political progress in Iraq', p. 10.
166. US National Security Council, *Benchmark Assessment Report*.
167. George W. Bush, 'President Bush visits Naval War College, discusses Iraq, War on Terror', 28 June 2007, www.whitehouse.gov/news/releases/2007/06/20070628-14.html.
168. Frederick Kagan, 'Reconcilable differences', *The Weekly Standard*, 12 November 2007.
169. Cockburn, *Muqtada al-Sadr*, p. 253.
170. Karen deYoung and Amit R. Paley, 'US plans to form job corps for Iraqi security volunteers', *Washington Post*, 7 December 2007.
171. Galbraith, 'Is this a "Victory"?', p. 75.
172. Ned Parker, 'The rise and fall of a Sons of Iraq warrior', *Los Angeles Times*, 29 June 2008; Ned Parker, 'Iraq seeks break-up of Sunni fighters', *Los Angeles Times*, 23 August 2008.
173. Woodward, *War Within*, p. 426.
174. Cockburn, *Muqtada al-Sadr*, pp. 244–6; Dawisha, 'The unravelling of Iraq'.
175. Ranj Alaaldin, 'Maliki's survival game', *The Guardian*, 6 December 2008, www.guardian.co.uk/commentisfree/2008/dec/06/iraq-kurds.
176. Galbraith, 'Is this a "Victory"?', p. 75.
177. Root, 'Walking with the devil'.
178. Massing, 'Embedded in Iraq', p. 36, n.
179. CBS/*New York Times* poll, 5–9 December 2007, www.graphics8.nytimes.com/packages/pdf/politics/20071211_poll.pdf.
180. Seamus Milne, 'Bush is trying to impose a classic colonial status on Iraq', *The Guardian*, 26 June 2008.

181. Amit R. Paley and Karen deYoung, 'Key Iraqi leaders deliver setbacks to US', *Washington Post*, 14 June 2008, A1.
182. Brookings Institution, *Iraq Index*, December 2008, p. 51.
183. *US–Iraq State of Forces Agreement*; Jonathan Steele, 'This is no sop: it's a vote to end the occupation of Iraq', *The Guardian*, 27 November 2008.

# CONCLUSIONS:
# AMERICAN HEGEMONY AFTER THE IRAQ WAR

Since 1979, American policy towards Iraq has been central to a wider effort to restore and maintain the hegemonic position of the United States in the Persian Gulf, an effort determined in turn by the import-ance of the Gulf to the international oil system and the importance of American hegemony in the international oil system to its wider global hegemony.

Iraq became an American preoccupation as a result of two develop-ments in the Persian Gulf regional sub-system. Firstly, the Iranian Revolution transformed America's regional proxy into a direct threat to the latter's regional predominance, completely undermining the 'twin pillar' strategy upon which American regional hegemony then rested. That development was soon followed by Saddam Hussein's decision to invade Iran, a decision whose unforeseen repercussions forced the Reagan administration to 'tilt' towards Iraq in order to prevent an Iranian victory in the resulting war. Over time, and with the growing influence of the 'pro-Arab' faction within the Reagan administration, that initial tilt was transformed into a more ambitious attempt to co-opt Iraq into the camp of pro-American, 'moderate' Arab states and, in doing so, to secure American hegemony on a more permanent basis. The policy of co-optation reached its peak during the first year of the administration of George H. W. Bush, but was then overthrown by the Iraqi invasion of Kuwait in August 1990. Saddam acted in an attempt to ensure his own survival and in the belief that the United States would not respond to his annexation of Kuwait. In doing so he underestimated the threat his action posed to American hegemony at all levels and the consequent willingness of the Bush administration to go to war.

America's crushing military victory in the resulting war, legitimated as it was by UN resolutions, supported by the vast majority of the international community, and demonstrating starkly the dependence of both core states and the Gulf oil monarchies on American military power, seemed to cement American regional hegemony. Saddam's survival, however, led the Bush administration to adopt an ad hoc strategy of containment, centred on a combination of sanctions and weapons inspections, which was ill-constructed for long-term use. Moreover, despite both having been degraded by major military conflicts, the United States now faced not one but two implacable opponents in the Gulf. The Clinton administration responded to this problem by renaming the policy it had inherited 'dual containment' but otherwise continued the effort to contain Iraq through a combination of sanctions, inspections and the threat and/or use of force. That policy was undermined, however, by the contradiction between a commitment to regime change in Iraq before containment could be lifted and an inability and/or unwillingness to take the measures needed to achieve that objective. The compromise that containment thus represented was unsustainable in the long term because of the absence of international support for the permanent exiling of Iraq from the community of nations and the suffering that the policy inflicted on Iraqi civilians.

By the end of the 1990s, therefore, American hegemony in the Gulf was once again beginning to fray at the edges. Iran remained unreconciled to America's regional influence and apparently bent on the development of nuclear weapons, whilst the containment of Iraq was crumbling by the day. With inspections already suspended and sanctions seemingly likely to follow, Saddam would soon be free once more to revive his WMD programme and pursue his goal of regional hegemony. Meanwhile, the combined suffering of the Iraqi and Palestinian people, for which most Arabs held the United States largely responsible, in combination with Washington's continued support for regional despots, was fuelling a toxic brew of anti-Americanism and radical Islam which manifested itself in the form of terrorist attacks and a growing threat to both the United States and its regional allies.

George W. Bush therefore entered the White House at a time when American regional hegemony appeared precarious. He also entered it aware that the varied strategies of his predecessors, from power-balancing, to co-optation, to containment, had failed to resolve that problem. Bush was different from his predecessors, however, in representing, both in his own person and in his appointments, the apotheosis of the 'conservative ascendancy' which had first manifested itself in Reagan's 1980 election victory. The significance of this development was that it meant the United States was now governed by an administration which saw rogue states armed with WMD as a mortal threat to America's global predominance, and one ideologically inclined to see unilateral military solutions as the most efficacious solution to that danger. The only thing the administration lacked was a plausible justification for military action against Iraq, and that was then provided in the form of the events of 11 September 2001.

George W. Bush was thus committed to regime change in Iraq from the moment he entered office, and 11 September was in that regard simply a facilitator to a pre-existing goal. Nevertheless, it is also clear that, between September 2001 and March 2003, some members of the administration, and most crucially the president himself, began to see regime change in Iraq as more than simply the means to eliminate a threat to America's ability to project its power in the Gulf. In addition, they came to see regime change in Iraq as the potential catalyst for the spread of market-democracy throughout the wider Middle East and thus as an opportunity to place American regional hegemony on a more stable, consensual, footing.

Such an objective was never likely to have been achieved in anything less than decades, given the manifold obstacles to its achievement both in Iraq and in the wider region. The chances of success were significantly reduced, nevertheless, by the Bush administration's deeply held antipathy to the concept of nation-building and the blithe, ideologically driven assumption of senior policy-makers that it would be possible to simply graft a new regime onto the still functional torso of the Iraqi state, hold elections and leave (apart from the forces who would remain under a SOFA), having created a grateful, pro-American market-democracy. Instead, when the United States invaded, the Iraqi state collapsed, leaving the Bush administration facing a massive task of state-building for which it was completely unprepared. The administration's response was to take a series of decisions, and implement a number of policies – including the reversal of the commitment to a swift transfer of sovereignty, the first two Coalition Provisional Authority orders, the attempted economic 'shock therapy', the sectarian construction of the Iraqi Governing Council and the failed reconstruction effort – which compounded the collapse of the Iraqi state and the fragmentation of the Iraqi polity, alienated Iraqis of all stripes and fuelled both the Sunni insurgency and sectarianism. When the administration subsequently abandoned Bremer's plans for a long occupation in favour of a return to a swift transfer of power, it found itself outmanoeuvred by Ayatollah Sistani and promoting a series of elections and referenda which cemented both the sectarian divide and the hold on power of the unpopular exile parties. Simultaneously, the administration responded to the growing insurgency by denying coalition military commanders the forces necessary to fight an effective counter-insurgency war. Only when Iraq descended into full-scale civil war in 2006 did the administration review its policy, after which the combination of the Surge and the Awakenings drew Iraq back from the brink.

By early 2009, nearly six years on from the American invasion, Iraq was certainly a good deal more peaceful than it had been in 2006. Nevertheless, it remained an extremely dangerous and violent country, with civilian deaths still running at approximately 500 per month. Moreover, many of those deaths were caused by al-Qaeda in Mesopotamia which, despite a series of setbacks, was still capable of launching twenty-four attacks in November 2008 alone.[1] Estimates of Iraqi civilian deaths ranged from an implausibly low 43,000 to anywhere between 426,000 and 793,000. The United States itself had lost 4,211 dead and 60,000–80,000 injured. Approximately 2 to 2.5 million Iraqis had fled into exile since the invasion and a further 2.7 million had been internally displaced. A fifth of the Iraqi population had thus been physically uprooted as a consequence of the war and subsequent events.[2]

Iraq also remained a deeply impoverished country in which five years of reconstruction had hardly begun to reverse the effects of two decades of war and sanctions. In early 2008, food rations were half what they had been under Saddam. Five million Iraqis remained dependent on those rations but half of them were unable to receive them because they had been displaced from their homes. Three-quarters of all doctors, nurses and pharmacists had fled abroad and even basic medicines were in short supply or non-existent. By the end of 2008, fuel supplies were at three-quarters of the government's target level, which was no better than in 2003. Electricity was still only available for half a day on average and unemployment rates remained unchanged at between 25 and 40 per cent.[3]

On 29 August 2002, George W. Bush had signed a National Security Directive entitled 'Iraq: Goals, Objectives and Strategy':

> US goal: Free Iraq in order to eliminate weapons of mass destruction, their means of delivery and associated programs, to prevent Iraq breaking out of containment and becoming a more dangerous threat to the region and beyond. End Iraqi threats to its neighbors, to stop the Iraqi government's tyrannizing of its own population, to cut Iraqi links to and sponsorship of international terrorism, to maintain Iraq's unity and territorial integrity. And liberate the Iraqi people from tyranny, and assist them in creating a society based on moderation, pluralism and democracy.[4]

Unstated in the NSD, but also prominent in the minds of policy-makers, were the objectives of facilitating a resolution of the Israeli-Palestinian peace process, coercing Iraq into foregoing its nuclear programme and spreading market-democracy across the wider Middle East.

Given that set of objectives, and viewed from the perspective of early 2009, the American invasion and subsequent occupation of Iraq would appear to represent 'a defeat of historic proportions for US foreign policy'.[5] The most immediate and long-standing of the administration's objectives had been the elimination of the threat posed to American regional hegemony by a WMD-armed Iraq. That threat, however, turned out not to exist. The combination of sanctions and inspections had worked. Iraq had been disarmed and Saddam had been unable to reconstitute his WMD programmes. Had the Bush administration not been so fixated on the goal of regime change, and so theological in its certainty that Saddam did have WMD, the return of the inspectors would likely have demonstrated that fact. Post-war investigations also confirmed that Iraq had no significant connection to al-Qaeda and nothing whatsoever to do with the attacks of 11 September.

The Iraq War was thus based on a false premise. Nevertheless, there were other objectives, and as it became clear that WMD would not in fact be discovered, so 'creating a society based on moderation, pluralism and democracy' became Bush's principal justification of choice for the war. In this regard, at least, the administration could find some crumbs of comfort. As it left office in early 2009, Iraq was indeed a democracy, of sorts, having managed to hold elections in January and December 2005 and again in January 2009. Moreover, whilst the first two elections had only deepened Iraq's sectarian divisions and fuelled the spiralling violence, some observers saw cause for optimism in the more recent provincial elections.[6] The elections took place with little violence, and the result was a significant victory for Maliki and his 'State of Laws' coalition which took 38 per cent of the vote in Baghdad and 37 per cent in Basra, as well as coming first in seven other governorates. Moreover, whilst Maliki had run on a relatively secular platform, the openly theocratic ISCI did badly, taking just 5 per cent of the vote in Baghdad and 12 per cent in Basra. The Sadrists, for their part, were virtually eliminated as a significant political force. In the Sunni provinces, parties running on secular and nationalist platforms did better than the Islamist parties.[7]

Nevertheless, there remained good reasons to be sceptical about the future of democracy in Iraq. The peacefulness of election day was only achieved through extraordinary security measures, with private vehicles banned from the roads and a curfew on anyone leaving their home except for the sole purpose of voting. Moreover, the supposed triumph of secularism in the elections was easily over-stated. Maliki may have been less overtly theocratic than ISCI but he was still committed to a state in which Islam played a central role and continued to consult Ayatollah Sistani before all major decisions. Voting, moreover, continued to be done on sectarian lines. Maliki's wins were all in Shia-dominated provinces in which he simply took Shia votes from ISCI and the Sadrists. Sunnis, meanwhile, voted for Sunni nationalist parties. The two genuinely secular parties, Iyad Allawi's Iraqi List and the Citizens' Coalition, made little headway.[8]

The pattern of voting thus reflected the fact that sectarian divisions remained deep in Iraq and that political reconciliation was still a long way from becoming a reality. Shia had voted for Shia and Sunni for Sunni. Kurds would no doubt also have voted for Kurds had growing tensions between them and Arab Iraqis not forced the postponement of the elections in the Kurdish governorates. Moreover, whilst Sunnis did engage with the political process rather than reject it, their objective in doing so was, for the most part, to drain power from the Maliki government and to secure the maximum degree of autonomy from Baghdad for their provinces.[9] The absence of legislation on the constitution, an oil law and the status of Kirkuk also confirmed the failure to achieve a cross-community consensus on fundamental political questions. Moreover, the security which had been achieved over the previous two years remained fragile and had, moreover, been bought at the cost of the physical segregation of the different ethnic and sectarian groups. The relative tranquillity of Baghdad came at the cost of the carving up of the city into religiously homogenous zones separated by concrete blast barriers and razor wire.

Whilst Iraq may have managed to maintain the electoral infrastructure of a democratic society, the pluralism, tolerance, secularism and other aspects of a democratic political culture which are equally, if not more, important to the development of a genuine liberal democracy, remained noticeable chiefly by their absence. Whilst Iraq did manage to score 5.05 out of 10 on the Index of Political Freedom, placing it equal fourth in the Middle East, it came 158th out of 173 on Reporters without Borders' Index of Press Freedom and 178th out of 180 in Transparency International's Annual Corruption Perceptions Index, suggesting that it still had a long way to go.[10] Iraqi society remained, to a great extent, both sectarian and tribal in nature. One of the most oft-stated objectives of both Bush and Bremer had been to create a society in which women's rights were respected and observed yet, if anything, those rights had been reduced as conservative Islamic parties and militias had gained in power and imposed 'traditional' norms on those areas they controlled. The election law for the 2009 provincial elections required that 25 per cent of the candidates were women, but the main problem for the parties was persuading women to stand in an environment in which to do so was to incur intimidation and death threats.

Iraqi democracy thus existed in a precarious state, with many of the preconditions for democratic development still non-existent or barely out of infancy. Iraqi society, moreover, remained riven with fault lines, all of which contained the potential to plunge the country back into violence. Even one of the developments largely seen as positive, namely the electoral victory of Maliki's coalition and the consequent strengthening of the central government, contained its own seeds of conflict, given the perception of ISCI, the Kurds and many Sunnis that

Maliki was bent on creating a dictatorship. Nor were their concerns entirely unfounded, given Maliki's clearly demonstrated tendency to utilise the growing power of the state to bolster his own position and to crush political opponents such as Sadr and the Awakenings leaders. If he continued down that path whilst also trying to recentralise political power in Iraq, there was a real possibility of conflict with the Sunnis and/or an ISCI-Kurdish alliance.

If the future of Iraqi democracy thus remained uncertain, the Bush administration might have tried to claim more success for the advance of the market. As security improved, so foreign direct investment increased, from less than $10 million per month in 2007 to $100 million per month in 2008.[11] More significant, however, were the terms under which Iraqi oil was being brought back into the global market. The production sharing agreements (PSAs) signed by the Iraqi government with the major oil companies marked a significant deviation from post-nationalisation norms whereby all 'upstream' activities were controlled by state-owned oil companies and the oil majors had had to confine their activities to marketing and selling. The PSAs, in contrast, gave the latter a share of the profits from production in return for investment in new productive capacity. The agreements thus provide the companies with benefits similar to those they used to receive from direct ownership of oil concessions.[12]

Nevertheless, the continued advance of the market, and the integration of the Iraqi economy into the WCS on the United States preferred terms both depend on continued stability and security in Iraq. Any renewed descent into violence will lead to the withdrawal of both the oil majors and FDI. Moreover, even if Iraq does remain stable, the leading role of the oil majors in Iraqi oil production is likely to depend on continued American influence in Baghdad. The PSAs were negotiated at a point at which the Iraqi regime was wholly dependent on the United States for its continued survival. If, in future, it is able to increase its autonomy from the United States, it may well seek to revisit the terms of the PSAs, or even renounce them, as the Russian government, the only other major oil producer to sign such agreements, has done.

If the future of market-democracy in Iraq was uncertain at best, that made its prospects a good deal brighter in that country than they were in most of the rest of the region. As far as the objective of making Iraq the catalyst for the spread of democracy in the rest of the region was concerned, the failure of American policy was unequivocal. Indeed, after having promoted the idea in 2004–5 by publicly calling on Arab regimes to reform, and creating the Middle East Partnership Initiative to help fund that process, the Bush administration soon began to retreat from its own vision, returning to the established mantra that Saudi Arabia, Egypt and the other Gulf monarchies were 'moderate' friends. That change of course reflected the administration's recognition that democracy might not turn out to be quite the panacea it had hoped. Elections in Lebanon, Egypt and the Palestinian Authority (PA) all saw gains for radical Islamist parties fiercely opposed to the American presence in the region. Those gains, and a failing policy in Iraq which appeared to be empowering Iran, led the Bush administration to abandon the democracy agenda in favour of a return to propping up reliable Sunni autocrats as the best means to contain Iran and maintain regional stability.[13]

One of the hoped for side-effects of the spread of market-democracy was to have been the isolating of Iran and the encouragement of democratic reform in that country. Even in the absence of that development, however, the administration believed that regime change in Iraq would put it in a position to coerce Iran into abandoning its nuclear programme and its challenge to American regional hegemony. Instead, however, in the view of most observers, 'of all the unintended consequences of the Iraq war, Iran's strategic victory is the most far-reaching'.[14] In defeating both the Taliban and Saddam Hussein, the Bush administration removed two of Iran's key enemies and, in the case of the latter, its most powerful regional rival. Iraq is now militarily weak and, thanks to the democratic process fostered by the United States, run by a Shia-dominated government with close ties to Tehran. The possibility that the United States might use military force to eliminate the Iranian nuclear programme was rapidly discounted by the entrapment of the United States in Iraq and Iran's consequent ability to make the American position in that country untenable. Iran is consequently in a stronger regional position after the Iraq War than it was before it.

Nevertheless, the fear of some that Iraq will become some kind of Iranian cats-paw in the region is surely over-stated. Nationalism is a powerful phenomenon, as was demonstrated in Eastern Europe under communism, and opinion polls show that 65–70 per cent of Iraqis view Iran in an unfavourable light.[15] Any Iraqi government will therefore pursue its own perceived interests and will have no desire to do Tehran's bidding where it conflicts with its own objectives, nor would it be politically wise for it to do so. Iran, in any event, does not seek to control Iraq, nor does it need to. It certainly desires to have influence in Baghdad, and more influence than the United States, but its main strategic objective, a weak and friendly Iraq, has already been achieved.

Many in the Bush administration (though not in the State Department) also believed that the road to an Israeli–Palestinian peace 'ran through Baghdad', whether through the evolution of democracy in the PA or simply because the elimination of a strong rejectionist state would demonstrate to the Palestinians that they had no choice but to accept whatever terms Israel was prepared to offer.[16] That this has not occurred hardly needs saying. Elections in the PA brought Hamas to power and rendered the Palestinians incapable of acting as a coherent interlocutor in any negotiating process. Israel, meanwhile, continues to show little interest in offering the Palestinians anything approaching a viable state and, as of early 2009, peace looked to be as far away as ever.

The Bush administration believed that regime change in Iraq would lead to the radical transformation of the Middle East and the reestablishment of American regional hegemony on a consensual basis. A decisive act of coercion would remove one WMD-armed rogue state and cow another into submission. It would also act as the catalyst for the spread of market-democracy across the region and the resolution of the Israeli-Palestinian conflict, developments which would in turn lead to a reduction in anti-American sentiment and terrorism and a consequent drawing down of the US military presence in the region.

Six years, and several hundred thousand deaths later, none of those goals had been achieved. The one ray of light was the possibility of democracy taking hold in Iraq, though a collapse into sectarian violence or evolution into a dictatorship looked equally likely. Whichever outcome did result, however, America's regional hegemony would remain precarious. Iran was strengthened and emboldened, and as unreconciled to America's regional presence as ever. Meanwhile, far from facilitating the spread of norms and values that would allow for hegemonic leadership to be exercised in a consensual fashion, the Iraq War had made anti-American sentiment more virulent than ever. The Zogby Poll of Arab public opinion in 2008 found that 83 per cent of respondents viewed the United States negatively and 70 per cent had no confidence in the United States. Another poll found that just 12 per cent of Saudis viewed Bush positively, putting him behind Osama bin Laden.[17] Far from eliminating the roots of terrorism, the Iraq War had poured fuel on the fire. The conclusion of the American intelligence community in April 2006 was that 'the Iraq jihad is shaping a new generation of terrorist leaders and operatives' and that 'the Iraq conflict has become the "cause célèbre" for jihadists, breeding deep resentment of US involvement in the Muslim world and cultivating supporters for the global jihadist movement'.[18]

Those 'jihadists' were a potential threat to the United States, but far more so to its regional allies, whose security, far from being enhanced by the removal of Saddam Hussein, was now more endangered than ever. In many cases they now faced increased domestic threats from angry populations and a new generation of terrorists. Leaders in Saudi Arabia, Egypt, Kuwait and elsewhere responded by reviving security systems that had been relaxed in the late 1990s and by ruthlessly stamping out dissent. Any tentative moves toward more democracy were abandoned or gerrymandered. Externally, these states now viewed with alarm the strengthening of Iran and significant advances for its Hizbollah allies in Lebanon, fearing that Sunni power in the Gulf was eroding. The Iraq War thus fuelled Sunni-Shia conflict in the wider region, as was seen clearly in Lebanon and also in Palestine where Fatah was backed by the Sunni states, the US and the EU and Hamas by Hizbollah, Syria and Iran.[19]

The American invasion of Iraq had thus strengthened the regional position of Iran and increased the hostility of most Arabs to the United States and its troop presence in the Arabian Peninsula. It compounded the security dilemmas of the United States and its regional allies and exacerbated the problems it was supposed to solve.[20] The Bush administration's response was to return to established norms and practices. In June 2007, it announced a $20 billion arms deal for Saudi Arabia and the other GCC states in order to counter the rising power of Iran.[21] The overall effect of the Iraq War was therefore to force the United States to maintain a direct military presence in the Gulf and the security relationships with the oil states that it was hoping the invasion would allow it to downgrade. In 2009, American policy was right back where it had started when the Bush administration came to power, and America's regional hegemony was as problematic as ever.

## NOTES

1. Toby Dodge, 'Despite the optimism, Iraq is close to the edge', *The Observer*, 21 December 2008.
2. Fischer, 'Iraqi civilian deaths estimates', Table 1, p. 3; Brookings Institution, *Iraq Index*, December 2008, pp. 16, 32.
3. Cockburn, *Muqtada al-Sadr*, pp. 240–1; Brookings Institution, *Iraq Index*, December 2008, pp. 40–2; Dodge, 'Seven questions'.
4. Woodward, *Plan of Attack*, pp. 154–5.
5. Dodge, 'Causes of US failure', p. 87.
6. William Shawcross, 'Democratic dawn in Iraq', *The Guardian*, 3 February 2009.
7. Tim Susman and Monte Morin, 'Maliki's party gains victory in Iraqi provincial elections', *Los Angeles Times*, 6 February 2009; Patrick Cockburn, 'Iraq's voters show faith in Maliki regime', *The Independent*, 6 February 2009.
8. Michael Jansen, 'Counting of ballots under way as elections pass off peacefully', *The Irish Times*, 2 February 2009.
9. Mark Chuvlov, 'Violence and intimidation mark run-up to Iraqi elections', *The Guardian*, 30 January 2009, www.guardian.co.uk/world/2009/jan/30/iraq-elections-violence-intimidation.
10. Brookings Institution, *Iraq Index*, December 2008, p. 36.
11. Ibid. p. 46.
12. 'Blood and oil: how the West will profit from Iraq's most precious commodity', *The Independent*, 7 January 2007.
13. Carothers, 'The democracy crusade myth'.
14. Galbraith, 'The victor?', p. 6.
15. Woodward, *The War Within*, p. 426.
16. Mann, *Rise of the Vulcans*, pp. 322–3.
17. Rami G. Khauri, 'America through Arab eyes', *International Herald Tribune*, 21 April 2008; Robin Wright, 'US plans new arms sales to Gulf allies', *Washington Post*, 28 July 2007, p. A1.
18. US, CIA, Declassified key judgements of the National Intelligence Estimate, 'Trends in global terrorism'.
19. Pelham, *A New Muslim Order*, pp. 215–23.
20. Alterman, 'Iraq and the Gulf States', p. 13.
21. Wright, 'US plans new arms sales'.

# BIBLIOGRAPHY

## PRIMARY SOURCES

*United States*

Albright, Madeleine K., 'A humanitarian exception to the Iraqi sanctions', *US Department of State Dispatch*, 6 (17), 24 April 1995.

Albright, Madeleine K., 'Preserving principle and safeguarding stability: United States policy toward Iraq', 26 March 1997, www.secretary.state.gov/www/statements/970326.html.

Commission on America and the New World, *Changing Our Ways: America and the New World* (Washington, DC: Carnegie Endowment for International Peace, 1992).

Commission to Assess the Ballistic Missile Threat to the United States, 'Report of Commission to Assess the Ballistic Missile Threat to the United States', 15 July 1998, www.fas.org/irp/threat/bm-theat.htm.

Indyk, Martin, 'The Clinton administration's approach to the Middle East', *Washington Institute for Near East Policy*, Report No. 84, 21 May 1993, Washington, DC.

Inspector General of the CPA, *Audit Report: management of personnel assigned to the Coalition Provisional Authority in Baghdad*, Report No. 04-002, 25 June 2004.

*Iraqgate: Saddam Hussein, US policy and the prelude to the Persian Gulf War, 1980–1994*, www.gwu.edu/~nsarchiv/nsa/publications/iraqgate/iraqgate.html.

*Iraq Study Group Report: The Way Forward, a New Approach* (New York, NY: Vintage Books, 2006).

Iraq Survey Group, 'Comprehensive report of the Special Adviser to the DCI on Iraq's weapons of mass destruction programs', 30 September 2004, www.lib.umich.edu/govdocs/iraqwar.html#duelfer.

Lake, Anthony, 'From containment to enlargement', *Vital Speeches of the Day*, 60, 15 October 1993.

National Commission on Terrorist Attacks upon the United States (9/11 Commission), *The 9/11 Commission Report: Final Report of the National*

*Commission on Terrorist Attacks upon the United States* (New York, NY: W.W. Norton, 2004).

National Public Radio, 'Article 15-6 investigation of the 800th Military Police Brigade' (Taguba Report), www.npr.org/iraq/2004/prison_abuse_report. pdf.

Petraeus, David H., 'Report to Congress on the situation in Iraq', 10–11 September 2007, www.defenselink.mil/pubs/pdfs/petraeus_testimony 20070910.pdf.

*Public Papers of the Presidents of the United States: George Bush, 1989–1993*, http://www.csdl.tamu.edu.bushlib/papers.

*Tower Commission Report* (New York, NY: Bantam and Times Books, 1987).

US Arms Control and Disarmament Agency, *World Arms Expenditures and Military Transfers* (Washingon, DC: USGPO, 1996).

US Central Command (CENTCOM), *Strategic Plan: 1995–1997*.

US, Central Intelligence Agency (CIA), 'Intelligence community experiment in competitive analysis: Soviet strategic objectives, an alternative view', Report of Team 'B', www.faqs.org/coa/docs/46/0000278531/Soviet-Objectives-An-Alternative-View-(Report-of-Team-%22B).html.

US, CIA, 'Iraq and Al-Qaida: interpreting a murky relationship', 21 June 2002.

US, CIA, 'Iraq's continuing programs for weapons of mass destruction', 1 October 2002, www.fas.prg/irp/cia/product/iraq-wmd-nie.pdf.

US, CIA, 'Iraqi support for terrorism', 29 January 2003.

US, CIA, Declassified key judgements of the National Intelligence Estimate, 'Trends in global terrorism: implications for the United States', April 2006, www.dni.gov/press_releases/declassified_NIE_key_judgements.pdf.

US Congress, House, Committee on Armed Services, Subcommittee on Seapower, Strategic and Critical Materials, *Hearings before the Subcommittee on Seapower, Strategic and Critical Materials*, 101st Cong., 1st Sess., 22 February 1989 (Washington, DC: USGPO, 1989).

US Congress, House, Committee on Foreign Affairs, Subcommittee on Europe and the Middle East, *Developments in the Persian Gulf, June 1984*, Hearings, 98th Cong., 2nd Sess., 1984 (Washington, DC: USGPO, 1984).

US Congress, House, Committee on Foreign Affairs, *United-States Iraqi relations*, Hearing before the Subcommittee on Europe and the Middle East, 101st Cong., 2nd Sess., 26 April 1990 (Washington, DC: USGPO, 1990).

US Congress, House, Committee on Foreign Affairs, *The Persian Gulf Crisis*, Joint hearings of the Committee on Foreign Affairs and the Joint Economic Committee, 101st Cong., 2nd Sess., 11 December 1990 (Washington, DC: USGPO, 1991).

US Congress, House, Committee on Foreign Affairs, *US Exports of Sensitive Technology to Iraq*, Hearing before the Subcommittee on International

Economic Policy and Trade, 102nd Cong., 1st Sess., 8 April and 22 May 1991 (Washington, DC: USGPO, 1991).

US Congress, House, Committee on Foreign Affairs, *Developments in the Middle East, November 1991*, Hearing before the Subcommittee on Europe and the Middle East of the Committee on Foreign Affairs, 102nd Cong., 1st Sess., 20 November 1991 (Washington, DC: USGPO, 1991).

US Congress, House, Committee on Foreign Affairs, *United-States Iraqi Relations*, Hearing before the Subcommittee on Europe and the Middle East, 102nd Cong., 1st Sess., 12 March 1991 (Washington, DC: USGPO, 1991).

US Congress, House, Committee on Foreign Affairs and the Committee on Armed Services, 'Statement of Ambassador Ryan C. Crocker, United States Ambassador to the Republic of Iraq, before a Joint Hearing of the Committee on Foreign Affairs and the Committee on Armed Services, US House of Representatives', 110th Cong., 1st Sess., 10 September 2007 (Washington, DC: USGPO, 2007).

US Congress, House, Committee on International Relations, *US Policy Toward Iraq*, Hearing before the Committee on International Relations, 106th Cong., 2nd Sess., 23 March 2000 (Washington, DC: USGPO, 2000).

US Congress, House, National Security Committee, 'Statement of Paul Wolfowitz, Dean of the Paul H. Nitze School of Advanced International Studies of the Johns Hopkins University for the House National Security Committee Hearings on Iraq', 105th Cong., 2nd Sess., 16 September 1998, www.globalsecurity.org/wmd/library/congress/1998_h/98-09-16wolfowitz.htm.

US Congress, Senate, Committee on Armed Services, *Crisis in the Persian Gulf, US Policy Options and Implications*, Hearings before the Committee on Armed Services, US Senate, 101st Cong., 2nd Sess., 11 and 13 September, 27, 28, 29 and 30 November, 3 December 1990 (Washington, DC: USGPO, 1991).

US Congress, Senate, Committee on Foreign Relations, *Chemical Weapons use in Kurdistan: Iraq's Final Offensive*, S. Rpt 100–48, 100th Cong., 2nd Sess., October 1988 (Washington, DC: USGPO, 1988).

US Congress, Senate, Committee on Foreign Relations, *US Policy in the Persian Gulf*, Hearings before the Senate Committee on Foreign Relations, 101st Cong., 2nd Sess., 17 October 1990 (Washington, DC: USGPO, 1990).

US Congress, Senate, Committee on Foreign Relations, *US Policy in the Persian Gulf*, Hearings before the Committee on Foreign Relations, US Senate (Part 1), 101st Cong., 2nd Sess., 4 and 5 December 1990 (Washington, DC: USGPO, 1991).

US Congress, Senate, Select Committee on Intelligence, *Postwar Findings about Iraqi WMD Programs and Links to Terrorism and how they Compare* to *Prewar Assessments*, 109th Cong., 2nd Sess., 8 September 2006, www.intelligence.senate.gov/phaseiiaccuracy.pdf.

US Congress, Senate, Subcommitee on Commerce, Consumer and Monetary Affairs, House Committee on Government Operations, *Strengthening the Export Licensing System*, 2 July 1991 (Washington, DC: USGPO, 1991).

US Department of Defense (DOD), 'Measuring security and stability in Iraq' (Washington, DC: DOD, December 2007).

US Department of State, 'Secretary Haig: news conference', *Current Policy*, 325, 7 October 1981.

US Department of State, 'Illustrative examples of omissions from the Iraqi declaration to the United Nations Security Council', *Fact Sheet* (Washington, DC: 19 December 2002).

US Department of State, 'Iraq: U.S./U.K./Spain Draft Resolution', 24 February 2003.

US General Accounting Office (GAO), 'US water and sanitation efforts need improved measures for assessing impact and sustained resources for maintaining facilities', Report to Congressional Committees, 7 September 2005.

*US-Iraq State of Forces Agreement* (SOFA), 'Unofficial transcript of the US–Iraq troop agreement from the Arabic text', www.mcclatchydc.com/iraq/story/56116.htm.

US National Security Council, *National Strategy for Victory in Iraq*, November 2005, www.whitehouse.gov/infocus/iraq/iraq_strategy_nov2005.html.

US National Security Council, *Benchmark Assessment Report*, 14 September 2007, www.whitehouse.gov/news/releases/2007/09/20070914.pdf.

US President, *A National Security Strategy of Engagement and Enlargement* (Washington, DC: The White House, February 1996).

*Other*

BP, *BP Statistical Review of World Energy: 1989* (London: BP, 1989).

International Advisory and Monitoring Board (IAMB), 'Development Fund for Iraq: report of factual findings in connection with disbursements for the period from 1 January 2004 to 28 June 2004', September 2004, www.iamb.info/auditrep/disburse101204.pdf.

International Committee of the Red Cross (ICRC), *Report of the ICRC on the Treatment by the Coalition Forces of Prisoners of War and other Protected Persons by the Geneva Conventions in Iraq During Arrest, Internment and Interrogation*, February 2004, www.globalsecurity.org/military.library/report/2004/icrc_report_iraq_feb2004.pdf.

Israel Ministry of Foreign Affairs, 'Memorandum of understanding between the government of the United States and the government of Israel on strategic cooperation', 30 November 1981, www.mfa.gov.il/MFA/Peace

+Process/Guide+to+the+peace+process/US+Israel+Memorandum+of+ Understanding.htm.

United Nations Development Programme (UNDP) and Iraqi Central Organization for Statistics and Information Technology, *Iraq Living Conditions Survey 2004* (Baghdad: UNDP and Iraqi Central Organization for Statistics and Information Technology, Ministry of Planning and Development Coordination, 2005), www.iq.undp.org.ILCS/overview.htm.

United Nations, Food and Agriculture Organization (FAO), *Evaluation of Food and Nutrition Situation in Iraq: Terminal Statement Prepared for the Government of Iraq* (Tome: UN FAO, 1995).

United Nations, International Atomic Energy Agency (IAEA), '4th consolidated report of the Director General of the IAEA under paragraph 16 of SCR 1051', www.globalsecurity.org/wmd/library/news/iraq/un/iaea-779.htm.

United Nations, IAEA, 'The status of nuclear inspections in Iraq: 14 February 2003 update', www.iaea.org/NewsCenter/Statements/2003/ebsp2003n006. shtml.

UNICEF, *The State of the World's Children* (New York, NY: UNICEF, 2001).

United Nations Monitoring, Verification and Inspection Commission (UNMOVIC), 'Briefing of the Security Council, 27 January 2003: an update on inspections', www.unmovic.org.

United Nations, UNMOVIC, 'Briefing of the Security Council, 14 February 2003: an update on inspections', www.unmovic.org.

United Nations, Security Council, 'Report of the specialists appointed by the Secretary General to investigate allegations by the Islamic Republic of Iran concerning use of chemical weapons', S/16433, 26 March 1984.

United Nations, Security Council, 'Report on the 7th IAEA on-site inspection in Iraq under SCR687, 11–22 October 1991', S/23215, 14 November 1991.

United Nations, Security Council, '8th report of the Secretary-General on the status of the implementation of the plan for the ongoing monitoring and verification of Iraq's compliance with relevant parts of section C of UNSCR 687 (1991)', S/1995/864, 11 October 1995.

United Nations, Security Council, 'Report of the Secretary General pursuant to Paragraph 7 of Resolution 1143', S/1998/90, 1 February 1998.

United Nations, Security Council, 'Letter dated 27 March 1999 from the chairman of the panels established pursuant to the note by the President of the Security Council of 30 January 1999 (S/1999/100) addressed to the President of the Security Council', S/1999/356, 30 March 1999, www.un.org/depts/unscom/unscmodc.html.

United Nations, Special Commission (UNSCOM), 'Report to the Security Council', S/1997/301, 11 April 1997.

SECONDARY SOURCES

Aarts, Paul, 'The new oil order: built on sand?', *Arab Studies Quarterly*, 16 (2), 1994, pp. 1–12.

Abrams, Elliot, *Security and Sacrifice: Isolation, Intervention and American Foreign Policy* (Indianapolis, IN: Hudson Institute, 1995).

Abramson, Paul R., John H. Aldrich and David W. Rohde, *Change and Continuity in the 1980 Elections* (Washington, DC: CQ Press, 1982).

Acharya, Amitav, *US Military Strategy in the Gulf: Origins and Evolution under the Carter and Reagan Administrations* (London: Routledge, 1989).

al-Khafaji, Isam, *War as a Vehicle for the Rise and Demise of a State-Controlled Society: the Case of Ba'thist Iraq*, Middle East paper no. 4 (Amsterdam: University of Amsterdam Research Center for International Political Economy and Foreign Policy Analysis, 1995).

Albright, Madeleine, *Madam Secretary: a Memoir* (London: Macmillan, 2003).

Alnasrawi, Abbas, *Arab Nationalism, Oil and the Political Economy of Dependency* (New York, NY: Greenwood Press, 1991).

Alterman, Jon B., 'Iraq and the Gulf States: the balance of fear', United States Institute of Peace, *Special Report 189*, August 2007.

Anderson, Liam, and Gareth Stansfield, *The Future of Iraq: Dictatorship, Democracy or Division* (Basingstoke: Palgrave Macmillan, 2004).

Ansell, Amy, 'Business mobilization and the New Right: currents in US foreign policy', in Ronald W. Cox (ed.), *Business and the State in International Relations* (Boulder, CO: Westview, 1996), pp. 57–77.

Axelgard, Frederick W., *A New Iraq: the Gulf War and Implications for US Policy* (New York, NY: Praeger, 1988).

Baer, Robert, *See No Evil: the True Story of a Ground Soldier in the CIA's War on Terrorism* (New York, NY: Crown Books, 2003).

Bailey, Kathleen C., *The UN Inspections in Iraq: Lessons for On-site Verification* (Boulder, CO: Westview, 1995).

Baker, James A. (with Thomas M. DeFrank), *The Politics of Diplomacy: Revolution, War and Peace, 1989–1992* (New York, NY: G. P. Putnam's Sons, 1995).

Baker, Russell, 'Condi and the boys', *The New York Review of Books*, 3 April 2008, pp. 9–11.

Baram, Amazia, 'The Iraqi invasion of Kuwait: decision-making in Baghdad', in A. Baram and B. Rubin (eds), *Iraq's Road to War* (Basingstoke: Macmillan, 1994), pp. 5–36.

Baram, Amazia, 'Neo-tribalism in Iraq: Saddam Husayn's tribal policies, 1991–1996', *International Journal of Middle East Studies*, 29, 1997, pp. 1–31.

Baram, Amazia, *Building Toward Crises: Saddam Hussein's Strategy for Survival* (Washington, DC: Washington Institute for Near East Policy, 1998).

Baram, Amazia, 'The effect of Iraqi sanctions: statistical pitfalls and responsibility', *Middle East Journal*, 54 (2), 2000, pp. 194–223.

Baram, Amazia, and Barry Rubin (eds), *Iraq's Road to War* (Basingstoke: Macmillan, 1994).

Barnes, Joe, and Amy Myers Jaffe, 'The Persian Gulf and the geopolitics of oil', *Survival*, 48 (1), 2006, pp. 143–62.

Batatu, Hanna, *The Old Social Classes and the Revolutionary Movements of Iraq: a Study of Iraq's Old Landed and Commercial Classes and of its Communists, Ba'thists and Free Officers* (Princeton, NJ: Princeton University Press, 1978).

Bellin, Eva, 'The Iraqi intervention and democracy in historical perspective', *Political Science Quarterly*, 119 (4), 2004–5, pp. 595–608.

Bengio, Ofra, 'Shi'is and politics in Ba'thi Iraq', *Middle Eastern Studies*, 21 (1), 1985, pp. 1–14.

Bengio, Ofra, *Saddam Speaks on the Gulf Crisis: a Collection of Documents* (Tel Aviv: Moshe Dayan Center for Middle Eastern and African Studies, 1992).

Bengio, Ofra, *Saddam's Word: Political Discourse in Iraq* (Oxford: Oxford University Press, 1998).

Bhatya, Shyam, and Daniel McGrory, *Brighter than the Baghdad Sun: Saddam's Race to Build the Bomb* (London: Little, Brown, 1999).

Bill, James A., *The Eagle and the Lion: the Tragedy of American-Iranian Relations* (New Haven, CT: Yale University Press, 1988).

Bina, Cyrus, 'The rhetoric of oil and the dilemma of war and hegemony', *Arab Studies Quarterly*, 15 (3), 1993, pp. 12–13.

Blix, Hans, *Disarming Iraq: the Search for Weapons of Mass Destruction* (London: Bloomsbury, 2005).

Bowker, Mike, and Phil Williams, *Superpower Detente: a Reappraisal* (London: Royal Institute for International Affairs, 1988).

Bowman, Steve, 'Iraqi chemical and biological weapons (CBW) capabilities', *CRS Issue Brief*, April 1998.

Bremer, L. Paul III (with Malcolm McConnell), *My Year in Iraq: the Struggle to Build a Future of Hope* (New York, NY: Simon and Schuster, 2006).

Brenner, Robert, 'Why is the United States at war with Iraq?', *New Left Review*, 185, January–February 1991, pp. 122–37.

Breyfogle, Todd, 'Some paradoxes of religion in the 2000 presidential election', *Reviews in Religion and Theology*, 8 (5), 2001, pp. 543–47.

Bromley, Simon, *American Hegemony and World Oil: the Industry, the State System and the World Economy* (Cambridge: Polity, 1991).

Bromley, Simon, 'Crisis in the Gulf', *Capital and Class*, 44, 1991, pp. 7–14.

Bromley, Simon, *Rethinking Middle East Politics* (Cambridge: Polity, 1994).

Bronson, Rachel, *Thicker than Oil: America's Uneasy Partnership with Saudi Arabia* (New York, NY: Oxford University Press, 2006).

Bronson, Rachel, 'Reconstructing the Middle East', *Brown Journal of World Affairs*, 10 (1), 2003, pp. 271–82.

Brookings Institution, *Iraq Index: Tracking Variables of Reconstruction and Security in Post-Saddam Iraq*, 2 July 2008, www.brookings.edu/iraqindex.

Brookings Institution, *Iraq Index: Tracking Variables of Reconstruction and Security in Post-Saddam Iraq*, 18 December 2008, www.brookings. edu/iraqindex.

Bruce, Steve, *The Rise and Fall of the New Christian Right: Conservative Protestant Politics in America 1978–1988* (New York, NY: Oxford University Press, 1988).

Brzezinski, Zbigniew, *Power and Principle: Memoirs of the National Security Adviser, 1977–1981* (New York, NY: Farrar, Straus, and Giroux, 1983).

Burke, John P., 'The contemporary presidency: Condoleezza Rice as NSC adviser, a case study of the honest broker role', *Presidential Studies Quarterly*, 35 (3), 2005, pp. 554–75.

Burnham, James, *Containment or Liberation? An Inquiry into the Aims of United States Foreign Policy* (New York, NY: The John Day Company, 1953).

Burnham, James, *The War We Are In: the Last Decade and the Next* (New Rochelle, NY: Arlington House, 1967).

Burnham, Walter Dean, 'The 1980 earthquake: realignment, reaction or what?', in T. Ferguson and J. Rogers (eds), *The Hidden Election, Politics and Economics in the 1980 Election* Campaign (New York, NY: Pantheon, 1981). pp. 98–140.

Busch, Andrew E., *Reagan's Victory: the Presidential Election of 1980 and the Rise of the Right* (Lawrence, KS: University Press of Kansas, 2005).

Bush, George (with Victor Gold), *Looking Forward* (London: The Bodley Head, 1988).

Bush, George, and Brent Scowcroft, *A World Transformed* (New York, NY: Knopf, 1998).

Butler, Richard, *The Greatest Threat: Iraqi Weapons of Mass Destruction and the Crisis of Global Security* (New York, NY: Public Affairs, 2000).

Byman, Daniel, 'After the storm: US policy toward Iraq since 1991', *Political Science Quarterly*, 115 (4), 2000–1, pp. 493–516.

Byman, Daniel, and Matthew Waxman, *Confronting Iraq: US Policy and the Use of Force since the Gulf War* (Santa Monica, CA: Rand Corporation, 2000).

Byman, Daniel, Kenneth Pollack and Gideon Rose, 'The rollback fantasy', *Foreign Affairs*, 78 (1), 1999, pp. 24–41.

Caridi, Ronald J., *The Korean War and American Politics: the Republican Party as a Case Study* (Philadelphia, PA: University of Pennsylvania Press, 1968).

Carmines, Edward G., and James A. Stimson, *Issue Evolution: Race and the Transformation of American Politics* (Princeton, NJ: Princeton University Press, 1989).

Carothers, Thomas, 'The democracy crusade myth', *The National Interest*, July–August 2007, pp. 8–12, www.nationalinterest.org/article.aspx?id=14826.

Center for Economic and Social Rights, *Unsanctioned Suffering: a Human Rights Assessment of the UN Sanctions on Iraq*, 12 May 1996.

Chandrasekaran, Rajiv, *Imperial Life in the Emerald City: Inside the Green Zone* (London: Bloomsbury 2007).

Chapman, Duane, and Neha Khanna, 'The Persian Gulf, global oil resources and international security', *Contemporary Economic Policy*, 24 (4), 2006, pp. 507–19.

Chubin, Shahram, 'The USSR and Southwest Asia', in Andrzej Korbonski and Francis Fukuyama (eds), *The Soviet Union and the Third World: the Last Three Decades* (Ithaca, NY: Cornell University Press, 1987).

Chubin, Shahram, and Charles Tripp, *Iran and Iraq at War* (London: I. B. Tauris, 1988).

Cigar, Norman, 'Iraq's strategic mindset and the Gulf War', *Journal of Strategic Studies*, 25, March 1992, pp. 14–18.

Cirincione, Joseph, Jessica Tuchman Matthews and George Perksovich (with Alexis Orton), *WMD in Iraq: Evidence and Implications* (Washington, DC: Carnegie Endowment for International Peace, 2004).

Clarke, Richard A., *Against all Enemies: Inside America's War on Terror* (London: Free Press, 2004).

Clinton, Bill, *My Life* (New York, NY: Knopf, 2000).

Clinton, Bill, 'The costs of action must be weighed against the price of inaction', in M. Sifry and C. Cerf, *The Iraq War Reader: History, Documents, Opinions* (New York, NY: Touchstone, 2003), pp. 205–9.

Cockburn, Andrew, and Patrick Cockburn, *Saddam Hussein: an American Obsession* (London: Verso, 2002).

Cockburn, Patrick, *The Occupation: War and Resistance in Iraq* (London: Verso, 2006).

Cockburn, Patrick, *Muqtada al-Sadr and the Fall of Iraq* (London: Faber and Faber, 2008).

Committee Against Repression and for Democratic Rights in Iraq (CADRI), *Saddam's Iraq: Revolution or Reaction?* (London: Zed Books, 1989).

*Congressional Quarterly Almanac, 1988* (Washington, DC: Congressional Quarterly Press, 1989).

*Congressional Quarterly Almanac, 1990* (Washington, DC: Congressional Quarterly Press, 1991).

Cordesman, Anthony H., *The Gulf and the Search for Strategic Stability* (Boulder, CO: Westview, 1984).

Cordesman, Anthony H., 'Inexcusable failure: progress in training the Iraqi army and security forces as of mid-July 2004', CSIS, Washington, DC, 20 July 2004.

Cordesman, Anthony H. and Ahmed S. Hashim, *Iraq: Sanctions and Beyond* (Boulder, CO: Westview, 1997).

Cottam, Richard W., *Nationalism in Iran* (Pittsburgh, PA: University of Pittsburgh Press, 1979).

Cottam, Richard W., 'Levels of conflict in the Middle East', in Joseph Coffey and Gianni Bonvicini (eds), *The Atlantic Alliance and the Middle East* (Pittsburgh, PA: University of Pittsburgh Press, 1989), pp. 17–72.

Coughlin, Con, *Saddam: the Secret Life* (London: Macmillan, 2002).

Cox, Michael, *US Foreign Policy After the Cold War: Superpower without a Mission?* (London: Royal Institute of International Affairs, 1995).

Cox, Robert W., 'Social forces, states and world orders: beyond international relations theory', *Millenium Journal of International Studies*, 10 (2), 1981, pp. 126–55.

Cox, Ronald W., and Daniel Skidmore-Hess, *US Politics and the Global Economy: Corporate Power, Conservative Shift* (Boulder, CO: Lynne Rienner, 1999).

Critchlow, Donald T., *The Conservative Ascendancy: How the GOP Right Made Political History* (Cambridge, MA: Harvard University Press, 2007).

Cumings, Bruce, 'Chinatown: foreign policy and elite realignment', in T. Ferguson and J. Rogers (eds), *The Hidden Election, Politics and Economics in the 1980 Election* Campaign (New York, NY: Pantheon, 1981), pp. 196–231.

Cumings, Bruce, *The Origins of the Korean War, Volume II: The Roaring of the Cataract, 1947–1950* (Princeton, NJ: Princeton University Press, 1990).

Cumings, Bruce, 'Is America an imperial power?', *Current History*, November 2003, pp. 355–60.

Daalder, Ivo. H., and James M. Lindsay, *America Unbound: the Bush Revolution in Foreign Policy* (Washington, DC: Brookings Institution Press, 2003).

Danner, Mark, *The Secret Way to War: the Downing Street Memo and the Iraq War's Buried History* (New York, NY: New York Review Books, 2006).

Dawisha, Adeed, 'The unraveling of Iraq: ethnosectarian preferences and state performance in historical perspective', *The Middle East Journal*, 62 (2), 2008, pp. 219–30.

Diamond, Larry, 'What went wrong in Iraq', *Foreign Affairs*, 83 (5), 2004, pp. 34–56.

Diamond, Sara, *Roads to Dominion: Right-Wing Movements and Political Power in the United States* (New York, NY: The Guilford Press, 1995).

Dobbins, James, John G. McGinn, Keith Crone, Seth G. Jones, Rollie Lall, Andrew Rathmell, Rachel M. Swanger and Anga R. Timilsina, *America's Role in Nation-Building: From Germany to Iraq* (Santa Monica, CA: Rand Corporation, 2003).

Dodge, Toby, *Inventing Iraq: the Failure of Nation-Building and a History Denied* (New York, NY: Columbia University Press, 2003).

Dodge, Toby, 'Iraqi transitions: from regime change to state collapse', *Third World Quarterly*, 26 (4–5), 2005, pp. 705–21.

Dodge, Toby, 'The Sardinian, the Texan and the Tikriti: the comparative autonomy of the state in the Middle East and regime change in Iraq', *International Politics*, 43 (4), 2006, pp. 453–73.

Dodge, Toby, 'Iraq: the contradictions of exogenous state-building in historical perspective', *Third World Quarterly*, 27 (1), 2006, pp. 187–200.

Dodge, Toby, 'The causes of US failure in Iraq', *Survival*, 49 (1), 2007, pp. 85–106.

Dodge, Toby, 'Seven questions: is the Surge working in Iraq?', *Foreign Policy*, September 2007, www.foreignpolicy.com/story/cms.php?storyid=3982.

Dodge, Toby, 'Coming face to face with bloody reality: liberal common sense and the ideological failure of the Bush Doctrine in Iraq', *International Politics*, 46 (2/3), 2009, pp. 253–75.

Dorrien, Gary, *The Neoconservative Mind: Politics, Culture and the War of Ideology* (Philadelphia, PA: Temple University Press, 1993).

Duelfer, Charles A., 'Why Saddam wants weapons of mass destruction', in M. Sifry and C. Cerf (eds), *The Iraq War Reader: History, Documents, Opinions* (New York, NY: Touchstone, 2003), pp. 412–13.

Duffy, Michael and Dan Goodgame, *Marching in Place: the Status Quo Presidency of George Bush* (New York, NY: Simon and Schuster, 1992).

Dumbrell, John, 'Unilateralism and "America First"? President George W. Bush's Foreign Policy', *The Political Quarterly*, 73 (3), 2002, pp. 279–87.

Dunn, David H., 'Myths, motivations and misunderestimations: the Bush administration and Iraq', *International Affairs*, 79 (2), 2003, pp. 279–97.

Edsall, Thomas B., *Building Red America: the New Conservative Coalition and the Drive for Permanent Power* (New York, NY: Perseus Books, 2006).

Ehrman, John, *The Rise of Neoconservatism: Intellectuals and Foreign Affairs, 1945–1994* (New Haven, CT: Yale University Press, 1995).

Eisenstadt, Michael, 'The Sunni Arab insurgency: a spent or rising force?', *Policywatch*, 1028, 26 August 2005, www.washingtoninstitute.org/templateco5.php?CID=2362.

Fallows, James, 'Blind into Baghdad', *The Atlantic Monthly*, 293 (1), 2004, www.theatlantic.com/doc/200401/fallows.

Farouk-Sluglett, Marion, '"Socialist" Iraq 1963–1978: towards a reappraisal', *Orient*, 23 (2), 1982, pp. 206–19.

Farouk-Sluglett, Marion, 'After the war: the debts pile up', *Middle East International*, 343, 3 February 1989.

Farouk-Sluglett, Marion, and Peter Slugglet, 'Iraqi Ba'thism: nationalism, socialism and national socialism', in Committee Against Repression and For Democratic Rights in Iraq, *Saddam's Iraq: Revolution or Reaction?* (London: Zed Books, 1989), pp. 89–107.

Fawcett, Louise (ed.), *International Relations of the Middle East* (Oxford: Oxford University Press, 2005).

Feaver, Peter D., 'Anatomy of the Surge', *Commentary*, 125 (4), April 2008, pp. 24–9.

Ferguson, Charles H., *No End in Sight: Iraq's Descent into Chaos* (New York, NY: Public Affairs, 2008).

Ferguson, Thomas, *Golden Rule: the Investment Theory of Party Competition and the Logic of Money-Driven Political Systems* (Chicago, IL: University of Chicago Press, 1995).

Ferguson, Thomas, and Joel Rogers (eds), *The Hidden Election: Politics and Economics in the 1980 Election* Campaign (New York, NY: Pantheon, 1981).

Ferguson, Thomas, and Joel Rogers, 'The Reagan victory: corporate coalitions in the 1980 campaign', in T. Ferguson and J. Rogers (eds), *The Hidden Election: Politics and Economics in the 1980 Election* Campaign (New York, NY: Pantheon, 1981), pp. 3–64.

Fischer, David Hackett, *Albion's Seed: Four British Folkways in America* (Oxford: Oxford University Press, 1989).

Fischer, Hannah, 'Iraqi civilian deaths estimates', CRS Report for Congress, 27 August 2008, www.cdi.org/pdfs/crs/%20on%20civilian%casualties% 202007.pdf.

Fisher, Louis, 'Legislative-executive relations and US policy toward Iraq', in John Davis (ed.), *Presidential Policies and the Road to the Second Iraq War: from Forty One to Forty Three* (Aldershot: Ashgate, 2006), pp. 62–91.

Fitzgerald, Frances, 'George Bush and the world', *New York Review of Books*, 26 September 2002, pp. 80–6.

Fleisher, Richard, and John R. Bond, 'Congress and the President in a partisan era', in Richard Fleisher and John R. Bond (eds), *Polarized Politics: Congress and the President in a Partisan Era* (Washington, DC: CQ Press, 2000), pp. 1–8.

Foote, Christopher, William Block, Keith Crane and Simon Gray, 'Economic policy and prospects in Iraq', *Journal of Economic Perspectives*, 18 (3), 2004, pp. 47–70.

Francke, Remd Al-Rahim, 'Political progress in Iraq during the Surge', United States Institute of Peace, *Special Report 196*, December 2007.

Freedman, Lawrence and Efraim Karsh, *The Gulf Conflict* (London: Faber and Faber, 1993).

Friedman, Alan, *Spider's Web: Bush, Saddam, Thatcher and the Decade of Deceit* (London: Faber and Faber, 1993).

Fry, Joseph A., *Dixie Looks Abroad: the South and US Foreign Relations, 1789–1973* (Baton Rouge, LA: Louisiana State University Press, 2002).

Fukuyama, Francis, 'The primacy of culture', *Journal of Democracy*, 6 (1), 1995, pp. 7–14.

Gaffney, Frank J., 'Making the world safe from VX', *Commentary*, October 1998, pp. 19–24.

Galbraith, Peter W., *The End of Iraq: How American Incompetence Created a War Without End* (New York, NY: Simon and Schuster, 2006).

Galbraith, Peter W., 'The victor?', *New York Review of Books*, 11 October 2007, pp. 6–9.

Galbraith, Peter W., 'Is this a "Victory"?', *New York Review of Books*, 23 October 2008, pp. 74–6.

Galula, David, *Counter-Insurgency Warfare: Theory and Practice* (New York, NY: Praeger, 1964).

Garfield, Richard, *Morbidity and Mortality among Iraqi Children from 1990 to 1998: Assessing the Impact of Economic Sanctions* (Goshen: Institute for International Peace Studies, University of Notre Dame, 1999).

Garfield, Richard, 'Health and well-being in Iraq: sanctions and the impact of the Oil-for-Food Program', *Transnational Law and Contemporary Problems*, 11 (2), 2001, pp. 278–97.

Gause, F. Gregory III, 'Iraq's decisions to go to war, 1980 and 1990', *Middle East Journal*, 56 (1), 2002, pp. 47–70.

Gause, F. Gregory III, 'The international politics of the Gulf', in L. Fawcett (ed.), *International Relations of the Middle East* (Oxford: Oxford University Press, 2005), pp. 263–81.

Gerson, Mark, *The Neoconservative Vision: From the Cold War to the Culture Wars* (Lanham, MD: Madison Books, 1996).

Goldberg, Jeffrey, 'A little learning', *The New Yorker*, 9 May 2005, pp. 36–41.

Gordon, Michael E., and Bernard Trainor, *The Generals' War: the Inside Story of the Conflict in the Gulf* (Boston, MA: Little, Brown, 1995).

Gordon, Michael and Bernard Trainor, *Cobra II: the Inside Story of the Invasion and Occupation of Iraq* (London: Atlantic Books, 2007).

Gordon, Murray (ed.), *Conflict in the Persian Gulf* (London: Macmillan, 1981).

Graham-Brown, Sarah, *Sanctioning Saddam: the Politics of Intervention in Iraq* (London: I. B. Tauris, 1999).

Greenstein, Fred I. (ed.), *The George W. Bush Presidency: an Early Assessment* (Baltimore, MD: Johns Hopkins University Press, 2005).

Gunter, Michael M., 'The KDP-PUK conflict in northern Iraq', *Middle East Journal*, 50 (2), 1996, pp. 225–41.

Haig, Alexander M., *Caveat: Realism, Reagan and Foreign Policy* (New York, NY: Scribner, 1984).

Halliday, Fred, *Threat from the East: Soviet Policy from Afghanistan and Iran to the Horn of Africa* (London: Penguin, 1982).

Halliday, Fred, *The Middle East in International Relations* (Cambridge: Cambridge University Press, 2005).

Halper, Stephan, and Jonathan Clarke, *America Alone: the Neo-Conservatives and the Global Order* (Cambridge: Cambridge University Press, 2004).

Hashim, Ahmed S., *Insurgency and Counter-Insurgency in Iraq* (Ithaca, NY: Cornell University Press, 2006).

Heikal, Mohammed, *Illusion of Triumph: an Arab View of the Gulf War* (London: HarperCollins, 1993).

Heller, Mark A., 'Iraq's army: military weakness, political utility', in A. Baram and B. Rubin (eds), *Iraq's Road to War* (Basingstoke: Macmillan, 1994), pp. 44–8.

Helms, Christine Moss, *Iraq: Eastern Flank of the Arab World* (Washington, DC: Brookings Institution, 1985).

Henry, Clement M., 'The clash of globalisations in the Middle East', in L. Fawcett (ed.), *International Relations of the Middle East* (Oxford: Oxford University Press, 2005), pp. 105–30.

Herring, Eric, and Glen Rangwala, *Iraq in Fragments: the Occupation and its Legacy* (London: Hurst and Co., 2006).

Herrman, Richard K., 'US policy in the conflict', in Alex Danchev (ed.), *International Perspectives on the Gulf Crisis, 1990–1991* (Basingstoke: Macmillan, 1994).

Herrman, Richard K., 'Coercive diplomacy and the crisis over Kuwait', in Alexander L. George and William E. Simons (eds), *The Limits of Coercive Diplomacy*, 2nd edn (Boulder, CO: Westview, 1994), pp. 229–66.

Hersh, Seymour M., 'Selective intelligence', *The New Yorker*, 12 May 2003.

Hersh, Seymour M., 'The stovepipe', *The New Yorker*, 27 October 2003.

Hersh, Seymour M., 'Torture at Abu Ghraib', *The New Yorker*, 10 May 2004.

Himmelstein, Jerome L., *To the Right: the Transformation of American Conservatism* (Berkeley, CA: University of California Press, 1990).

Hinnebusch, Raymond, *The International Politics of the Middle East* (Manchester: Manchester University Press, 2003).

Hiro, Dilip, *Desert Shield to Desert Storm: the Second Gulf War* (London: HarperCollins, 1992).

Hiro, Dilip, *Neighbours not Friends: Iraq and Iran after the Gulf Wars* (London: Routledge, 2001).

Hooglund, Eric, 'Reagan's Iran: factions behind US policy in the Gulf', *Middle East Report*, 151, March 1988, pp. 28–31.

Hunter, Shireen, 'Islam in power: the case of Iran', in Shireen Hunter (ed.), *The Politics of Islamic Revivalism: Diversity and Unity* (Bloomington, IN: University of Indiana Press, 1988).

Hurst, Steven, *The Foreign Policy of the Bush Administration: in Search of a New World Order* (London: Cassell, 1999).

Hurst, Steven, 'The rhetorical strategy of George H. W. Bush during the Persian Gulf crisis 1990–1991: how to help lose a war you won', *Political Studies*, 52 (2), 2004, pp. 376–92.

Hurst, Steven, *Cold War US Foreign Policy: Key Perspectives* (Edinburgh: Edinburgh University Press, 2005).

Ikenberry, G. John, 'Power and liberal order: America's postwar world order in transition', *International Relations of the Asia-Pacific*, 2005 (5), pp. 133–52.

Iraq Body Count, 'No longer unknowable: Fallujah's April civilian toll is 600', 26 October 2004, www.iraqbodycount.net/press/index.php#pr.9>.

Jabber, Paul, 'US interests and regional security in the Middle East', *Daedalus*, 109 (4), 1980, pp. 67–80.

Jentleson, Bruce W., *With Friends Like These: Reagan, Bush and Saddam, 1982–1990* (New York, NY: W. W. Norton and Co., 1994).

Judis, John B., 'War resisters', *American Prospect*, 7 October 2002.

Judis, John B., and Spencer Ackerman, 'The selling of the Iraq war: the first casualty', *New Republic*, 30 June 2003.

Kagan, Robert, and William Kristol (eds), *Present Dangers: Crisis and Opportunity in American Foreign and Defense Policy* (San Francisco, CA: Encounter Books, 2000).

Kagan, Robert, and William Kristol, 'Introduction: national interest and global responsibility', in R. Kagan and W. Kristol (eds), *Present Dangers: Crisis and Opportunity in American Foreign and Defense Policy* (San Francisco, CA: Encounter Books, 2000), pp. 3–24.

Kahl, Colin H., Brian Catulis and Marc Lynch, 'Thinking strategically about Iraq: report from a symposium', *Middle East Policy*, 15 (1), 2008, pp. 82–110.

Kaplan, Lawrence F., and William Kristol, *The War over Iraq: Saddam's Tyranny and America's Mission* (San Fransisco, CA: Encounter Books, 2003).

Karsh, Efraim, and Inari Rautsi, *Saddam Hussein: a Political Biography* (New York, NY: Grove Press, 2002).

Katzman, Kenneth, 'Iraq: politics, elections, and benchmarks', CRS Report for Congress, 21 November 2008.

Katzman, Kenneth, and Jennifer Elsea, 'Iraq: transition to sovereignty', CRS Report for Congress, 21 July 2004.

Kelly, John H., 'Lebanon: 1982–1984', in Jeremy R. Azreal and Emil A. Payin, *US and Russian Policy-making with Respect to the Use of Force* (Santa Monica, CA: Rand Corporation, 1996), available at www.rand.org/pubs/conference_proceedings/CF129/CF-129.chapter6.html.

Kennedy, Paul, *The Rise and Fall of the Great Powers: Economic Change and Military Conflict from 1500–2000* (London: Fontana, 1989).

Keohane, Robert, *After Hegemony: Cooperation and Discord in the World Political Economy* (Princeton, NJ: Princeton University Press, 1984).

Khalidi, Rashid, *Resurrecting Empire: Western Footprints and America's Perilous Path in the Middle East* (London: I. B. Tauris, 2004).

Khalilzad, Zalmay, 'A geo-strategic overview: stability or new aggressive coalitions?', *Proceedings of the Washington Institute*, 3rd annual policy conference, 'US policy in the Middle East: toward the next administration', 16–18 September 1988 (Washington, DC: Washington Institute for Near East Policy, 1988).

Khalilzad, Zalmay, 'The United States and the Persian Gulf: preventing regional hegemony', *Survival*, 37 (2), 1995, pp. 95–120.

Klare, Michael, 'Have RDF, will travel', *The Nation*, 8 March 1980, p. 266.

Klare, Michael, *Rogue States and Nuclear Outlaws: America's Search for a New Foreign Policy* (New York, NY: Hill and Wang, 1995).

Klinker, Philip A., *Midterm: the Elections of 1994 in Context* (Boulder, CO: Westview, 1996).

Krauthammer, Charles, 'The unipolar moment', *Foreign Affairs*, 70 (1), 1991, pp. 23–33.

Krauthammer, Charles, 'Why America must not go into Bosnia', *Weekly Standard*, 4 December 1995, pp. 15–17.

Kristol, Irving, 'Foreign policy in an age of ideology', *National Interest*, 1, Fall 1985, pp. 6–14.

Kristol, William and Robert Kagan, 'Toward a neo-Reaganite foreign policy', *Foreign Affairs*, 75 (4), 1996, pp. 18–32.

Kupchan, Charles A., *The Persian Gulf and the West: the Dilemmas of Security* (Boston, MA: Allen and Unwin, 1987).

Ladd, Everett C., 'The 1994 Congressional elections: the postindustrial realignment continues', *Political Science Quarterly*, 109 (5), 1994–5, pp. 1–23.

Lake, Anthony, 'Confronting backlash states', *Foreign Affairs*, 73 (2), 1994, pp. 45–55.

Lemann, Nicholas, 'The next world order', *The New Yorker*, 1 April 2002.

Lemann, Nicholas, 'How it came to war: when did Bush decide that he had to fight Saddam', *The New Yorker*, 31 March 2003.

Lesch, David W., *1979: the Year that Shaped the Middle East* (Boulder, CO: Westview, 2001).

Lieber, Robert J., 'Iraq and the world oil market: oil and power after the Gulf War', in A. Baram and B. Rubin (eds), *Iraq's Road to War* (Basingstoke: Macmillan, 1994), pp. 85–99.

Lind, Michael, 'The weird men behind George Bush's war', *New Statesman*, 7 April 2003, pp. 10–13.

Lynch, Marc, 'Smart sanctions: rebuilding consensus or maintaining conflict?', *MERIP Online*, 28 June 2001, www.merip.org/mero/mero062801. html.

Mahdavy, Hossein, 'The patterns and problems of economic development in rentier states: the case of Iran', in M. Cook (ed.), *Studies in the Economic History of the Middle East* (Oxford: Oxford University Press, 1970).

Mahdi, Kamil, 'Neoliberalism, conflict and an oil economy: the case of Iraq', *Arab Studies Quarterly*, 29 (1), 2007, pp. 1–20.

Malone, David, 'US–UN relations in the UN Security Council in the post-Cold War era', in Rosemary Foot, S. Neil MacFarlane and Michael Mastanduno (eds), *US Hegemony and International Organizations* (Oxford: Oxford University Press, 2003), pp. 73–91.

Malone, David, *The International Struggle Over Iraq: Politics in the UN Security Council 1980–2005* (Oxford: Oxford University Press, 2006).

Mann, James, *Rise of the Vulcans: the History of Bush's War Cabinet* (London: Penguin, 2004).

Markusen, Ann R., Peter Hall, Scott Campbell and Sabina Deitrick, *The Rise of the Gunbelt: the Military Remapping of Industrial America* (Oxford: Oxford University Press, 1991).

Marr, Phoebe, *The Modern History of Iraq* (Boulder, CO: Westview, 1985).

Marr, Phoebe, 'Iraq in the 1990s', *Middle East Executive Report*, June 1990.

Massing, Michael, 'Embedded in Iraq', *New York Review of Books*, 17 July 2008, pp. 33–6.

McCormick, Thomas, '"Every system needs a center sometimes": an essay on hegemony and modern American foreign policy', in Lloyd C. Gardner (ed.), *Redefining the Past: Essays in Diplomatic History in Honour of William Appleman Williams* (Corvallis, OR: Oregon State University Press, 1986), pp. 195–200.

McCormick, Thomas, *America's Half Century: United States Foreign Policy in the Cold War and After* (Baltimore, MD: Johns Hopkins University Press, 1995).

McGirr, Lisa, *Suburban Warriors: the Origins of the New American Right* (Princeton, NJ: Princeton University Press, 2001).

McNaugher, Thomas L., *Arms and Oil: US Military Strategy and the Persian Gulf* (Washington, DC: Brookings Institution, 1985).

Mead, Walter Russell, 'God's country?', *Foreign Affairs*, 85 (5), 2006, pp. 24–44.

Miles, Michael W., *The Odyssey of the American Right* (Oxford: Oxford University Press, 1980).

Miller, Arthur H., and Thomas F. Klobucar, 'The role of issues in the 2000 presidential election', *Presidential Studies Quarterly*, 33, 2003, pp. 101–23.

Mines, Keith, 'On fighting a 16-division war with a 10-division force', Foreign Policy Research Institute, 8 March 2005, www.fpri.orglenotes/20050308.military.mines.16dwar10dforce.html.

Mitchell, John V. (with Peter Back and Michael Grubb), *The New Geopolitics of Energy* (London: RIIA, 1996).

Morgan, Iwan, and Philip Davies (eds), *Right On: Political Change and Continuity in George W. Bush's America* (London: Institute for the Study of the Americas, 2006).

Mueller, John, *Policy and Opinion in the Gulf War* (Chicago, IL: University of Chicago Press, 1994).

Mufti, Malik, *Sovereign Creations: Pan Arabism and Political Order in Syria and Iraq* (Ithaca, NY: Cornell University Press, 1996).

Muravchik, Joshua, *Exporting Democracy: Fulfilling America's Destiny* (Washington, DC: AEI Press, 1991).

Muravchik, Joshua, 'What to do about Saddam Hussein', *Commentary*, June 1998, pp. 37–41.

Murphy, Cullen, and Todd S. Purdum, 'Farewell to all that: an oral history of the Bush White House', *Vanity Fair*, February 2009, www.vanityfair.com/politics/features/2009/02Bush-oral-history200902?currentpage=1.

Mylroie, Laurie, 'The Baghdad alternative', *Orbis*, 32 (3), 1988, pp. 339–64.

Mylroie, Laurie, 'US policy toward Iraq', *Middle East Intelligence Bulletin* (3) 1, January 2001, www.meib.org/articles/o1o1_irl.htm.

Nash, Gerald D., *The American West Transformed: the Impact of the Second World War* (Bloomington, IN: Indiana University Press, 1985).

Nichols, John, *The Rise and Rise of Dick Cheney: Unlocking the Mysteries of the Most Powerful Vice President in American History* (New York, NY: New Press, 2004).

Nonneman, Gerd, *Iraq, the Gulf States and the War* (New York, NY: Ithaca Press, 1986).

Noorbaksh, Mehdi, 'Shiism and ethnic politics in Iraq', *Middle East Policy*, 15 (2), 2008, pp. 53–65.

O'Ballance, Edgar, *The Gulf War* (London: Brasseys, 1988).

Odell, Peter, *Oil and World Power*, 8th edn (London: Penguin, 1986).

Odell, Peter, 'International oil: a return to American hegemony', *The World Today*, November 1994, pp. 208–10.

Ottaway, Marina, 'Iraq: without consensus democracy is not the answer', Carnegie Endowment for International Peace, *Policy Brief 36*, March 2005.

Owen, Roger, *The Middle East in the World Economy 1800–1914* (London: Methuen, 1981).

Packer, George, *The Assassin's Gate: America in Iraq* (London: Faber and Faber, 2007).

Painter, David S., 'Explaining US relations with the Third World', *Diplomatic History*, 19 (3), 1995, pp. 525–48.

Palmer, Michael A., *Guardians of the Gulf: a History of America's Expanding Role in the Persian Gulf, 1833–1992* (New York, NY: Free Press, 1993).

Parmet, Herbert S., *George Bush: the Life of a Lone Star Yankee* (New York, NY: Scribner, 1997).

Pelham, Nicholas, *A New Muslim Order: the Shia and the Middle East Sectarian Crisis* (London: I. B. Tauris, 2008).

Pelletiere, Stephen, *Iraq and the International Oil System: Why American Went to War in the Gulf* (Westport, CT: Praeger, 2001).

Perle, Richard, 'Iraq: Saddam unbound', in R. Kagan and W. Kristol (eds),

*Present Dangers: Crisis and Opportunity in American Foreign and Defense Policy* (San Francisco, CA: Encounter Books, 2000), pp. 99–110.

Perry, William J., 'Gulf security and US policy', *Middle East Policy*, 3 (4), 1995, pp. 10–11.

Pfiffner, James P., 'Did President Bush mislead the country in his arguments for war with Iraq?', *Presidential Studies Quarterly*, 34 (1), 2004, pp. 25–46.

Pfiffner, James P., 'Intelligence and decision-making before the war with Iraq', in George C. Edwards and Desmond King (eds), *The Polarized Presidency of George W. Bush* (Oxford: Oxford University Press, 2007), pp. 213–44.

Pillar, Paul R., 'Intelligence, policy and the war in Iraq', *Foreign Affairs*, 85 (2), 2006, pp. 15–27.

Pimlott, John, and Stephen Badsey, *The Gulf War Assessed* (London: Arms and Armour Press, 1992).

Podhoretz, Norman, *The Present Danger* (New York, NY: Simon and Schuster, 1980).

Podhoretz, Norman, 'Appeasement by any other name', *Commentary*, July 1983, pp. 25–38.

Podhoretz, Norman, 'Neoconservatism: a eulogy', *Commentary*, March 1996, pp. 19–27.

Pollack, Kenneth M., *Arabs at War: Military Effectiveness, 1948–1991* (Lincoln, NE: University of Nebraska Press, 2002).

Pollack, Kenneth M., *The Threatening Storm: the Case for Invading Iraq* (New York, NY: Random House, 2002).

Pollack, Kenneth M., *A Switch in Time: a New Strategy for America in Iraq* (Washington, DC: Saban Center for Middle East Policy at the Brookings Institution, 2006).

Pollack, Kenneth M., 'The seven deadly sins of failure in Iraq: a retrospective analysis of the reconstruction', *Middle East Review of International Affairs (MERIA)*, 10 (4) 2006, www.meria.idc.ac.il/journal/2004/ossue4/jv10no4a1.thtml.

Pomper, Gerald M., F. Christopher Arterton and Ross K. Baker (eds), *The Election of 1992: Reports and Interpretations* (Chatham: Chatham House Publishers, 1993).

Posen, Barry L. and Andrew L. Ross, 'Competing visions for US grand strategy', *International Security*, 21 (3), 1996–7, pp. 5–53.

Powell, Colin (with Joseph E. Persico), *A Soldier's Way: an Autobiography* (London: Hutchinson, 1995).

Prados, Alfred B., 'Iraq: post-war challenges and US responses', CRS Report for Congress, 31 March 1999.

Prados, John, *Hoodwinked: the Documents that Reveal how Bush Sold us a War* (New York, NY: New Press, 2004).

Project for the New American Century (PNAC), *Rebuilding America's Defenses,* www.newamericancentury.org/RebuildingAmericasDefenses.pdf.

Przeworski, Adam, Michael Alvarez, Jose Cheibub and Hernando Limongi, *Democracy and Development* (New York, NY: Cambridge University Press, 2000).

Quandt, William B., 'The Middle-East crises', *Foreign Affairs*, 58 (3), 1979, pp. 540–62.

Rabil, Robert G., 'Operation "Termination of traitors": the Iraqi regime through its documents', *MERIA*, 6 (3), 2002, www.meria.idc.ac.il/journal/2002/issue3/jv6n3a2.html.

Rae, Nicol C, *The Decline and Fall of the Liberal Republicans from 1952 to the Present* (Oxford: Oxford University Press, 1989).

Rahimi, Babak, 'Ayatollah al-Sistani and the democratization of post-Saddam Iraq', Nathan Hale Foreign Policy Society, Working Paper Series, www.foreignpolicysociety.org/workingpapers/wp6-Rahimi.pdf.

Ramazani, Rouhollah, *Revolutionary Iran: Challenge and Response in the Middle East* (Baltimore, MD: Johns Hopkins University Press, 1986).

Randall, Stephen J., *United States Foreign Oil Policy since World War One: For Profits and Security* (Montreal: McGill-Queen's University Press, 2005).

Rathmell, Andrew, 'Planning post-conflict reconstruction in Iraq: what can we learn?', *International Affairs*, 81 (5), 2005, pp. 1013–38.

Reagan, Ronald, *An American Life: an Autobiography* (New York, NY: Simon and Schuster, 1990).

Rice, Condoleezza, 'Promoting the national interest', *Foreign Affairs*, 79 (1), 2000, pp. 45–62.

Ricks, Thomas E., *Fiasco: the American Military Adventure in Iraq* (London: Penguin, 2007).

Ritter, Scott, *Endgame: Solving the Iraq Crisis* (New York, NY: Simon and Schuster, 1999).

Robins, Philip, 'Iraq in the Gulf War: objectives, strategies and problems', in Hans W. Maull and Otto Pick (eds), *The Gulf War: Regional and International Dimensions* (London: Pinter, 1989), pp. 45–59.

Root, Hilton L., 'Walking with the devil: the commitment trap in US foreign policy', *The National Interest*, 88, March–April 2007, pp. 42–5.

Rubin, Barry, 'The Reagan administration and the Middle East', in Kenneth A. Oye, Robert J. Lieber and Donald Rothchild (eds), *Eagle Defiant: United States Foreign Policy in the 1980s* (Boston, MA: Little, Brown, 1983), pp. 367–89.

Russett, Bruce, *Grasping the Democratic Peace: Principles for a Post-Cold War World* (Princeton, NJ: Princeton University Press, 2003).

Schurmann, Franz, *The Logic of World Power: an Inquiry into the Origins, Currents and Contradictions of World Politics* (New York, NY: Pantheon, 1974).

Shafer, Byron E., and Richard Johnston, *The End of Southern Exceptionalism: Class, Race and Partisan Change in the Postwar South* (Cambridge, MA: Harvard University Press, 2006).

Shaffer, Ed, *The United States and the Control of World Oil* (London: Croom Helm, 1983).

Shultz, George P., *Turmoil and Triumph: My Years as Secretary of State* (New York, NY: Charles Scribner's Sons, 1993).

Sick, Gary, *All Fall Down: America's Tragic Encounter with Iran* (New York, NY: Random House, 1985).

Sifry, Micah, and Christopher Cerf (eds), *The Gulf War Reader: History, Documents, Opinions* (New York, NY: Times Books, 1991).

Sifry, Micah, and Christopher Cerf (eds), *The Iraq War Reader: History, Documents, Opinions* (New York, NY: Touchstone, 2003).

Simon, Steven, 'The price of the Surge: how US strategy is hastening Iraq's demise', *Foreign Affairs*, 87 (3), 2008, pp. 57–65.

Skidmore, David, 'Understanding the unilateralist turn in US foreign policy', *Foreign Policy Analysis*, 2, 2005, pp. 207–28.

Sluglett, Peter, 'The Kurds', in Committee Against Repression and For Democratic Rights in Iraq, *Saddam's Iraq: Revolution or Reaction?* (London: Zed Books, 1989), pp. 177–202.

Sluglett, Peter, 'The Cold War in the Middle East', in L. Fawcett (ed.), *International Relations of the Middle East* (Oxford: Oxford University Press, 2005), pp. 41–58.

Stork, Joe, 'Saudi oil and the US', MERIP Report no. 91, October 1980, Washington, DC.

Summers, Harry G., *On Strategy II: a Critical Analysis of the Gulf War* (New York, NY: Dell, 1992).

Suskind, Ron, *The Price of Loyalty: George W. Bush, the White House and the Education of Paul O'Neill* (New York, NY: Simon and Schuster, 2004).

Suskind, Ron, *The One Percent Doctrine: Deep Inside America's Pursuit of its Enemies since 9/11* (New York, NY: Simon and Schuster, 2006).

'Symposium on dual containment', *Middle East Policy*, 3 (1), 1994, pp. 1–26.

Taremi, Kamran, 'Iranian foreign policy towards occupied Iraq, 2003–5', *Middle East Policy*, 12 (4), 2005, pp. 28–48.

Tarnoff, Curtis, 'Recent developments in reconstruction assistance', CRS Report for Congress, 12 May 2005.

Taylor, C. II (ed.), *Alerting America* (Washington, DC: Pergamon-Brasseys, 1984).

Teicher Howard, and Gayle Radley Teicher, *Twin Pillars to Desert Storm: America's Flawed Vision in the Middle East from Nixon to Bush* (New York, NY: William Morrow and Co., 1993).

Thompson, John B., 'The theory of structuration', in John B. Thompson,

*Studies in the Theory of Ideology* (Cambridge: Polity, 1984), pp. 148–72.

Timmerman, Kenneth, *The Death Lobby: How the West Armed Iraq* (Boston, MA: Houghton Mifflin, 1991).

Trevan, Tim, *Saddam's Secrets: the Hunt for Iraq's Hidden Weapons* (London: HarperCollins, 1999).

Tripp, Charles, 'The foreign policy of Iraq', in Raymond Hinnebusch and Anoushiravan Ehteshami (eds), *The Foreign Policies of Middle East States* (Boulder, CO: Lynne Rienner, 2001), pp. 167–92.

Tripp, Charles, *A History of Iraq* (Cambridge: Cambridge University Press, 2002).

Tripp, Charles, 'The United States and nation-building in Iraq', *Review of International Studies*, 30 (4), 2004, pp. 545–58.

Trubowitz, Peter, *Defining the National Interest: Conflict and Change in American Foreign Policy* (Chicago, IL: University of Chicago Press, 1998).

US Public Broadcasting System (PBS), *The Gulf War: Oral History Interviews*, www.pbs.org/gulf/oral.

US Public Broadcasting System (PBS), *Frontline: Spying on Saddam*, 27 April 1999, www.pbs.org/wgbh/pages/frontline/shows/unscom.

Vance, Cyrus, *Hard Choices: Critical Years in America's Foreign Policy* (New York, NY: Simon and Schuster, 1983).

Vasiliev, Alexei, *The History of Saudi Arabia* (London: Saqi Books, 1998).

Vitalis, Robert, 'Black gold, white crude: an essay on American exceptionalism, hierarchy, and hegemony in the Gulf', *Diplomatic History*, 26 (2), 2002, pp. 185–213.

Waas, Murray, and Craig Unger, 'In the loop: Bush's secret mission', *The New Yorker*, 2 November 1992.

Wallerstein, Immanuel, *The Capitalist World Economy* (Cambridge: Cambridge University Press, 1979).

Waltz, Kenneth, 'Structural realism after the Cold War', *International Security*, 25, 2000, pp. 5–41.

Waxman, Henry A., and Byron L. Dorgan, 'Halliburton's questioned and unsupported costs in Iraq exceed $1.4 billion', 27 June 2005, www.democrats.reform.house.gov/documents/20050627140010-82879.pdfbidding.

Weinberger, Caspar W., *Fighting for Peace: Seven Critical Years in the Pentagon* (New York, NY: Warner Books, 1990).

West, Bing, *No True Glory: a Frontline Account of the Battle for Fallujah* (New York, NY: Bantam Books, 2005).

Wheeler, Nicholas J., *Saving Strangers: Humanitarian Intervention in International Society* (Oxford: Oxford University Press, 2000).

Wheelock, Tom, and Robyn McGuckin, 'Iraqi power sector: CPA's legacy and lessons', *Middle East Economic Survey*, 18 July 2005.

Wilcox, Clyde, *Onward Christian Soldiers? The Religious Right in American Politics* (Boulder, CO: Westview, 1996).

Wilson, Ernest J. III, 'World politics and international energy markets', *International Organization*, 41 (1), 1987, pp. 125–49.

Wimmer, Andreas, 'Democracy and ethnic-religious conflict in Iraq', *Survival*, 45 (4), 2003–4, pp. 111–34.

Wohlforth, William, 'The stability of a unipolar world', *International Security*, 24, 1999, 5–41.

Woodward, Bob, *The Commanders* (New York, NY: Simon and Schuster, 1991).

Woodward, Bob, *Bush at War* (London: Pocket Books, 2003).

Woodward, Bob, *Plan of Attack* (London: Pocket Books, 2004).

Woodward, Bob, *State of Denial* (London: Pocket Books, 2006).

Woodward, Bob, *The War Within: a Secret White House History, 2006–2008* (New York, NY: Simon and Schuster, 2008).

Wooten, James P., *Rapid Deployment Force*, Congressional Research Service (CRS) Issue Brief no. IB80027, May 1985.

Wright, Susan, 'The Hijacking of UNSCOM', in M. Sifry and C. Cerf (eds), *The Iraq War Reader: History, Documents, Opinions* (New York, NY: Touchstone, 2003), pp. 186–90.

Yergin, Daniel, *The Prize: the Epic Quest for Oil, Money and Power* (New York, NY: Pocket Books, 1993).

Yousif, Bassam, 'Economic restructuring in Iraq: intended and unintended consequences', *Journal of Economic Issues*, 41 (1), 2007, pp. 43–60.

# INDEX